THE HUNTER AND THE HUNTED

Also by Robin Page:

Down Among The Dossers
The Decline of an English Village

The Hunter and the Hunted

A Countryman's View of Blood Sports

Robin Page

DAVIS-POYNTER
London

First published in 1977 by
Davis-Poynter Limited
20 Garrick Street London WC2E 9BJ

ISBN 0 7067 0203 4

Printed in Great Britain by
Bristol Typesetting Co. Ltd
Barton Manor, St Philips, Bristol

Contents

Illustrations

Introduction

It has not been easy to write this book, for it is about the countryside, and the relationship between the people who live, work, and play in it, and the wild creatures that depend on it for their survival, and which add much colour and character to country life. Many of the pastimes and sports encountered arouse strong emotions, and there have been numerous pitfalls, all well concealed, that I have tried to avoid. It has also been difficult because of the political, moral, and social issues and implications, which for many years have led to bitter disputes and controversies. It has not been my intention to be controversial; all I have wanted to do is to describe the various animals and birds of the countryside, and to show how 'civilized' people co-exist with, control, kill, and compete with them. In addition, my purpose has not been to produce a definitive scientific or sociological study of British wildlife and rural pursuits, but an attempt to see each activity in its country context and to deal with the visual facts and personal feelings, which are usually far more accurate than figures and clinical assessment.

My interest in the phenomenon of affluent, educated, Western man acting as a primitive predator goes back several years, for the taking of wild foxes, pheasants, and fish, with dogs, guns, and hooks, at first glance seems to be anachronistic in our largely urban twentieth century society. It is a society in which 'progress' and the worship of technology seem to predominate. Few people have to bother with the once basic tasks of gathering fruit and vegetables, and rearing animals for food, and when hunger comes, pre-packed peas, pulverized mashed potatoes, and frozen fish fingers are all readily available in attractive wrappers on supermarket shelves. Yet despite this, several million people regularly feel the need to go out and search for wild places; there they adopt the role of the hunter, pursuing various birds, animals, and fish, and seeming to act out a distant part of their evolutionary past. For although development and superficial sophistication appear to have moved man on to a position far divorced from his animal and tribal background, the urges that helped his ancestors to survive still seem to be surprisingly close at hand.

Because the subjects of hunting, shooting, and fishing are so often accompanied by anger and outrage, and because those who object and those who participate are so vociferous and highly organized, before proceeding further it seems only sensible to make my own position clear, for I would not wish to be seen as an apologist for one side or the other. My own attitude towards field/blood sports is a simple one; normally I take no part in hunting, shooting, or fishing, but have done so for the purposes of this book, to feel for myself the emotions involved, and to see what skills, if any, are required. All my life I have been surrounded by a variety of wild and domestic animals and birds, and from observing them has grown a concern for the conservation of our wildlife and countryside. Indeed my own relationship with animals has been so personal, as I have described in some detail in *The Decline of an English Village*, that in certain instances it has probably been too sentimental and I have tended to give my animals the thoughts and feelings of human beings. Like most people, before I started writing this book I had certain prejudices against some of the activities, formed from what I had heard and read, and I had also been put off shooting, when, as a boy, I saw roe deer cruelly shot by men with guns and cartridges designed for killing birds. Living in the country, however, I also accept that most of our larger mammals need to be controlled. And, furthermore, I enjoy eating pheasant.

Unfortunately the complications and contradictions arising from hunting for food and killing for pleasure can not be avoided; beauty and brutality, humour and harassment, hope and fear, are all there, in both the natural and the unnatural cycles of life and death. I have tried to observe them and write about them honestly, in the hope that the ways and problems of the country will become more real to those who live in it, and in the hope also that some of those who make up the large urban majority will understand them better. The British countryside is currently under great pressure, and its fascinating ways and wildlife will only survive if they are first understood.

Chapter One

Wild and Free

As the landscape has changed, with progress and the passing of time, so too has Western man; from a nomadic wanderer and hunter to, in the most part, an urban dweller, with each individual playing a minute part in a highly organized and complex industrial society. At first glance many people have been tamed by the new environment and way of life, for the supermarkets, central heating, the factories, and the four walls of a brick-built house not only separate them from the hardships, traditions, the pastimes, and the community spirit of the past, but they also separate them from the realities of the present; the basic needs for life, and the inevitability of death. Man the hunter has been domesticated and imprisoned and programmed to perform a number of simple tasks and functions, the accomplishment of which those who organize and direct society call 'life'.

But appearances are deceptive, for in the countryside wild creatures continue to flourish, untamed and free, having survived the changes by processes of adaption and adoption of both habits and habitat. Most are common and welcome parts of the rural scene, yet the very features that have allowed them to continue have also hidden several aspects of their behaviour, and although animals such as hares and rabbits, foxes and deer, are common, many of their ways remain unknown and rooted firmly in folklore.

Much wildlife is watched and hunted by a large number of men and women, for despite affluence, comfort, and social change, many people, both rich and poor, continue to get drawn into the countryside with binoculars or guns, fishing rods or field guides, to hunt out wild things, or simply to seek solitude and beauty; all are manifestations of the old hunting instinct and the wandering of the free spirit that enabled earlier men to survive and sow the seeds of today's civilization.

Even a normal country walk over a piece of common countryside, in winter or in summer, can enkindle refinements of the old sensations; for movement is still dictated by the sights, sounds, and scents of open places, and the reflexes of the body continue to respond automatically to movement, new smells, or a sudden sound. Each week, at least once, I walk in a large circle to cover the boundaries of our small farm, accompanied by three dogs, two labradors, Tinker and her fat daughter Tirra, and Foss, a young border collie. We pass through a spinney and onto arable fields, then across grass by a small brook, until a field of wasteland and summer weeds is reached. Then under a minor road along the bed of the brook, and into more long standing meadowland, before returning to arable and home. Yet each stroll, despite the fact that I have covered the same ground many times before, is stimulating and worthwhile; for there is always the unexpected to encounter and an ever changing beauty and struggle to absorb; the flowering and dying of seasons; a bird suddenly flushed onto wing, or a whirl of water as a moorhen or a water vole dives for safety.

On one such walk, in early summer, a pigeon sat tightly on its dishevelled stick nest above me as I waded waist deep through the cow parsley of the spinney; it was balanced precariously in a stunted hawthorn bush, dwarfed by the elms around it and shaded by branches dappled with the down of new leaves. On the large arable field beyond, the spring crops looked lawn-like in their drills of fresh green, and the weathered winter soil crumbled into footprints with every stride as the land dried and warmth allowed growth. Skylarks sang, but were barely visible in the bright sky and there were signs of rabbits in a well established piece of winter wheat where the dew still lingered and dampened boots; the full force of regeneration could be felt in the air and heard in the birdsong. Walking close to the high hedge of the brook meadow I called the dogs to me; it was sheltered, warm, and still, as the gentle breeze was deflected upwards by the leaves; mosquitoes danced and two turtle doves, tiring of their purred message of intimate love, clatttered off jerkily into flight, their rufous wings reflecting summer rays and their black tails, edged with new whiteness, fanning out and feeling for air as they flew down to drink. Ahead and upwind of me, a blackbird scolded, but the reason for its alarm never showed. A cuckoo called from a group of brookside elms, and the clarity of its voice matched the cleanliness of the air. Insects searched busily to the gentle hum of working wings along the laden boughs of bursting whitethorn, and in the long grass by a ditch, indignant squeaking betrayed the presence of some fighting shrews or voles. All was quiet at a fox earth among the tangled trunks and branches of bulldozed willows, but from the flattened patches of growing corn and the scattered bones of pheasants, rabbits, and domestic hens, it was clear that a vixen and her cubs were there. From the next parish a bird-scarer fired, and a grey cloud of pigeons took to the air, leaving a field of newly planted peas. The cuckoo flew off, its rounded wings and long narrow tail giving it the appearance of a hawk. The similarity was apparent to others too, for three small birds flew up to worry it; the cuckoo remained unconcerned and was soon flying on to the spinney alone.

Several months later, the same journey on an ordinary January afternoon made a complete contrast; the trees and fields had lost their life; the branches were bare and the soil was cold and much of it lay in upturned furrows; but there were still many surprises and features of interest. As I passed through the spinney with the dogs it was drafty and inhospitable; a damp west wind whistled through, and black twisting ridges of cloud, with rain streaming from their edges crossed the sky at regular intervals. The drops of rain were large and cold but the visual promise of a heavy downpour was not fulfilled. The wide troughs of open sky between the clouds were of a watery pastel blue and already, in a wide south-westerly arc patches of lighter cloud and blue were being flushed with the rubicund rays of the early-setting sun. The large field was wet and cold with patches of ploughed land, waterlogged stubble, and one small piece of lighter gravelly soil already sown. On it a hare's half eaten body lay, its head and forelegs gone and its intestines lying as if heaved out and partially gulped down to satisfy hunger; it had fed a fox, and the remains were left to become carrion for rooks and crows, or for another meal that night. Beyond the grass field by the brook, the sinking sun had travelled into open sky and a strangely soothing copper light lit the landscape; the dark recesses in the ragged bark of a row of weather-worn willows ran with bronze, and only the tractor wheelings in winter wheat beyond the far bank remained dark and out of light.

Great flocks of starlings flew in from all directions to a field where rain had caused thirty acres of a neighbour's barley to rot unharvested. They flew in great dark clouds with the edges of each flock flowing and changing in regular and rounded shapes; the movement of bodies and wings in air held the same symmetry as oil on water, and as each wave landed, the birds behind flew on like water over a fall. The field of summer weeds that bordered the battered barley was briefly given life, as the drab brown of thistles and teasles took on a new bronze richness, for as the sun dropped lower it seemed to glow white hot, of almost magnesium intensity, and the light transformed everything it touched to gold. The wings of winter midges flashed, and even branches of dead wood briefly glowed. The trees cast shadows far longer than themselves and a willow silhouetted in front of the sun blazed, and reflected the brilliant rays in shafts of streaming clarity along the same path as the cutting wind. The blues and pinks of the setting sun gradually merged into gentleness, and the low clouds were edged with silver. But still the birds poured in, not in thousands, but in tens of thousands, and some flew on to the spinney and along a hedge where they perched in a black, murmuring mass. For several weeks they had met at the same time and place, before flying off towards the sun. Some old villagers had seen the phenomenon before: 'They'll stay until they stink themselves out and then they'll find somewhere else until it gets sweeter again'.[1]

A kestrel that had been perching at the top of one of the willows suddenly planed off towards a mass of feeding starlings. The entire flock flew up in a black swirling cloud, with the wind of wings mixing with cries of fear and anger. The kestrel seemed confused, or alarmed, for it turned and flew back. Soon it made off along a hedge and began to hunt by hovering over some rabbit holes. With danger gone, the starlings settled again, and still more flew in. At one end of the field birds rose and flew a few yards further on; others followed, making a black rolling wave which travelled from one side of the field to the other.

As still more starlings flew in, the three dogs began to hunt for rabbits, causing the kestrel to fly off, and then they went down to the brook. I followed them, stepping over stones and travelling under the road bridge to the grassfields beyond where a few cattle were still wintering out without harm. The light was quickly fading

[1] This strange meeting and flight of starlings is said to be 'a pre-roost flight', with the main roost for the night usually being two or three miles away. Those that fed were not eating barley, but the ruined crop was an ideal place for many grubs and insects. A few days later all the birds disappeared, as suddenly as they had arrived.

and the sun dulled into a clear yet gentle ball of brilliant crimson in a darkening sky. Gradually it slid away behind a small lowland ridge of chalk that forms its winter setting place, and looking back I could see that the starlings had started to move once more. As they left the field and the spinney they streamed over and through the elms and willows of the brook, and flew off towards the dusk. They formed a great river of meandering movement, well over two miles long, curving round and flying directly away from me. They were like a huge swarm of giant bees, twisting and curling into the night. Their method of mass communication was inexplicable, and their numbers and behaviour created a sense of wonder and of awe.

A rabbit fled from the brook, where the dogs were working in a small clump of brambles; it ran lazily, alert, but in no great hurry, as if aware that the dogs had not yet seen it go. By the time the old labrador, Tinker, had picked up its trail it had reached the safety of the hedge and ditch where rabbit holes and drain pipes afforded refuge. Plovers changed position on the ploughed land beyond the brook, their white tail bars betraying their presence, and another larger flock travelled higher, in the lighter air, from west to east. A heron flew over and wheeled away towards the water, its legs trailing out, its feet heavy with mud, and its long neck hunched up. It flew directly over a tattered bundle of grey feathers that had rested in the same place for three weeks; it was the headless body of another heron, lying as if killed by a fox and left. It might have been taken by the water's edge as it waited patiently for food, or it might have died where it lay. Half way across another field of grass, returning home, a snipe flew up, letting out its rasping cry of alarm as it fled away in zig-zagged spiralling flight. A blackbird began to sing in an old greengage tree near the farm, being both late in the day and early for the time of the year. The lights of the cow yard shone brightly, where milking was well under way, and Foss ran hard to my pet fox's winter shed where the vixen whined and wagged her brush to greet our return.

To those made insensitive by city living, such wanderings through ordinary English countryside have little to commend them, for many people seem unaware of the beauty, the tragedy, the peace, and the conflict which join together in the natural cycle of life and which were so important and obvious to earlier generations. But even now this strange union of opposites can attract and fascinate, and it still creates a balance which is essential for the survival and well being of all.

Although it is easy to romanticize about country life and wild things, the strong element of conflict and competition can not be avoided. Yet there is usually a dignity and a purpose to natural death, and amid the violence and trauma, there is also much tranquillity and harmony. The conflict and competition can be seen in simple things; in the fighting shrews, the kestrel wanting to hunt, the headless heron, the half-eaten hare, the pigeons feeding on planted peas and in the stolen hens at the fox's earth. At other times, too, glimpses of this never ending struggle can be seen; a stoat crossing a road, carrying in its mouth the body of a mouse, or a heron being mobbed by rooks as it follows in flight the bends of the brook. One afternoon I watched two kestrels as they flew at one another as if to fight. But they always veered away at the last moment to settle again on the wooden posts of a barbed wire fence. The aerial manoeuvring went on for several minutes until one of the birds misjudged its flight and crashed into the top strand of wire. It hung there, impaled, with a barb struck deep into its wing; but as it fluttered helplessly, the other did not rest in victory, but attacked it violently and repeatedly, and cries of rage and pain mewed across the field. I ran towards them to intervene and the attacker flew off; soon the held bird managed to release itself and fluttered to the ground. Surprisingly its wing was apparently undamaged, for after a pause, it ruffled its feathers and flew away, low and fast, and the only sign of battle was the blood covered barb.

This violence, creature against creature, is not cruel, but fundamental and essential, and concerns the securing of mates, the defence of territory, and the taking of food. By involving themselves in this violence many of those who participate in country sports take on the mantle of predator, and in so doing they seem to be resisting the present and responding to the past. Each week thousands of men and women from town and country hunt, shoot, and fish, either to control numbers, or for enjoyment, in a way that some people find deplorable, and from which others derive reassurance. It is the abundance of wildlife that generally permits these pursuits to flourish; in fact some animals are so numerous that Man has an obligation to act as predator, to allow a natural balance to continue in the unnatural surroundings that he has created. Foxes, rabbits, and rats can be found in such large numbers that they have to be controlled, and pheasants, ducks, and deer are carefully managed to provide both sport and food, and even many waterways have been cleaned and restored so that people can go in search of wildfowl and fish.

The killing of animal by animal is inevitable, and there is no doubt that early Man was omnivorous. He ate meat through necessity, both to supplement his summer diet of nuts, fruit, leaves, grasses, and roots, and also to get him through the winter. He used knives, spears, arrows, and hunting dogs; he built traps and snares and acted in a way that ensured survival and protection.

As wandering ceased and cultivation and the domestication of animals became important, there was still a need for extra meat, and hunting continued, to supply food and to kill those predators that preyed on people and livestock. As time passed and society and agriculture developed, the larger predators thought to be harmful to Man were tracked down and destroyed; wolves and bears were harassed into extinction,[2] and by the time hunting had ceased to be a necessity, it had become established as a sport, to provide entertainment and game for the nobility and their friends. Organized hunting with horses, hounds, falcons and, later, with guns, became the pastimes of the privileged classes; the aristocracy and the landed gentry who had time and money in abundance. They hunted, shot, or went fishing for pleasure, and for the social status that such pursuits were thought to give. But even so, while the upper classes shot and rode for fun, many ordinary labouring people still relied on rabbits and birds to provide most of the meat for their large families. They could not purchase meat with the meagre wages given for work on the land, and rabbits, sparrows, song birds, and game birds all became important supplements to the diet of country people, well into this century.

Consequently trapping, and poaching became popular necessities for many, and while rituals and social rivalries developed with hounds, horses, and guns, traditions and techniques of equal strength grew up among those who laboured on the land, with gin

[2] It is thought that wild bears could still be found in Britain during Saxon times and various accounts suggest that the last wolf was killed in Sutherland at the end of the seventeenth century, or in the middle of the eighteenth century.

traps, snares, working dogs, ferrets, cunning, and ingenuity. As a result country sports are still popular with people from all social classes and from widely differing backgrounds.

Those who hunt, shoot, or fish today, refer to their interests as 'field sports'; while those who oppose them always prefix the word 'sports' with 'blood'. But to understand the sports as they now exist it is important not only to see how they developed from the hunting of history, but also to appreciate how important they have been in country life to ordinary people, right up to the comparatively recent past. For the roots and traditions of blood or field sports are very deep and apply equally to those who ride to hounds and shoot grouse, and to those who poach, trap, and enjoy rough shooting. Indeed there are many old countrymen who remember as the highlights of their early lives the hours spent in search of rabbits and hares for food and sport. Work on the land was hard, and opportunities for organized games, leisure, and recreation were scarce, and so the pursuit of wild animals played an important part, not only in filling the cooking pot, but also in providing much enjoyment at a time when transistor radios and television sets were not on hand to provide instant entertainment.

Jim, the old First World War veteran who worked for many years on Father's farm, was never happier than when he had a gun under his arm and a dog at his heels, and it made his day to shoot something for his Sunday dinner. He was not a cruel man, but he waged a never ending battle with cock pheasants, and shooting, for him, was his greatest and simplest pleasure. In their earlier days a large number of men of Jim's generation depended on their guns and snares for their meat supply and their sport. One such man was Arthur Sewell, who lived in a neighbouring village, and whose involvement with country sports was typical of those in lowland farming regions. He was one of a breed of sturdy and resilient countrymen who were born at the turn of the century into ordinary labouring homes, and he learnt many of his ways and skills from his father. His whole life was linked closely to the land, apart from a short break when he went to fight in Europe and beyond. While 'on the Somme' he was wounded by shrapnel and a bayonet, and he rode in some of the last horse cavalry charges in the history of warfare. He returned to his home, and resumed where he had left off, on the land. His struggle on low wages was made worse by the arrival of a large family, caused he believed by the curse of a gypsy from whom he had refused to buy clothes pegs, and so he took to poaching and catching game. During his life he developed techniques and a knowledge of the countryside that those born into future generations will never be able to match, and a simple conversation with him was like listening to living history.

Many poachers started their work when no farmers could be persuaded to let them wander over their fields in search of rabbits, or game. Although the law meted out severe punishments for poaching, those engaged in it viewed it almost as a sport. For some it was a way of earning extra money by selling rabbits and skins, but it also meant that the men and their families could eat better, as farm wages allowed few luxuries, and to most families meat was a luxury. Those who poached usually went out when the moon gave just enough light to see, but left sufficient shadows and darkness to hide in; they experienced the primitive urge and the excitement of the hunter, but with policemen, farmers, and gamekeepers for ever on the look out, they also felt the fear, and developed the furtiveness of the hunted.

Arthur Sewell's poaching career started slightly differently, after he had been reported for shooting a pheasant out of season. His employer had not reported him, but the local policeman had been informed of the misdeed by a neighbouring farmer, who had been passing the field and heard the shot; as a result Arthur was fined 'four quid or a month in clink'.

The fine was reported in the local papers and was noticed by Ruff, a poacher of gypsy descent who lived a few miles away; he poached as 'a one-man gang' and needed an assistant. When Ruff knocked on Arthur's door for the first time he told him that all poachers belonged to a club, and if one of their number got fined, their first duty was to recoup the value of the fine from the person who had 'shopped' them, and their second, was to help the wife and family of any poacher who was sent to prison.

The next suitable night, armed with guns and snares, they visited the neighbouring farmer's land, and Arthur often enjoyed telling of his experiences. 'To start orf with we 'ad a go at the ol' pheasants and got fifteen; that paid for the fine, and then we set snares round a heap of bloody ol' swedes. In the mornin' there were nine ol' hares an' a blinkin' fox'. Fox furs were then very fashionable and many women wore them draped over their shoulders, complete with brush, feet, head, and glass eyes; furriers did a brisk trade curing the skins and Arthur could get a pound for every one. Because of this he rarely shot a snared fox, instead he would pick up one end of the snare and swing the lassoed animal around his head until the wire pulled tighter and the fox was dead; a practice that the local hunt would not have appreciated, particularly as Arthur had often been allowed to ride a hunt horse to help with the 'whipping-in'.

Arthur and Ruff worked so well together on their first night that they decided to keep in partnership, and the next fine evening they went netting rabbits. That involved setting up a net, three feet high and between 70 and 120 yards long, in front of rabbit holes, so that those rabbits out feeding in the fields could be frightened, in the hope that they would bolt and become entangled in the net. The site they chose was in the grounds of a large hall, where a party was in progress, and the noise of laughter, dancing and enjoyment filled the night air and drowned the surreptitious sounds of poachers at work. Ruff went off into one of the adjoining fields to make the rabbits bolt, and Arthur stayed by the net, holding a line at the top to feel for the vibrations that would tell him when a rabbit was caught up. 'They'd got a party goin' on in the 'ouse, an' the butler kept on a comin' to the door to put tins in the dustbin. I'd got hold of this net, when all of a sudden it went coooor'd like this. It didn't arf shake and I thought to myself: "There's a bloody man fell in it". I goo runnin' out about two fields to find Ruff, 'cause I knew where he was. He said: "What's the matter?" I says: "Some bugger's fell in the net". He swore at me, mate, he said: "You bloody fool", he said, "they're only rabbits", he said, "you int frightened of a rabbit are you?"' Each time the net shook after his initial fright, Arthur ran along it until he came across the caught-up rabbit; they netted twenty-five that night.

In another nearby park they went for a much bigger prize and when Ruff was safely up a tree with his twelve-bore shotgun at the ready, Arthur drove some fallow deer under him. One was killed instantly with a single shot, and before the gamekeepers could locate them in the dark, they cut up the carcass and made off; the following week they both had money in their pockets and joints of venison appeared in the window of a local butcher's shop.

In addition to nets, snares, and twelve-bore guns, they also sometimes used a small .410 walking stick gun. It looked just like a walking stick, but when the handle was twisted, a hinged trigger sprung out, and if the ferrule was removed it showed that the shaft was in fact a barrel. Ruff used it quite a lot: 'He's used it until he's 'ad a snout on 'im as big as a cauliflower, 'cause you 'ad to hold it right in front of yur face and it didn't arf have some kick in it mate; lookin' at his nose now I don't reckon its gorn down since.'

They were never caught, always managing to keep 'two jumps of a flea ahead of the law', but one night they did think that their poaching partnership was at an end. They were going through a small covert: 'We was goin' up some ol' whitethorn trees when Ruff sees an ol' bird. He 'ad a shot at the ol' bird an' when he shot orf something ran out of these trees and we thought it was some bugger after us, or a watchin' on us. I turned round sharp and a bloody briar caught hold of my cap and took it orf. We went down this ol' cow walk and Ruff says: "Where's yur bloody cap?" I said: "I've lorst it." "One of the worst things you can ever do, lose anything," he said, "they'll find you if you lose anything; you might as well send them a postcard saying you've been." So we went creeping back, when all at once I sees this bloody cap. I says to 'im: "There he stands," it looked just like a man standin' there, but it was my cap hangin' from the briar. So I quickly went an' got the buckin'[3] ol' thing down, and he didn't swear at me again.'

But as well as poaching with Ruff, Arthur also poached with others, especially when he went netting partridges – 'partridge trundlin''. It involved pulling a large net, between thirty and fifty yards across, over fields where partridges skulked at night. On feeling the net over them, the birds would try to fly, and whole coveys would get tangled up. 'When we went trundlin' we first went and 'ad a look a couple of days before we were agoin'. One day we see a bit of clover and we thought, cooor'd that will be a nice place; the partridges will set on here tonight. Because of that we went that night; we got the ol' trundle net orf, and started goin' mate, an' do you know, the ol' keepers had been an' stuck briars all about. We got caught up in them and it took us two hours to get the net orf.'

He also went poaching on his own or with a dog, and he even

[3] A word often used by old country men, instead of actually swearing.

managed to snare pheasants and pike. When the pike were basking in the sunlight in a brook or pond, it was possible to use a pole on which a length of copper wire was fitted as a snare. Carefully the wire was drawn up over the fish's tail and along its body until it was just behind the gills. If it was yanked upwards the wire slipped behind the gills and the fish was hoisted out. Snaring pheasants was based on a similar principle: 'If you get a fairish dark night, not too dark, so that you can see what you're doin' and see where they're a sittin', you can snare 'em. Where we was they used to get in these ol' whitethorn bushes. I've seen five, or as many as seven in one of these ol' bushes. Well you creep along on your hands and knees an' set underneath 'em an' you have a stick with a snare on the end. You can put it up if they're arf asleep, an' you give 'em a little touch on the breast and they'll shove their head forward an' when you know you've got one over you give your ol' stick a pull an' it pulls tight round their neck and pulls 'em down. But mostly that would frighten the others and they would fly out; you would only get one or at the most two.'

The best dog he ever had working with him was a lurcher[4] that he bought from an old scissor grinder. The old man had said: 'I've got a good ol' dog, mate an' I only want five bob for it. I've got to get rid of it 'cause they're after me'. Apparently his dog, a cross between an Irish terrier and a greyhound, was too well trained and the old man had been preying on the local stocks of pheasants and hares at such a rate that the gamekeepers were keeping a special watch out for him. Despite suspecting that as soon as he released the dog for his own use, it would return to its original master, Arthur bought it, and tied it up for a week in the hope that it would settle down and work for him. 'Then I said to the missus: "We'll take ol' Grinder out tonight", I said, "an' let him goo, an' if he goos he goos". We took him and let 'im orf agin a field, an' away the ol' dog went and we were there about arf an hour. I said: "Grinder's gorn, we shan't see no more of 'im." We was makin' orf towards home, when over the top of a gate come Grinder, with a grert ol' hare. Then we 'ad 'im rabbiting; one of the best blinkin' rabbiting dogs mate anybody could ever wish to see. He would just pick 'em up mate, you wouldn't hear him, you wouldn't know where he was. He'd p'raps be gone three-quarters

[4] A dog usually obtained by crossing a greyhound, for speed, with a collie or a labrador for intelligence.

of an hour an' you'd never know where he was, but he'd know where he left you. An' I bet if he turned a hare up mate he was goin' to have it. I've seen an ol' hare two fields in front of him an' still he's kept a goin'.'

Because of his poaching, Arthur developed such a knowledge of game and the 'vermin' that preyed on it that he was offered a job as a gamekeeper; when instead of poaching pheasants he protected them from both human and four-legged predators. As his employer liked shooting as well as fox-hunting this proved difficult, for when fox numbers increased, he wanted them reduced for the sake of his pheasants, but at the same time he did not wish members of the hunt to find out; consequently he left it up to Arthur to get rid of the foxes quietly and unobtrusively. Unfortunately this was easier to order than to accomplish. When one night sixteen turkeys were killed and their headless corpses were left behind, Arthur could think of only one solution; he put a hen in a crate, and left it in the middle of a field, surrounded by hidden gin traps. By the next morning he had caught a fox, but in their eagerness to get at it, two of his own terriers also became caught in the traps; such a commotion of yelping and snarling followed that the news quickly spread and was not well received in hunting circles. His employer was annoyed again when crows and jackdaws started to visit the hen runs, and he asked Arthur once more to put a stop to it without too much fuss. Because of the request Arthur constructed a wire jackdaw trap, and at the end of the day there were thirty-six jackdaws and seven crows fluttering inside. His employer was not pleased yet again, and as Arthur was not sure how he was supposed to get rid of pests, without actually damaging them, he eventually left. But even after that, both at work and in his long retirement, his interest in animals and game continued, and much of his knowledge and many of his skills he passed on to his sons who continue to seek rabbits, hares, pigeons, and pheasants quite legitimately.

A few miles north of where Arthur lived and worked, the soil turns black, most of the trees disappear from the landscape, and the desolate flatness of the Fens stretches for as far as the eye can see. But there too men of his generation remember vividly how their lives were made easier by the creatures of the drains, 'dykes',[5]

[5] The word dyke is used to describe virtually any water course between two banks, from ditches to quite large drainage channels.

and fields around them. Pheasants, deer, and foxes were scarce, and so they went in search of fish, waterfowl, eels, and wild marsh hares. One elderly 'fen tiger', Bill, still has nets, traps, and ancient implements hanging in his garden shed, but they are now rarely used as necessity has gone. He lives comfortably on his pension and from his seven-acre plot; his 'garden'. What he grows in excess he sells, and he has no need to go out to the marshes and waterways to provide a decent living, as did his ancestors; yet whenever he talks of his childhood he pulls his cap down over his eyes and remembers some of the enjoyment that accompanied hardship.

His father was a ferryman, living in a parish house and working a rowing boat as the village ferry, which was the only way of getting many of the landworkers over the river to the farms beyond. When time permitted, his uncles, as well as his father would go wildfowling and fishing to get extra money, and one of their favourite winter pastimes was netting green plovers.[6] They went after the plovers when the washes were in flood and they took with them a wooden frame, some twenty yards long and ten feet wide, which was floated on the water. The frame was covered with wire mesh which was hidden by grass cuttings, so that the raft looked like a small island. It was floated and anchored close to a few tame birds that had been taken as chicks and reared through the summer, and they were tethered to clumps of grass, or small islets, to act as decoys. When wild plovers landed on the raft a string was pulled which sent a net over them, shooting them into the water. The plover men, who were usually 'hid in a holt', a clump of willows over the bank, would then rush out in their thigh boots to get the plovers before they could escape from the net. They would get about sixpence for each bird, and could catch up to twenty at a time. Bill did not like eating them, however, 'for they tasted very wormy, like'. The practice of netting plovers died out between the two World Wars.

His father also went fishing, not with a rod and line, but with a net about forty yards long. It took five men and a boat to use the net properly. A stop net was put 'up the dyke', and then the long net was put across the river and pulled along, with three men pulling two ropes on one bank, and a boat and another rope

[6] Lapwings or peewits.

pulling man on the far side to keep the net open. The fish were caught in a bosom net, which was like a large keep net in the middle of the long net; it was called a bosom net because when fishing was in progress it looked like an elongated nipple on a large female breast. They normally caught roach, bream, and pike, and could land up to a hundredweight each time.

In July 1907, there was a stir when they landed only one fish, but that by itself weighed well over a hundredweight; it was an eight-and-a-half-foot-long sturgeon weighing 294 pounds. A photographer travelled five miles in a horse and cart to get a record of the catch and of the men; the pictures were taken in a nearby 'gig house',[7] with the fish laid out on the horse's manger. Although by law the monarch was, and still is, supposed to have any landed sturgeon, the King did not receive it, for it was sent to Billingsgate fish market where it was sold for five pounds. Later Bill's father landed a 'porpoise pig' (a porpoise), which he shot with a rifle. 'It was a big'n. I know, 'cause I had to dig the bloody great hole to bury it. It was such a hot summer that it soon started to stink.'

Some local men also used nets for purposes other than fishing. They would find the gateways through which hares usually fled from the fields when disturbed, and they would suspend a net between the gateposts. The hares would then be put up by dogs, and would run straight into the nets. Others also used them for 'trundlin' ', but in the dampness of the Fens, partridges were not common, and larks were the main catch.

As a boy Bill also contributed to the family income by catching sparrows for local farmers. 'Me an' another ol' boy would go round the stacks with a clap net[8] after sparrows, and we got a ha'penny for each bird. One day me mate decided to hang on to 'em and said to the farmer when we went for our money: "We'll throw them out", and he threw them behind some bushes. After we got outside and the door was shut we picked 'em up again for the next night. But he eventually tumbled to it, and afterwards he took a leg off each bird he paid for'. With the clap net they also went along the hedgerows after dark and caught sparrows, blackbirds, 'and ol' mavis's' (thrushes), and the breasts of the birds would end up in crusty pies.

[7] A gig was a light, two-wheeled, one-horse carriage. Both the horse and the gig were often housed in the 'gig house'.
[8] A clap net was a net held upright and aloft on poles.

Later on, when Bill left home and went to work in the wet Fen fields he earned extra money by catching eels in wicker 'hives', woven out of willow.[9] He could make three hives a day, but he never used as many as one of his uncles, who would set up to a hundred at a time. He normally caught six or seven pounds of eels in each trap, although on a few occasions they weighed as much as a stone. He used to skin them himself and he sold them at 8d per pound. The biggest one he ever caught weighed three and a half pounds. He also used his skill with his hands to make five-bar-gates; these too he would sell for extra money at twelve shillings each.

In addition to these activities he went out frequently with his shotgun, made from a converted rifle, to try and shoot duck for dinner. If he saw an otter he would shoot that too, for in the twenties he could get five pounds for every otter skin. Otters were quite common in the Fens at that time, and one day as a friend of his rowed to the bank an otter ran across the front of the boat and leapt into the water; in his eagerness to shoot he nearly shot through the bottom of his craft.

Now life in the Fens is easier, yet the traditions for fishing and fowling are still very strong, and they are carried on by ordinary fenmen using conventional guns and ordinary rods and lines. In other areas, too, the habits and customs of the past continue to be very much alive and involve creatures from red deer and mountain game, to salmon and trout in freshwater and the sea. Some people still pay much money for their sport, and others gain theirs for nothing or just for the risk of getting caught; but in most cases with affluence and the breakdown of social barriers, field sports continue to flourish among new generations of participants from a variety of backgrounds.

The wide appeal of field sports can best be seen at an annual Game Fair, which is organised by the Country Landowners' Association, and held each summer in the grounds of a stately home, or country house. There, lords, ladies and upper crust sportsmen who like 'good sporting shots', rub shoulders with cowmen, common law wives, and men who would shoot virtually anything with feathers or a tail. Although it has an ancient sounding name, the Fair was not started until 1958, when it was established to

[9] Another trap was also used in the Fens, a 'grig', again made of willow, thin in the middle and wide at the ends.

encourage land owners and farmers to bring the management of game birds into their farming systems, to enable them to get recreation, or profit, as a by-product of their work. Then, the Fair attracted 8,500 visitors and fifty-eight trade stands and exhibitions; by 1974 when it was held in the grounds of a large country estate in southern England, it attracted over 63,000 people, and in excess of 300 stands of various kinds for its two days; by then it had also grown to cover all blood sports, as well as many aspects of wildlife conservation, not directly related to hunting, shooting, and fishing.

Even as I drove towards the Fair it was possible to see the great social mix, for as the traffic jams started seven miles out, there were Bentleys with well groomed occupants, and drivers sporting gloves, sun glasses and fat cigars, and there were also clapped-out Fords and Austins filled with people who looked as if they had arrived straight from some muddy farmyard. But the large majority of people were in ordinary cars, wearing ordinary clothes, who in normal circumstances could have been going anywhere and would have attracted no attention. Once safely arrived and mingling with the large crowd among the stands, demonstrations, the fishing, the falconry, the pheasant breeding, and the run containing two Great Bustards, the extremes of class, bearing and way of life were more marked, for there were people with baggy tweeds, plus fours, and superfine accents, and there were others with dirty jackets, wellington boots, and who spoke and laughed with the regional ring of deep country.

Language and laughter formed a distinct line of demarcation, for there were many visitors who described everything as being 'awfully', 'frightfully', or 'super', and even the names of their children showed their social background. 'Oh Rupert, poppet where are you?' 'Come here, Julius', and 'Jason' seemed popular with both boys and well-bred dogs. One man of obvious good breeding greeted another like a long lost friend: 'Oh John, awfully lovely to see you', he bellowed with an accent and at a volume that suggested he was an Old Etonian stockbroker with an extra large larynx.

In the Country Landowners' refreshment tent there were a large number of ordinary farmers seeking liquid and more substantial refreshment, but there were also many 'awfully', 'frightfully', 'super' people, who somehow seemed to drift together. There were men with red faces, sharp features, and round patches of whiskers on their upper cheeks, one wore a monocle, and several looked like gin-soaked ex-military men with large country estates. There too, eating at tables, or out of hampers, were 'frightfully nice' upper class young men and monied young ladies; the young men were self-conscious as they sipped their half pints of lemonade shandy and ate their salmon sandwiches, and when they laughed they seemed to hang open their bottom jaws to whinny politely. Some of the young ladies were immaculate; straight from the beauty parlour or from the pages of *Vogue* or *Vanity Fair,* with their faces, characters, and vital statistics hidden beneath hair lacquer, cosmetics, and expensive fashions. Indeed, looking at some they seemed so sleek and genteel that I wondered how they managed to perform the normal and essential functions of the body, without losing their dignity. And how did such creatures breed? Surely not in the same coarse way as rabbits, ferrets, or even pedigree gun dogs; for they seemed sheltered from such unseemly things, pure, and untouched by human hand; perhaps, I thought, they reproduced by budding, or even with the help of a star in the East.

At the other end of the scale there were also voices and manners to match appearances. There were scruffily dressed couples dragging with them sweet stickied children, and at the public refreshment tents there were men swilling beer, eating cheese and onion crisps, and setting off bouts of raucous laughter with anecdotes and dirty stories. 'Bloody' this and 'bloody' that were littered lavishly in every sentence, together with a liberal sprinkling of other common words, used to give inaccurate and often obscene description to every individual, incident, and circumstance, and they were all having a 'bloody good time'. Just as the salmon sandwiches and salads were popular in some circles, so were the hot dogs and hamburgers in others, and one stall holder counted out £83 as she emptied her till.

But, regardless of background and behaviour, to all who take their sport seriously, sporting language is most important, and snatches of the approved jargon could be picked up from assorted conversations, in accents from both the public school, and the public bar. For in 'sport' the right words have to be used, and just as in cricket and football there are terms such as 'maiden over', 'boundary', and 'the back four', for field sports at the Game Fair the talk was of 'a right and left', 'a brace of foxes', 'a flight of duck', and 'a couple of hounds', and of course no mention was heard of hounds barking or wagging their tails; they 'speak' and 'wave their sterns'. The correct vocabulary is particularly important when referring to deer, for with red deer the talk is of stags, hinds, and calves,[10] with fallow there are bucks, does, and fawns, while roe are bucks, does, and kids. Even deer footprints are called 'slot marks', and to use the wrong word, or to lapse only for a moment, is thought to betray either great ignorance or only an assumed and superficial interest.

Strangely, the language of sport also extends to the droppings of some of the sporting animals, and it is an odd fact, that in the English language there is no one polite word to describe the faeces of man, beast, and bird; for those generally used are either excessively prudish, or else thought to be extremely rude, and there is nothing in between. Consequently to the sportsman, the fox deposits 'scats', otters drop 'spraints', and deer leave 'fewmets'. One old man informed me: 'I call it all shit, and everybody knows what I'm talking about.'

The many displays and stands showed the wide cross section of people and interests. There were top quality guns on view at £7,000 each, and cheap guns from Spain to suit all but the emptiest of pockets. Information was available on grouse and the flying of hawks, as well as on snares, killing rats, and 'electronic ferrets'. Fine art and literature could be viewed and purchased, as well as souvenirs, tea cloths, and assorted cheap-jack junk. There were competitions for shooting clay pigeons, gun dog control, and casting dry flies, and there were also plenty of entrants for the 'World Pigeon Plucking Contest'. There was even one stand designed to bring together two of the warring factions of the country sports fraternity; those who hunt foxes, and those who shoot pheasants, and the aim of the 'Hunting and Shooting' stand was to convince both sides that foxes can co-exist with gamebirds. When some Dorset gamekeepers went in to view the display of photographs and statistics they were met by an upright, military-sounding gentleman who greeted them with: 'Come on in; this is to show you how to look after foxes.' 'We look after they buggers alright', one of them replied, as he put his newly purchased snares into his pocket.

10 The names for the males, females and young of the red deer.

The sheer numbers at the Fair and all the different sports and pastimes represented, demonstrated the real interest there seems to be for many people in field sports, with or without blood. But it also demonstrated something more; for to some people and organizations, the taking of rabbits, fish, and wild game has gone beyond necessity, sport, and genuine enjoyment; what they seem to be creating is a high turnover, mass production, impersonal killing industry, in which the participants, the wild creatures, the guns, horses, and hounds, are simply seen as pieces of machinery or replaceable spare parts.

Chapter Two

To Hunt a Fox

The animal most people associate with blood sports is the fox; a creature that is both hunted, and hunts. For many years it has been pursued and persecuted by country people, and when Jim worked on the land his one big disappointment was that foxes were so few; to him the only good fox was a dead one, and he would have welcomed the opportunity of increasing the number of 'good foxes'. But although he spoke of them disparagingly he also told tales of their cunning and skill, and it seemed that secretly he held their independence and expertise in high regard. His attitude was typical of those who worked on the land, or who kept poultry at the bottom of their gardens; it was a view of the fox that had been handed down through many generations, and which time did not change. Indeed the war waged against foxes was so fierce at one time that, if their pursuit had not developed into a booming sport in the eighteenth century, it is likely that fox would have become extinct many years ago in most parts of the British Isles. As a result the only wild foxes free today would have been confined to a few remote and mountainous areas in Scotland and Wales. Even so, their numbers were reduced to such a level that hunts had to carefully preserve their quarry, and a flourishing trade in live foxes developed, including many animals imported from the continent.

Fox hunting as an organized sport usually involves the following of foxes by huntsmen on horseback, using a pack of hounds; at the present time there are 206 such packs in England, Scotland, and Wales, making a total of over 8,000 working hounds. As with all sports which depend on scent and which pit animal against animal, it is the subject of a great deal of misrepresentation, both from opponents who insist that the fox is a harmless creature, wrongly accused and callously abused, and by some hunters who suggest that the fox actually enjoys being hunted.

Part of the problem in getting a realistic view of foxes and their place in the countryside and country life stems from the fact that although they have been hunted for many years, and they are now common in most areas of both town and country, a surprisingly small amount is known about their habits and way of life. The situation is made worse by the fact that many of our attitudes towards them are governed by impressions gained as children, for the fox has become almost a folk-hero, and features in story and picture books in many homes and most primary schools. Although foxes are depicted as being regular farmyard thieves, stealing hens, ducks, and geese, they are also shown as intelligent, clever, and resourceful animals, with almost human feelings and powers of reasoning. Their physical beauty also helps to hide their natural instincts and their liking for fresh raw meat covered with feathers or fur. When a fox is shown hunting, it is the beauty of movement that attracts; the purpose of its stealth and artistry are ignored, as are the tearing jaws, breaking bones, and the conclusion of violent death. The illustrations and photographs that are most commonly seen are of the pointed ears and nose testing the air for scent and sound, the deep brown eyes with their cat-like elliptical pupils, quizzical, watchful, and enquiring, and the long flowing brush. All combine to give the impression of comparative harmlessness, domesticity, and peace. Pictures too, of cubs playing at the entrance of their earth, or romping with their mother in apparent harmonious play, add to an image which does not seem to warrant persecution.

I have had a number of pet foxes, all have been delightful creatures, but it is unfortunately true that even captive foxes never completely lose their wildness, or the innate urge to kill,[1] and wild foxes living in the countryside can do a great deal of damage in farmyards and along hedgerows, if their numbers get too high. Those people who retain the picture-book image of the fox as a fun loving, harmless creature usually do so through ignorance, self-deception or, for political, social, or intellectual reasons, they choose to be dishonest; they are clearly unaware, or they decide to ignore, the evidence of fox damage that can be obtained from reliable sources in most rural communities where poultry or sheep are kept. If they were to visit a fox's earth in the spring or early summer, they would see numerous carcasses scattered about the entrances; ample practical proof of the resident's diet. At one time it was even

[1] **My current vixen, Rusty, is no exception, and has killed a number of hens, several rats, blackbirds, and a half grown hedgehog.**

the habit of some countrymen to make regular visit to earths in their parish or on the farm where they worked, to collect the bodies that had been freshly killed but not yet eaten; by so doing they could sometimes enjoy eating pheasant lawfully, but out of season, and they also found domestic fowl, headless, and sometimes bruised, but which were perfectly fit to eat.

Even with only an elementary knowledge of foxes it is possible to see the delicacies on a fox's menu, and so it is surprising that some seemingly responsible organizations and people, who claim to be interested in animal welfare, continue to show the fox as an animal that does little harm. One survey stated that the majority of farmers were not troubled by foxes, implying that fox damage was grossly exaggerated or just a figment of fox hunters' imaginations; but of course if arable farmers were asked from some of our large hedgeless cereal lands, this would be the case, for although foxes have a very varied diet, they do not yet consume vast quantities of oats, barley, and wheat.

Foxes eat whatever is readily available to them, and in eating rats, mice, and even stray cats, they can do some good.[2] They eat other things too; during harvest they consume large numbers of black beetles, and beetle wings and blackberry pips appear in the fox droppings that are deposited on heaps of bales after the corn has been combined. From the number of droppings on bales, foxes seem to enjoy climbing, although I have only seen them in trees. At the other end of my parish however, the Trinity Foot Beagles are kennelled, and the former kennelman has seen a vixen and her cubs playing on bales of hay in broad daylight. Although the hounds are immediately behind the house, and the baying of beagles can be heard all over the parish at feeding time when the wind is right, each year a vixen has her cubs in an earth at the bottom of the kennel's garden. Recently another vixen had her litter in a small, isolated graveyard in front of the house, and so the hounds had foxes on two sides of them.

The garden foxes are surrounded by rabbits, but they all appear to live together in harmony, and when the cubs are half grown they often walk up the garden and through the main gate with

[2] Some 'experts' deny that foxes eat cats. This year, 1976, I have seen the carcass of a large black cat outside the entrance of an earth on the farm where three cubs were successfully reared. It could have been killed, or the body could have been scavenged, but there is no doubt that the foxes ate it.

their mother, and the beagles ignore them completely. When the large field opposite had been sown with pink flowering trefoil, and the crop had been cut and baled for hay, the kennelman watched the family of foxes from his bedroom window as they played around the bales in late afternoon. They would run, climb, and leap on them, trying to catch butterflies with their paws. He even saw one of the cubs stalking beetles in the grass verge right next to the road, occasionally pouncing, and then chewing its victim; it was so intent on its sport that it seemed oblivious of the traffic rushing past, and the car drivers were completely unaware of its presence.

On an adjoining field, as a farmworker ploughed stubble, a fox actually started to follow the plough. It would follow the tractor half way across the field catching mice, rats, and beetles that had been disturbed, and then it would return to some rough grass by a ditch and wait for the tractor to return. While cultivating another field close by, a tractor driver had a surprise when he drove right over a resting fox and rolled it over several times with his spring-tined-harrows. Apparently undamaged, the fox slowly stumbled off, it was not sick or injured, but bloated, for a nearby farmer had lost fifteen turkeys the night before; fourteen had been left dead and uneaten, and the fox had gorged itself on the other.

It is this last habit of killing domestic poultry, as well as game birds, that makes the fox such a persecuted animal; for although foxes undoubtedly do much good, they also cause much damage to stocks of pheasants, farm hens, and lambs, and their numbers have to be controlled if possible. It is an odd fact that fox numbers now appear to be higher than for many years, and their increase seems to date back to the early Fifties and the onset of myxomatosis[8] which killed off most of the rabbit population. Because of the introduction and spread of 'mexy', many people forecast the end of the fox, as an important item of food was suddenly removed from its diet and it was expected that many foxes would starve, as did many buzzards that could not find any alternative sources of food. Instead, fox numbers have increased and one of the most feasible explanations is that myxomatosis caused a rapid decline in the amount of snaring and trapping, and it is also coincided with the banning of the gin trap; for it seems likely that gin traps and rabbit

[8] Pronounced 'mexomatosis' in Cambridgeshire.

catchers were responsible for the death of many foxes. This easing of pressure, and also the fox's varied diet and adaptability, has meant that it has flourished. It has also come to terms with agricultural change as well as with the growing encroachment of land by semi-detached suburbia; and now with the availability of agricultural land-drainage pipes and suburban gardens, the fox can live, breed, and find refuge where it is least expected.

Apologists for the fox say that mass slaughter takes place only when the animal has been driven into a panic by the flapping wings of frightened birds in an enclosed space. Again this does not appear to be borne out by facts; gamekeepers have found pheasants taken from their nests and killed for no apparent reason, and early one morning there was such a disturbance in our deep litter shed that the door burst open and several hens flew out. I woke up because of the commotion to see a fox tearing through the horse-radish, thoroughly enjoying itself, and later we found sixteen dead hens scattered over a large area.

Because of examples like this there is no doubt that foxes have to be controlled; the problem is how to keep numbers down to a reasonable level without causing undue suffering and without causing them to become too scarce. Today various methods are used; all are unpleasant, yet all are described as 'humane' by those who use them and by many of those who are opposed to hunting. One day a few months ago when Father went to feed some pullets that were on 'the point of lay', he found that a hole had been scraped underneath the hen house door and inside twenty-eight birds were scattered about dead; some headless, and others with broken necks. A few nights later I was disturbed by hens in the deep litter crying out and two eyes reflected back through the window of the shed when I shone my torch. The fox jumped up and scrambled through the already barred window, and inside another twenty-nine hens were dead. Most of the fifty-seven birds killed were in a good enough condition to pluck and eat, and we gave many of them away to friends, but it meant a significant loss in eggs and income, that neither Father, nor brother John could afford. Consequently they decided that the fox had to be killed; a decision taken with reluctance, for no fox had been killed on the farm before, but they felt that they had no other alternative. Previously both sheds were thought to have been fox proof, and it is a strange fact that many of those who blame fox damage on the farmers themselves for not keeping their fowl shut up, are often the same ones who protest bitterly about methods of factory farming and the scarcity of free range eggs.

John stayed up several nights with his rifle and shotgun, but in the darkness it was impossible for him to see the fox properly as it sniffed around the buildings, and so Father decided to break the law; he found an old gin trap and set it behind the door under which the fox had burrowed. The next morning the trap had claimed a victim, a rat, which Tinker enthusiastically shook and killed. At 2.30 am the following night I again stumbled out of bed to the cries of a hen in distress. Out of the darkness John appeared with his gun; he had heard the fox sniffing about for an hour, but with no moon he had not seen it. The sound of a rattling chain came from the hen house and we immediately thought that the fox must be in the gin trap. I carefully opened the door, and there sitting quietly was the victim, our house cat Tigger, with one of her front paws held in the steel jaws of the trap. She let me release her without much fuss; no bones were broken, although she limped slightly, and the trap was put away, not to be used again. On shining a light over towards the spinney, the fox's eyes shone brightly back as it sat looking at us, but the range and the darkness made it impossible to shoot, and it got away once more.

The only other alternative seemed to be to set a snare; again a method of fox control very much disliked; but they had no other choice. A wire snare was purchased and set on a fox path up to the deep litter shed. Several foxless nights followed and then early one Saturday morning John woke me at first light, shouting up to my bedroom window, asking me to get him the rifle, as a vixen was in the snare. She was in excellent condition with a sleek, rich chestnut coat, but no white tip to her tail, and she sat looking at us, with that picture-book expression that destroys anger and makes them seem harmless. As we went closer she struggled and jumped about in fear, but the snare held her tightly around the neck. Her movements were so violent and frenzied that John missed with his first shot and only wounded her with the second, and it took one more bullet to kill her. It was a sad end. She weighed ten pounds.

Three nights later another fox was in the snare by 11.30 in the evening. It was a big dog fox and it was terrified; a heavy drizzle was falling, and from the flattened ground around the 'wire', and the animal's mud plastered coat, it was clear that it had been pulling and jumping in a frenzied struggle to break free for some time. It was a less attractive fox than the vixen, larger, plainer, and darker, again with no white tip to its tail, and as we got nearer, and Father loomed out of the darkness in his wellington boots and pyjamas, the frightened animal struggled more furiously. John shot it in the forehead, but for some reason it did not die, it just crouched down looking at us, its soft brown eyes and its fearful expression filling me with an irrational guilt. He shot it again and it rolled over on its side twitching violently. An eye popped out of its socket horrifically and John pushed it back in place with his boot, and its upturned ear gradually filled with oozing blood that finally overflowed and trickled into the mud. The snare had only just held and with a few more minutes of struggle the fox would have broken free; it weighed seventeen pounds[4] and had a hairless nick in its brush about one and a half inches long.

It is strange that although most people refer to every large fox they see as 'a big old dog fox', it is virtually impossible to tell the sex of a single fox as it goes about its daily business. Yet many still insist that they can tell the difference and even huntsmen will claim to have hunted 'a fine dog fox'. One upper-class Master of hounds was annoyed by a village roadman during one hunt when the hounds had run out of scent, for the old man, who had been watching the proceedings while leaning on his broom, suddenly shouted: 'A dog fox over there. A dog fox over there', and he pointed away from the hounds. The Master evidently considered that a non-hunting roadman was incapable of sexing foxes and he asked with disdain: 'How do you know it's a dog fox?'

'Because it jumped the gate and I heard its balls rattle', came the instant reply.

There is no doubt that snaring foxes is unpleasant; but it is the simplest and most practical way of catching them. If a badger or a domestic cat is caught, it is possible to put a forked piece of wood or a pitchfork over its neck to hold it down and prevent bites while the wire is taken off. Another type of snare is also used by some

[4] The average weight of a vixen is about twelve pounds, while that of a dog is about fourteen pounds. It is not uncommon for dog foxes to go over twenty pounds.

gamekeepers, which, when the animal pulls, the wire tightens and a self-locking device prevents it slackening off when the animal ceases to struggle. The animal held is usually dead, strangled, by the time the snare is inspected, and it is odd that even some animal welfare organizations claim that these snares are 'humane'. Yet simply because a death is not seen it does not become 'humane', and in my view these snares are the cruellest instruments of 'control' currently available, crueller even than gin traps. If the snares are set badly, animals such as deer, dogs, and badgers, as well as foxes can get their legs caught in them, and foxes and badgers can easily be held around the waist or hips, and each time the animal pulls, the wire is drawn tighter, and the victim can almost be cut in two while still alive. If badgers are caught there is rarely any chance of release, and the sooner this type of snare is made illegal the better.

It is a peculiar fact that the other method of control in which the actual death is not seen, is also described as 'humane' and gassing is advocated by many of those who object to other methods of killing foxes. Yet how an animal with a highly developed sense of smell and which is terrified when trapped, can be said to have a humane end when gassed and all its routes of escape are sealed up is beyond my comprehension. To make matters worse there is plenty of evidence from those who use gas of its inhumanity; 'right kerfuffles' are sometimes heard underground as the foxes try to dig themselves out as the gas advances and gets stronger, and foxes that have managed to dig themselves free have been found dead on the surface in conditions that suggest that their end was far from pleasant. It is also quite easy to mistake a badger's sett for an earth, especially when foxes have been using it as a temporary shelter, and so there is always the additional danger that badgers could be gassed by accident, or design, by someone claiming to be after foxes.

Another method frequently advocated by those opposed to hunting, is shooting, and some pompously urge the use of 'expert shots'. I have seen foxes shot at by 'expert shots', and many are missed or wounded, with the result that death is often slow and painful. Shooting people are rather like fishermen in the stories they tell, for they only seem to remember the good days. Most will claim to have shot foxes, but they rarely say how many cartridges they used for each fox, and how many escaped wounded and full of lead. It seems to me that far fewer than 50 per cent of the foxes shot at are killed cleanly with one cartridge. To be reasonably certain of killing a fox with a twelve-bore shotgun it needs to be within twenty yards, and of course the very nature of the fox makes such an ideal situation uncommon; even shooting with a rifle becomes a matter of chance, because of movement, or the slight deflection of the bullet caused by a twig or other obstruction. One method of shooting is to shine a powerful torch down an earth when the cubs are about the size of small cats; they are said to be drawn out to the light by their enquiring natures, and they can be shot quite easily; but that too is not very practical or safe, and I dislike the idea of shooting cubs. Large numbers of foxes are shot each year, but to suggest that their end is humane is to dwell in the world of fantasy and wishful thinking.

Hunting is the other commonly used method of trying to kill foxes, and although field sports objectors claim that the number of foxes killed by hunts is insignificant, in fact it is estimated that between 15,000 and 18,000 foxes are killed in a normal season by the various hunts, and that the overall number of foxes killed each year is between fifty and sixty thousand, although many people think that this is a very conservative estimate.[5]

Although I have always been close to foxes, and familiar with the various methods used to control them on the farms in the neighbourhood, the one exception has been hunting, and in order to attend a hunt, and to see it on horseback, I learnt to ride. Previously, as a small boy, I had only ridden an old grey donkey as he had walked around the farmyard and garden, and so getting on a horse was a new experience, and far more difficult than I had expected. After my first lesson, lasting only an hour, of walking, and briefly trotting on a lethargic horse called Jason, my legs and backside were stiff and sore; on trotting, instead of rising gracefully out of the saddle, I bounced rapidly every time a hoof hit the ground. Over the next few lessons I did everything wrong; I put my wrong foot in the stirrup when trying to mount, which if I had continued would have meant sitting on the horse backwards; I put my correct foot in the stirrup but forgot to tighten the girth, so that when I went to mount, both the saddle and I

[5] Another very conservative estimate concerns the overall fox population for the United Kingdom; a minimum figure is thought to be in the region of 200,000.

descended rapidly, and once, with Jason out of control and cantering back to his stable I baled out when faced with the choice of either jumping off or being thrown.

My first actual fall was not from the horse but from my bike. For dressed in smart new riding boots and hat purchased from Moss Bros and clutching a crop, I somehow managed to ride into the verge and headlong to the ground, in full view of the stables and my riding teacher.

By the time I could manage an undignified rising trot, and could hang on grimly for a canter, a neighbour offered me the use of his horse Remo. For some reason I had imagined that horses were friendly and amenable, but Remo soon taught me differently. In fact he soon showed me that the most important rule in riding is, 'first catch your horse', which in a two acre paddock of heavy clay is not easy. Several times I lured him with lumps of sugar, but then he developed a method of taking the sugar and retreating rapidly. After that it was a waste of time trying to catch him, and the only thing that I could do was phone Linda, a girl at the other end of the village. With no trouble at all she would make as if to feed him and catch him easily. Yet when I tried the same ruse Remo would gallop away. One day when I was discussing horses with an old farm worker he told me not to worry, because even in the old days some of the regularly worked farm horses had their awkward moments. He told of one mare who, when she could not be caught, the horsekeeper had to go home and put on his collar and tie. The horse would then go right up to him, thinking it was Sunday and her day off.

Once I fell off at speed and thought that my hip had broken. Fortunately everything was still intact, although for several nights it took me a long time to get from the sitting to the lying position in bed. After that Remo developed the habit of suddenly dropping his head and raising his haunches, simply to throw me off, but each time my Moss Bros headgear saved me from damage.

Eventually I learned to stay on when trotting and galloping, and even when Remo shied at the approach of gypsies and dustcarts, or at the appearance of a fresh piece of litter or at a newly hung gate. I had discovered that far from being easy, horse riding was an extremely difficult skill to master, and that it was also a very pleasant way of seeing the countryside. I was still far from being an expert and any large jump would have caused disaster, but nevertheless I decided that with luck I could keep on long enough to follow the local hunt.

The day of the fox hunt dawned mild but overcast, I was to go out with the local hunt; a hunt considered by those who ride with it to be a 'farmers' hunt', a description used to suggest that anybody can ride, and that hunting has nothing to do with class, privilege, or money. The impression gained by those who are stopped in their cars by wandering horses and wayward hounds is different, however: 'Bloody snobs, do they need all the road?' 'Who do they think they are?' 'Tally-ho off the blinking road', and 'Jorrocks to you too', are the normal reactions. Despite this a large number of ordinary country people continue to accept hunting and huntsmen as part of the normal rustic scene, and they enjoy the meet held once or twice each year in their particular parish, and many follow the progress of the hunt in their cars.

On arriving at the stables I was disappointed to find that Jason had been saddled for me; he looked in superb condition, black, 14.3 hands high,[6] with a red tail bandage and his mane braided, but then I remembered his earlier lethargy, and assumed that after the first five minutes I would not see the hounds again as the horse would be exhausted. I need not have worried, for once there, and after seeing other horses and hearing the hounds, Jason's mood changed; his eyes brightened, his ears pricked, and his stride became eager.

The hunt was to take place around a small village in a large island of land hemmed in by two main roads. It is an attractive part of gently undulating clayland, with mixed corn and grass and a large number of woods and spinneys which make a welcome change from the fen lands to the north and the arable land to the east, where many hedges and trees have been sacrificed to the demanding God of agricultural efficiency. Just outside the village horse-boxes were parked in a line opposite an old mill that had been converted into a house, and a man with grey hair and a camera stood in the gateway taking photographs. I walked Jason past the horses and their transport and along the High Street where the meet had attracted riders, hounds, and onlookers. Up on Jason's back, with hat, boots, and crop, I felt definite feelings

[6] A 'hand' is equal to four inches. A horse's height is measured to the shoulder.

of arrogance and self-satisfaction, gained through the additional height, the horse's power, and the fact that most pedestrians wisely seem to distrust horses. My feelings were aided by the fact that I had progressed from jeans to my mother's 'ski' trousers (normally used for gardening), and with my donkey jacket, and my Moss Bros accoutrements, I felt the part, even if I did not look it.

The stirrup cup was being taken to the riders, drinks on a silver tray, and I took a large sherry; my feelings of superiority continued until it was pointed out to me that Jason's tail bandage was meant only for the journey in the trailer. The hounds, and the pink-coated huntsman and 'whippers-in', seemed eager to get away as horsemen and spectators milled around. There were 'good mornings', smiles and laughter, 'frightfullies', 'awfullies', and 'supers'; there were trim girls in black coats on smart horses, men of all shapes and sizes wearing bowlers, a well-padded auctioneer with a moustache and a top hat, a university lecturer, far from his books on German history and philosophy, an eighty-two-year-old retired butcher on his long-serving horse, and a working farmer with a sports jacket and a broad accent. In addition, as it was holiday time, there were several children on ponies, and the grey van of the terrier man was also there, with two terriers shut in a secure wooden box, several spades, and a set of chimney rods to push any hiding foxes out of drains.

The huntsman blew his horn and moved onto the road, and with the hounds and whippers-in close behind he made off at a trot towards the centre of the village. The lady Master in her black coat followed, and putting the strap of my hat under my chin, to make it secure, I moved off with the rest of the field. As the horses clattered down the road, excited children, some still wearing pyjamas, peered out of windows and doors, frosted and snow-covered in Christmas decoration. We rode past new houses and old cottages, clean brick and pebble-dash, to a junction where we veered left along a minor road which ran by the side of a sluggish stream. Kerb stones gave way to grass verge and the feeling of the old village replaced the 'mod cons' and pretension of the new; the houses were larger, with wooden beams, reed-thatched roofs and whitewashed walls. At one smaller cottage a thatcher was pegging new straw onto old, pausing on his ladder to watch us pass the church, with its square tower of flints and clunch; the scene was saturated with tradition and antiquity.

By the time we moved away from the road and through a farmyard, Jason had already pushed his way almost to the front; it was clear that he was so eager to be off that the reins were going to provide a very inefficient braking system. One hound went to sniff some bales in a covered barn and a cat took refuge high above. The huntsman took the hounds along a narrow hedgerow which they worked with their noses down and their 'sterns waving', and as we followed I fought with Jason to prevent him from overtaking the Master. Such a situation is considered to be very infra dig and she cast several glances of surprise in my direction but said nothing. I eventually beat him, by periodically steering him towards the hedge so that he had to stop, or occasionally by taking him around in a circle and tucking in behind another horse, so that when that stopped, Jason had to follow suit. No fox was found in the hedge and the hounds were taken into a wood while the riders stopped and waited; one young hound rushed out in full cry, chasing a rabbit, but its quarry easily evaded capture and the other hounds found nothing.

After a lengthy and fruitless search the pack was brought out and we cantered to a large grass field, jumping a small fence on the way; my hat went over my eyes, but the strap held it on. No sooner had we started than we stopped; Jason was restless to keep going, but he had to be content with quietly walking about like the other horses and riders. It was dull, cold, and boring. Somewhere, apparently, the terrier man was digging to bolt a fox from an earth, but it was taking a long time. We moved off again at a gallop towards an open gate; Jason was frustrated and in top gear, and as the other horses slowed to go through the opening, he overtook them, out of control, and went between the opened gate and a litter of rusting farm implements straight for the barbed wire fence. He pulled up with his head over the wire and as we circled back I reprimanded him and gave him a sharp whack with the crop, to make him briefly more responsive. Again we waited, with the terrier man in view and digging. Suddenly there was a shout, the fox had gone, but nobody had seen it go, not even the hounds. We queued up to jump over a fence with oozing black mud on both sides, but the hounds made little noise and the fox had vanished. I was again up with the Master, and steered Jason into the hedge. We then turned back and queued up to jump out of the small field once more and waited in the large field where the terrier man was still digging. It seemed an odd sport.

Suddenly the hounds started up in full cry, and Jason seemed to boil. We were off again, another fox had been flushed from the hole and this time the hunt was really on; one large horse refused at the small fence, almost throwing its rider into the mire, but Jason jumped it with no hesitation and we were immediately galloping furiously. The sun came out as the late morning cloud melted away, catching the colours, the movement, and the sleek coats of the horses. The hounds streamed out along the edge of ploughland, still in full cry and we followed, well to the fore. We ran in a wide arc, through some farm buildings and out onto the road, to gallop along the verge, away from the village and past the mill; the grey haired man was still taking photographs and his daughter held a banner proclaiming 'Ban Hunting'; he obviously objected to the hunt being anywhere near his plot of twenty acres, with its small grassfields, cattle and sheep.

The hounds turned into a large field of winter wheat, running fast and steadily. Jason was going well, although the ground was very heavy, and he cleared several ditches easily and eagerly: some were narrow and shallow, and others were wide and cavernous. We followed a ditch onto stubble, still galloping hard. The sun was in my eyes but I could see that far from tiring, Jason was actually looking for the hounds. I was sweating, but having taken the advice of several old men who had dealt with military horses and ridden in earlier days – 'keep your knees in and your heels down' – I had experienced no difficulty in staying on; but still the hooves pounded, water squelched, mud flew, and the wind cut into and cooled my cheeks.

The pack disappeared into a large block of unharvested sweet corn; hares fled from the far side and ran off over grass, and one ran towards us until it stopped, looked, and doubled back in alarm. Way over on our right a fox was running directly over a ploughed field, disappearing into a ditch that cut the land in two. Aching thighs and legs were rested and some stretched their feet forwards as their horses steamed. The hounds picked up the scent again and appeared from the far end, crying out in full and enthusiastic pursuit. The chase started once more, where rain had turned tractor wheelings into waterways, and more mud flew into faces and onto coats. Jason began to slow, but he was still trying hard as the pack went back onto grass and we followed along a farm road. After jumping and climbing over sheep netting, topped with barbed wire, the hounds scrambled down a bank and over a steep-sided stream. It slowed them down, and as they climbed the far bank and jostled and bumped in their eagerness to get over more sheep wire their barking and baying reached a frustrated crescendo. One caught a front paw in the wire and howled chillingly with pain, as if suffering great agony and I imagined that its leg must be broken. The huntsman leapt from his horse to help but could do nothing as the leg was held so tightly; still the hound howled and the huntsman called for his wire cutters; the paw fell free, but the dog did not wait for inspection or sympathy, it was immediately off, without even a limp.

The hounds were hunting almost as one and the scent carried them in a straight and purposeful line, through a farm, over a road, and into a field of old pasture; it contained a large flock of sheep and old pollard elms with thick trunks and tall, upright, and slender branches that had remained uncut for many years. The sheep moved together in the far corner as the hounds clambered over the wire; the scent was much weaker for they loped across the grass with no great purpose. Despite the smell of sheep and tarmac the leading hounds quickly found where the fox had left the field, and as they began to 'speak' the other hounds ran to them with new urgency as they again moved onto arable. They ran in a straggling line along the narrow thread of scent and it was clear that the fox had started to run in a wide half circle, to take it back towards its starting point. The horses crossed the road and moved onto stubble to try and catch up with the hounds, but as the pack continued running we met a solid block of winter wheat with no rough headland, or ditch side, along which we could follow and so all the horses and riders had to turn back.

The tail-enders became the leaders, and in his eagerness to catch up, and with his second wind, Jason stumbled and almost fell in a hock-deep hole of slurry, nearly pitching me over his head and into the mud; but we both just recovered. By the time we could see the hounds again it was obvious where they were going; the fox had again made for sheep and had run straight across the grass paddocks of the old mill where the blood sports objector had his flock. As the hounds struggled over his fence, he ran towards them shouting angrily, taking more photographs. It was a bizarre sight; the fox being pursued by the hounds; the hounds being followed by horses and riders, and the riders being chased by an irate man with a camera; the sort of comedy scene that could only take place in Britain; the 'uneatable', the 'unspeakable', and the unthinkable, all engaged in a hectic ritual.

'I really am very sorry', the huntsman shouted to the land owner, more in annoyance than apology, as he stopped at the boundary fence.

'Yes, I'm sure you are', the landowner replied, more in sarcasm than honesty, as he glared back from his side of the wire.

All the riders were now completely separated from the hounds and we had to make a wide detour to take us out past the front of the mill again and along the road. There we could see the hounds running away over a large block of hedgeless arable, making towards woodland and another small village that almost grew from the side of a low brook valley, half hidden by trees. We turned back once more to get on to another minor road, passed the mill again for more photographs and a banner proclaiming 'Cruel People', and then it was a steady canter along grass verge to catch up with the pack. Over more ploughland the scent was weaker and the hounds 'feathered' out, searching for scent, their tails ('sterns'), and noses ('bows?') working vigorously. They crossed the road and ran over more wet furrows down towards the slowly flowing brook. We had to follow in single file, so that the land was not cut up by the horses' hooves; Jason had again carried me close to the front and he was still impatient to get on. The brook had to be crossed by a small bridge of rotting railway sleepers; the wood beneath the horse in front began to give way as the sleepers splintered; but it scrambled to safety. I had still got no brakes and Jason continued eagerly forwards despite my protestations and somehow we too got across, although no other horse managed to follow. The few who made it walked on into a large wood in single file until we came to the end of the hunt. Hounds were milling around excitedly on a large mound, looking and barking; they had not made a kill, for the fox had outwitted them and taken refuge down a large badger sett. Several hounds were looking headlong into the holes, but the fox was safe and despite a long and hard chase I had not even seen it. We returned to the road another way, through boggy ground and muddy water. Back at the mill a new notice had appeared proclaiming: 'The League Against Cruel Sports'.

The hounds and a greatly reduced number of riders moved off to begin another hunt, but with the sun beginning to sink I decided to ride the twelve miles back to the stables. Jason was reluctant to go, and whenever he heard the horn his ears twitched and he turned his head towards the sound. The sun was bright and warm for the time of year and the air felt fresh and clean. A low thorn hedge was still decorated as if in autumn, with clusters of copper-gilded leaves, strings of brilliant red bryony berries, and clumps of hips and haws that gave sprays of orange and crimson to the dormant winter wood. Some ridges and furrows in a field of old grassland dazzled with luminosity and even the ploughland seemed slightly iridescent. As the sun fell in a ball of white light, the sky passed through its soothing shades of sunset and the woodland elms and oaks seemed to glow with deep purple. The moon was almost full and slowly the stars dotted the sky; close to the stables Jason lost a shoe, but it was too near home to cause concern. There was little traffic, it was still and clear, it was Christmas night, and as the horse plodded into the stable yard I was filled with an inner warmth of contentment.

The actual hunt had consisted of sixty-five minutes of almost non-stop galloping, not knowing where or how far we would go. Some people maintain that hunting is only indulged in for the social status that it is thought to give, yet I found all the clichés about 'the thrill of the chase' to be true; it was 'exhilarating', 'exciting', 'thrilling' and 'hectic', and, come to that, it was 'frightfully super' too. It was also dangerous, with jumps, deep ditches, mud holes, barbed wire, and the rotten bridge, and it is easy to understand why there are fatalities every year on the hunting field.

It is true that I did not see a fox killed, but it seems to me that one of the great advantages of hunting is that if a fox evades the hounds it is left quite unharmed, and many hunted foxes have been seen to resume their own hunting as soon as danger has passed. It is also likely that the fox only feels real fear over the last few yards, or when cornered, for they can not anticipate failure and some have even been seen to turn and run into a pack of hounds as if confident of survival. The actual death, although not picturesque, is very quick, simply because of the number of hounds and their size, and suffering is minimal. If a few hounds are out in front when the fox is caught then the death may take several seconds, but if the fox is engulfed by the whole pack its end is almost instantaneous. In the Fells, where hounds kill many foxes, even small groups, or single hounds will kill a fox extremely quickly; in fact Fell hounds kill so many foxes that they often just kill them and leave the bodies intact. Because of this, if hunting is looked at purely from the point of view of animal suffering, then when compared with other forms of fox control it is the most humane way of killing foxes.[7]

But although the element of cruelty in fox hunting is exaggerated by those who oppose it, there are some unpleasant aspects. Earth stopping is one practice that seems unreasonable, for the foxes are 'stunk out' of their earths with diesel oil, creosote, or even moth balls, to get them onto the surface, and then the holes are blocked up with soil, plastic bags, paper, or wood, so that they can not seek refuge underground during a hunt. The actual 'stinking out' is not so cruel, for many foxes lie on the surface anyway, which again makes hunting more realistic than other methods of control, but a hunted fox must experience great fear if it retreats to an earth that has been sealed up. Many foxes are actually killed as they try to dig themselves to safety, and a terrier man from a well-known pack told me of a fox that he saw have a narrow escape. 'We saw this fox run to the blocked-up hole and it tried to get in, although the hounds were close to him. He did look a Charlie. He looked; he sat on his arse and looked back, listening to the hounds coming and wanting to go down the hole. He scrapped, and then away he went and the hounds never got him.' Others are not so fortunate.

The flushing out of an already hunted fox that has gone to earth, or sheltered up a drain, just so that it can be hunted again also seems regrettable. If a fox beats the hounds it should either be left alone, or, if a farmer wants it killed it should be dug or pushed out and then shot at close range. Most terrier men kill many foxes this way, with help underground from their dogs. Terriers are often ill-tempered and aggressive animals, yet they do have courage, and although a fox will defend itself, a terrier will not let one pass and will keep a fox at bay until it is dug out. If a

[7] Some people have suggested that poison could be used, but the danger to other forms of wildlife is obvious. It has also been said that foxes could be sterilized by the introduction of hormones to bait. No such oral method has yet been developed, however, and there would again be risks to both domestic and wild animals.

young terrier does not automatically bark at a fox, then several fox brushes are suspended just out of reach, and in its frustration the young dog will learn to yap. Once the terrier man has dug down to his dog and the fox can be seen, a spade or a piece of wood is used to hold the animal still, pushing it against the earth wall, and it is shot. When a fox is dug out in this way the animal is obviously extremely frightened, but there is no chance of it being left maimed or disabled. One old West Country terrier man killed 102 foxes using two terriers during a recent season, and to get one, he had to dig for eight hours; his interest in fox hunting started when he was eight; he is now well over seventy and retired, and most of his time is taken up with terriers, foxes and hunting.

Many of those who use terriers become very attached to them, and when a dog is lost underground they will go to almost any lengths to try and recover it. When a terrier vanished in a maze of tunnels in a very sandy Hampshire earth, its owner dug down to a depth of over fourteen feet until he was in great personal danger from the possible collapse of the unstable walls; but the dog was not found. Another even obtained the use of a mechanical digger to try to recover his dog, but although he moved a large mound of earth, his working companion and pet was never seen again, and his sorrow was as great as if he had lost a close friend.

Another unfortunate aspect of hunting is that there is no definite and clearly defined season; it starts in late summer with cubbing,[8] and gradually drifts to a halt in the early spring. Yet to avoid the possibility of hunting pregnant vixens it is unreasonable to hunt on into March and April, and terriers ought not to be put down earths during those months. Some 'antis' maintain that hunts actually breed foxes in captivity which they release as the hunting season approaches. This is most unlikely, for foxes are notoriously difficult to breed in captivity and at one time it was thought to be impossible. Even some zoos and wildlife parks that have bred rare animals, in danger of extinction, have failed to induce foxes to mate, and I have only come across one man connected with a hunt who has managed to breed foxes easily.

He is a retired publican and smallholder who lives in Devon

8 'Cubbing' is an unsporting part of the sport in which hounds, including fresh young ones, are put into coverts containing foxes while the riders ring the wood to keep the foxes in. It is done to kill some of the cubs and to 'introduce' the new hounds to hunting.

and who has bred foxes for many years; but it is likely that similar examples are very few and far between. He now spends most of his time breeding pheasants, and instead of breeding foxes he catches them. Listening to him talk and walking with him in his back yard was like going back in time. The small muddy farmyard was cluttered with bits of old wood and metal that he thought might come in useful one day, as were all his sheds, and in one of them he had a twelve-bore shotgun that had once had a rifle barrel fitted between and beneath the two main barrels. His eyes sparkled mischievously beneath the rim of his battered trilby as he showed me his traps and the stuffed head of a fine red deer stag, that he had snared and shot many years ago on a nearby area of rolling common, covered with bracken, gorse, and heather. In his younger days he also went badger digging, and he still snares them. He and his friends from his village pub would dig the badgers out and take them back to a large house or barn and there they would hold badger fights, with one badger against two terriers.

On the day before I met him a vixen and her cubs had visited the pheasants he was rearing and had killed fourteen. He had already snared one of the cubs, which was three-quarters grown, and he had put it in a shed with his vixen; a pet that he had kept for sixteen years. She was in fine condition, well fed, but moulting: 'Hallo therrr Tiny', he said to her in his rich Devonshire accent, 'them are slippin' therrr jackets now.' He snares foxes by setting the 'wires' in their runs: 'You got to see where 'ee runs, arn' 'ee; yu'm got to see wherrr 'ee comes through the 'edge see. Where a fox goos larss yerr 'e'll go this yerr; thas a funny thing. It won't be the same fox 'cause you'll catch un wont 'ee. I'm eighty-eight, an' I was trappin' when I was twenty. I started breed'n' them about 1925. I've 'ad as many as sixteen ol' ones in a pen, an' I've 'ad a badgerr in wi' 'em, an' a terrier. I neverr used to stake 'em out, I'd let a vixen stop in the pen an' one of the dogs would line 'err. They 'ave three to eight cubs; some might have three, an' anotherr might have eight.' He had a large collection of photographs, faded and brown with age, of adult foxes, cubs, and vixens suckling litters of various sizes and ages, with the vixens behaving like dogs and standing up to let the larger cubs feed. When I asked him what he had done with all his foxes he replied: 'Oh I in't tellin' on you that', but later he said that he had occasionally let some out when he used to hunt, especially for the Boxing Day hunt, and others he had killed for their skins; for any foxes he catches now he can still get £3 a skin.[9] He said that the way to handle a live wild fox was to pick it up by the brush, and then to work a hand up under its chin and hold its nose and jaws fast. In all his years of handling tame and wild foxes he has only ever been bitten once, when he pulled a hunted fox out of a drain: 'An' 'ee only bit me 'cause I were pissed. I was huntin' pissed.'

But although in general foxes are not bred, there is a thriving trade in cubs. If a litter of cubs appears on a shooting estate, or in areas that are not good for hunting, they are often dug out and taken to a place where there is a shortage of foxes, or to good hunting country. They are then placed in an artificial earth, or in a dry drain, and food and water are left for them until they are old enough to look after themselves. In cases of genuine fox shortages this action could be justified on conservation grounds, but often it takes place only because of the conflict between shooting and hunting interests, and so is indefensible. If areas of hunting land and shooting land are situated side by side, the foxes are drawn to the pheasant coverts because of the abundant supply of food, and the gamekeepers snare them; consequently unless foxes are brought in, there would be few to hunt, and there is no doubt that many of the cubs transported to, and reared on hunting farms, with shoots surrounding them, are often quickly caught in snares. Some of those who shoot say that cubs reared in this way are often marked by the hunt, so that it can be seen whether the reared cubs are caught by the hounds; the mark is said to be a cut made in the tail. If this is correct it would explain the strange but definite scar on the brush of the dog fox that we caught on the farm.

In the early Sixties one ex-terrier man made a definite effort to preserve foxes when many adults were found dead with a disease thought to be a type of hepatitis. He feared that foxes might be exterminated, and so he decided to intervene. He dug out eighteen cubs and arranged for a 'hunting vet' to inoculate them; they were then kept in a corn silo until the late summer, when he released them in various places around his district. He need not have worried, however, for the next spring, instead of fox litters averaging about three and a half cubs each, many litters were found with six, seven, and even eight cubs. He now thinks that

[9] In East Anglia at the same time in 1974, the price was £4.

animals can automatically adjust after being hit by a disease or a natural disaster, probably because fewer individuals means less competition for territory, food, and mates, and so the animals that survive reach the breeding season in prime physical condition.

Another very questionable practice that still takes place is the transportation of trapped, live, adult foxes. Although most hunting people deny all knowledge of such activities and trade, it seems highly likely that it is quite widespread, and I find it difficult to believe that it goes on without the knowledge and the approval of the officials of the hunts concerned. In the middle of the 1974–75 hunting season a horse box was said to have left Newmarket early one morning with eleven foxes in the back, to be released in an adjoining area where there was a shortage of foxes, and on the edge of the Fens where old Bill works his garden, he actually catches foxes in a large cage behind his house. For many years he has kept hens and has been troubled by foxes and because of this he decided to build a device so that when foxes went to steal bait, 'they went and shot their bloody selves'. After some experiments he decided that his contraption was too dangerous and so he built a cage instead. He made it from wood, corrugated iron, and wire, and it is about the size of two tea chests joined together. He leaves it permanently baited, with a dead hen or a rabbit tied to a wooden peg; when a fox tries to take the bait, the string pulls a wooden peg from a hole, and a heavily weighted door crashes down behind it. At one time he would shoot the foxes he caught with a .410 shotgun, but now he sells them at £1.50 each to a man with hunting connections who says that he takes them for release in Hertfordshire where foxes are scarce. The arrangement suits Bill, as shooting caged animals is unpleasant and messy; it also gives him pocket money at regular intervals 'and it saves me digging bloody holes'. Some people suggest that trapping foxes in cages is 'humane', but Bill showed me some wire that he had been forced to replace; it had been bent, bitten, and scrapped, as if the fox had gone almost berserk in an effort to get out. Although many hunters consider themselves to be 'fair' and 'sporting', it is miserable and distinctly 'unsporting' to hunt a carted fox. A fox caught and then released and hunted on unfamiliar land has little chance of evading capture and can only run aimlessly about until it is killed; the animal is used purely as a sporting accessory and the practice is offensive and objectionable.

If hunting is carried out properly, it can be said with all honesty that it is probably the most humane way of controlling foxes, and certainly better than gas, guns, snares and traps, although it is also the most expensive and the most inefficient. But if hunting is carried on with deception and carted live foxes then it is a sorry spectacle and a sad reflection on some of those huntsmen who pretend that they care for the traditions and character of country life.

Chapter Three

The Harried Hare

Surprisingly, the antecedents of the hare as an animal of the hunt go back into history far further than those of the fox, and for many centuries it has been pursued by huntsmen and sportsmen with a variety of dogs and weapons. Even in the sixteenth century the hare was considered to be a far more noble quarry than the fox and Elizabeth I had her own pack of beagles.

Today the brown hare is still thought to be an animal worthy of sport, and it is found widely distributed throughout England, Scotland, and Wales. Physically it has remained unchanged since the last Ice Age,[1] and for its survival it relies on its natural camouflage and speed. Despite its nature and its wide distribution, however, many of its habits and ways remain rooted in tradition and folklore, and even less is known about the hare than the fox. I came into contact with hares from a very early age, for during most months of the year wild hares could be seen in the fields around the farm and I was always fascinated by the sight of hares in their March madness. It was said that their behaviour was due to their eagerness to acquire a mate, yet after their antics became more normal they continued to breed, and before the arrival of the first combine harvesters, young leverets[2] were often found skulking under sheaves of corn in the harvest fields of late summer.[3] From tractors pulling ploughs, cultivators, drills, rollers, balers, and grass-cutters, the modern-day farm workers still see leverets skulking, or hurrying off on long uncoordinated legs, during most seasons of the year, and with the threat from natural predators, sportsmen, and heavy agricultural implements, it is

[1] As has the roe deer.

[2] Leverets are the young of hares; they are born fully furred and with their eyes open.

[3] Hares have several litters a year. The gestation period of a hare is just over forty days. One old country saying is: 'A hare and a mare go a year', meaning that the period of pregnancy for a mare is about eleven months, and for a hare about a month.

astonishing that the hare continues to survive at all.

To Jim on the farm, the hare was both a help and a hindrance, for it was said that 'winter wheat should cover a hare in March', but ten hares 'eat as much as a sheep', and so he felt obliged to shoot them. During his dinner break, when no pheasants were in sight, he would wander with his old single-barrel twelve-bore shotgun after an 'ol' Sally',[4] with Peter our spaniel eagerly helping him in his search. Often over ploughed land it was difficult to tell the difference between a clod of earth and a hare, but Jim had a foolproof method of recognition: 'As you walk towards a piece of dirt it seems to get bigger, but as you walk towards a hare it gets smaller, skulking into the ground.' As Jim entered a field at one end, a hare, with Peter yapping many yards behind it, would usually disappear out of the other. Once he saw a hare skulking in some long grass and he tried to put his foot on it: 'It struggled and I was slightly off balance and over I went. That ran too and it's a wonder it did. It's a wonder it didn't singe all its hair off its back for what I was saying to it.' Although he liked shooting them, he would never eat a hare, as he considered the meat to be too strong; instead he would give each one to us and we would enjoy eating them jugged, with plenty of redcurrant jelly.

Many country people refused to eat hares for other reasons; the meat of a bucking hare was said to cause diarrhoea, and there are still those who believe that hares can bring on miscarriages in pregnant women; a belief that probably stems from the high volume of blood in the body of a hare which makes the meat very dark. Injured hares also seem to bleed more than most other animals, and when in pain or experiencing fear they scream with the pitch and anguish of a despairing child. Again, because of this it was a belief that witches turned themselves into hares; a theory that was reinforced in springtime when hares could often be seen sitting in circles, their heads inwards as if attending some strange meeting or witches' coven. Another peculiar belief in some areas suggests that if a hare runs through a village street, a fire will break out shortly afterwards. Looking at a hare it is easy to

[4] The local name for a hare. They are also known as Sarahs. In some other areas the names Puss and Horrey are used. Most country people refer to hares as 'she' as it is difficult to tell the difference between the sexes, even when dead and cut up. At one time they were believed to be hermaphrodites.

see how they have become associated with the supernatural, for when one just crouches and watches, or lopes over a field with its five inch ears upright and its large bulging eyes staring, it can look wild, mad, and uncanny. As I was passing through part of the Breckland forests early one morning with two forest rangers, two large hares sat watching us; one of the rangers commented: 'They look really evil old buggers don't they, sitting down there with their eyes bulging as if they're going to put a spell on you.'

Jim believed many of the stories about hares, and states with complete conviction that if a leveret is found with a white mark on its forehead it is one of a litter of three, and that if it has no mark then it is the only one born. Arthur Sewell also believed that the white mark indicated that there was more than one in a litter, and both men were adamant that they had come across plenty of examples. Despite this, when I mentioned the phenomenon to an 'expert', he dismissed it as fantasy, and gave the impression that the life of the hare is simple, quite ordinary, and uninteresting.[5]

Most countrymen are also sure that hares spend much of their time sitting in forms,[6] looking behind them, which means that they can only be approached from the front. Foxes are said to take hares in their forms by approaching them from the front, not only because of the hare's habit of looking backwards, but also because a hare can only leave its form by going forwards. The habit and ability of hares to look behind them was confirmed at a shoot when a spaniel set off in pursuit of a hare, ignoring the shouts of its master to 'sit'. The hare was so intent on following the movements of its pursuer that it ran straight up to a large black labrador which eagerly closed its jaws around it, as if it couldn't believe its luck.

But other beliefs are contradictory and confusing; some gamekeepers and farmworkers believe that the doe has her litter in one place, and then disperses her young as a precaution against predators, carrying each infant in her mouth like a dog with a puppy, but others state that she gives birth to each leveret separately, in different parts of a field. Some say that the mother suckles her young singly, but a gamekeeper (who worked for many

[5] Despite this there is a Ministry of Agriculture publication, *Wild Animals and the Land*, in which the author, Mr F. Howard Lancum, writes that each leveret 'has, in its early days, a white spot in the middle of its forehead'. I don't know whether it is true or false.

[6] A form is a depression in the ground in which the hare crouches. A good form gives the animal a surprising amount of shelter from the elements.

years on the estate of a Socialist lord) once saw a doe call her young; five leverets then went to her from different parts of a hedge to feed, and after they had fed the mother drove them off again into cover.

There are also conflicting views about the intelligence and courage of hares. Some, particularly huntsmen, consider hares to be more cunning and difficult to pursue than foxes; and others think that they are about the most stupid of all our wild animals, and there certainly appears to be plenty of evidence to support the latter view. When hunted, it is claimed that some hares will run through sheep or take to water like foxes;[7] but others will skulk down until the hounds almost fall over them. Some hares are said to leap out of their forms so that their resting places remain undetected, yet others run predictably over the same route on every journey and take few precautions. One such hare had a regular escape route over a ditch, yet after a heavy rain it went the same way and instead of jumping or swimming, it disappeared down one bank, and emerged up the other, seemingly oblivious of the fact that the ditch was full of water. Despite the stories of the hare's cowardice and stupidity there are also authentic accounts of does showing great courage defending their young against dogs and birds of prey.

Their behaviour during the springtime madness is even more difficult to understand; sometimes as many as twenty hares can congregate together, chasing, boxing, or just watching. Once, on entering a small grassfield, a woman who had hunted hares almost all her life came across a great 'lump of hares', with hares climbing over one another in a large heap, a sight she had not seen before or since. Another keen huntsman has seen a hunted hare stop in its flight to stand up and fight another buck while being pursued by a pack of beagles. As the hounds caught up and engulfed them they were still fighting, completely oblivious to all that was happening around them. During the spring it is also possible to shoot hares with rifles, for often they remain quite unconcerned by a sudden shot, and bucks have even been seen trying to mount does that have been twitching and quivering in death. Because of the sexual habits and appetites of hares there are some gamekeepers

[7] Both foxes and hares can swim well, but for some unaccountable reason their scent sometimes seems to hang over the water at the exact place of their crossing.

who dislike them, they say that they are 'full of pox, but this is usually untrue as the hares are simply suffering from skin trouble.[8]

Due to their erratic and strange behaviour it is said that, unlike rabbits, hares can not be tamed and kept as pets. Even zoos rarely have hares on display, partly because it is difficult to get them to breed in captivity, and partly because they are so highly strung that they will often keep running into the wire of their enclosures. Yet even so there are numerous people who have found leverets pressing themselves down into the ground and who have picked them up to keep as pets. William Cowper, the poet, became very attached to some hares that he was given, and on the death of one he wrote an emotional 'Epitaph on a Hare'; he also wrote an article on keeping hares for *The Gentleman's Magazine*.

One woman who works at some riding stables, from which horses are hired out to go hare hunting, became very involved with a pet leveret. She had it when it was very small, after her labrador, trained as a retriever, had brought the animal into her house from the fields and left it on the carpet. Because of the dog's soft mouth the leveret was quite unharmed. It lived with her, having a complete run of the house for six months, before she decided to give it back its freedom. It visited the garden several times after release and still let her stroke it, and although she does not know of its fate she is sure that she did the right thing. Now, although she does not condemn hunting, she has a great sympathy and liking for hares and has convinced herself that hare hounds rarely catch a hare.

As with most animals and birds around the villages where he worked, Arthur Sewell learnt much about hares, but his experiences do not really help to clarify any of the inconsistencies and contradictions in the stories and beliefs about them. He saw hares run from dogs and jump fenland dykes fifteen feet across without touching the water, and yet he saw others swim to safety; indeed one fenland hare was seen to swim the tidal river at Wisbech with nothing pursuing it at all. But he also saw hares seize up through stupidity or fear and thus easily be caught. He often caught hares using a method that is described by many countrymen: 'If you see a hare sittin' in a field, in a form, an' you want this 'are an' you've got nothing to get it with. You take

[8] Leporine Ulcerative Dermatitis.

your coat orf an' lay it down or hang it on a hedge and go an' fetch something, a gun to shoot it, an' that hare will still be there when you come back, sittin', watchin' yur coat. An' another way of pickin' an ol' hare up, if you want to pick an hare up, that's if a hare is sittin'. You start walkin' round in a big circumference and keep getting nearer and nearer, an' that hare'll sit there until you can crack it; I've done it so I know that's right. They sort of get mesmerized and they don't pay no notice of you walkin' round, thinking to themselves he's walking round and round, but still you're getting nearer to it an' he don't realize that you're getting nearer to it.' Another common variation of that method was for a coat to be put down before the circling began, and the hare was said to watch the coat until it could be hit with a stick. Even though they were apparently stupid in this way Arthur saw does defend their young: 'I've seen a hare goo for ol' birds, but I've never seen them tackle a stoat or a dog or anything like that. They'll go for ol' 'awks though. They'll 'fend their young uns when there's 'awks about. They box 'em with their feet; they sit up and box 'em.

'I wouldn't like to say that they have more than three leverets. If you see a leveret up to a month old and that's got a star on its fore'ead, you can bet there's three in the litter, an' I don't care who contradicts that. It's white hair on the fore'ead, but it goes away as they grow older. They have the leverets round about in the circumference of a few yards, but when they come to feed 'em they have 'em all up to feed at the same time. So they're not far apart in the day time.

'When I was a keeper, keeperin', I picked a young hare up, a little leveret, an' that was quite young, an' that spun round an' round an' its ears dropped orf; they screwed off. An' that went on right up till harvest time. An' I was with an ol' man when we were cutting a bit of corn, and he says: "Arthur, I believe there's an ol' monkey in 'ere." An' I said: "An ol' monkey?" He said: "Yes, it's got a head just like a monkey an' it keeps stickin' it out of this corn." An' I went an' stood agen him, an' the binder went round agen an' that stuck its head out of this corn agen, an' I said to him: "Well that's an ol' hare that's what that is." An' he said: "An ol' hare be blowed, that ain't no hare it's a monkey." An' that was this ol' hare you know, growed up, an' he hadn't got no ears, an' that looked exactly like a monkey.'

Arthur also coursed hares with his dog Grinder, and because of the hare's predictable behaviour he would sometimes try to shorten the chase: 'One day I got in this run, 'cause I knew this ol' hare would go through this run, once he got goin' round a hedge. He'd go through, then run up one side of the hedge and then back down this side again, and so he kept goin' round the same bit. So I thought to myself, well I'll stop you ol' mate. I jumped down in the ditch an' got in this run, an' he came through this gap an' hit me in the chest an' cut me back. That never hurt the blinkin' hare mate, but he went through me hands quicker than ever a football would go through. If you set a snare in a run, out in an open field, you won't get the hare unless the 'are is runnin'. If the 'are is runnin' he'll go through it; but if 'es just joggin' along on his own, he sees it and jumps over it an' knocks it down. But if you get a snare in the 'edge where there's grass over the top, you can get one every time. When anything's after them – when Grinder's been after 'em they've broke their necks. They will mate, but the snare's got to be set in an open field. You see an 'are's comin' along this run at such a triffic buckin' pace mate, an' you're staked down, an' that snare pulls up tight quick mate an' that chucks that 'are right over.

'But the best way if you want to catch a hare out in the field is to put a ploughshare on your snare. Leave a ploughshare layin' there an' 'ave your snare set. An' when you come in the mornin' you can see where 'es been trundlin' this ploughshare about you see, an' you get the ol' hare alive if you want them for greyhounds or anything like that. I used to catch 'em and send 'em up to London to Harringay for training these dogs, an' we used to put on the crates "Tame rabbits", an' so I have rabbits. They'd pay you anything for live rabbits up there, to train the dogs. I used to go out with the long net and get ten or twenty or whatever rabbits I could, an' put them all in this crate, shove 'em on the train an' they'd go up to Harringay an' they used to pick them up there. They used to pay me about fifteen bob for a live rabbit, and a live hare they'd give you anything for them blighters. You may depend it still goes on.' Another thing that still goes on in greyhound racing circles is the purchasing of live domestic rabbits to 'sharpen' up the dogs for competition running.[9]

[9] Live rabbits can be purchased at many cattle markets.

It is the running of hares against greyhounds at coursing meetings that has, over the years, been condemned more than any other sport. It is a practice that dates back to 4,000 BC and the ancient Egyptians; although in this country the history is shorter, with organized meetings dating back to the eighteenth century. Men coursed their dogs at informal gatherings long before that, however, and at the turn of this century it was still common for ordinary country people to set their dogs after hares on Boxing Day morning. Indeed it is thought that coursing was so popular in East Anglia that the coursing by greyhounds of the Great Bustard was the main reason why that bird disappeared from Britain as a breeding species.

The thought of dogs chasing hares and ripping them apart simply for the benefit of sportsmen and bookmakers is not pleasant, and so when I went to a coursing meeting near Huntingdon I anticipated a very unedifying spectacle. Whereas the idea of Jim shooting the odd hare 'for the pot', or Arthur Sewell using his lurcher to get a dinner seemed reasonable and acceptable; coursing dog against dog, and both against the hare seemed unfair, and I imagined that each course would be over very quickly with the hare standing no chance and being pulled apart in the process. Newspaper headlines and film extracts had already suggested to me that it was a pointless, cruel pastime, and from the outrage and condemnation that also seemed to accompany it, I assumed that the hares were released from captivity quite close to the greyhounds, and that those watching somehow derived pleasure from the spectacle of a wild animal running confusedly in front of dogs over strange ground.

The morning of the coursing meeting was bitterly cold, with a biting February wind blowing from the east. About 300 people and two bookmakers had gathered and it was immediately clear that my mind had been wrongly programmed, for there were no signs of caged, trapped, or handicapped hares; they were completely free and being driven by beaters towards a large field about a hundred acres in size. The surrounding land was really rural, with farms, smaller fields, and more hedges than in many areas. On a small rise a Norman church stood out from a cluster of tall bare elms, their trunks green with clinging ivy. Lapwings were flying in large flocks and throughout the day ragged flights of mallard cut through the wind on hard-working wings. Sheep were still in some of the fields and tufts of wool were caught on the hedges and strands of wire.

The first hare after my arrival loped through the hedge and as it passed the Land Rover, behind which the slipper crouched,[10] it saw the two held dogs through its large, bulging, and backward looking eyes and accelerated quickly away. The second surprise followed immediately afterwards for without too much trouble the hare beat the hounds after being given a start of about a hundred yards. On two or three occasions as the dogs closed in it twisted or suddenly turned and the unexpected change of direction was sufficient to keep it safe. With the hare running fast, its ears flat and its tail down, and the greyhounds chasing with both power and grace in their movements, it was not an unpleasant sight, and until the hare got away the spectacle held me with a compelling tenseness. As greyhounds follow by sight alone the hare is usually safe once it passes through a hedge into an adjoining field or along a ditch. One dog wore a red collar and the other a white, and the judge who watched from horseback signalled the winner by waving the appropriate coloured handkerchief. The winning dog is not the one that kills the hare, or get the closest to seizing it, it is the dog that follows most skilfully and forces the hare to take evasive action. The courses that immediately followed ended as the first, with the hares escaping, and when one hare ran in a straight line across the field it was the dogs who were hopelessly humiliated. One finished panting, well beaten, and the other gave up half way. Some striking coal miners who were standing nearby were not impressed. 'That old dog couldn't even catch a hare if it was put on a plate in front of him', one of them complained as he saw that he had lost his money.

As more people arrived, some moved towards a thin hedge that divided the top half of the field in two: 'Get away from the stuff,' an official cried impatiently, or so I thought, 'get away from the stuff, or you'll frighten the hare.' I couldn't understand what he meant, but the people obeyed him without question and moved away. During the next course it seemed that I would see my first kill, for the hare was forced to twist and turn, but still the two dogs kept close to it. Once the hare turned at ninety degrees and gained a brief respite, for the change in direction sent one dog

[10] The slipper is the person who releases the dogs for each course. Both he and the judge wear 'pink' coats.

cartwheeling over, impeding the other, but they both quickly recovered and made up the lost ground. As the hare approached a small mound it was clear that the end was near; it ran straight towards the hillock with the dogs almost on it; then, much to my amazement it disappeared. The greyhounds ran around the mound looking cheated and the course was over. In fact the official had not shouted 'stuff', but 'sough',[11] and the refuge, made of old railway sleepers covered with soil, had allowed the hare to take shelter through its small entrance, while the greyhounds remained outside. There were two soughs altogether and both were used by hares during the meeting. Not only did this throw new light onto coursing, but it also created one more mystery about the habits of the hare; for how did the hares know that the soughs were there and that they would give them protection, because in normal circumstances they would not use them? Although this action suggests high intelligence, an onlooker informed me that on one occasion he had seen a hare run out of a sough and straight into a pair of beaten greyhounds; it was killed instantly, while the coursed hare got away.

About ten courses took place before I saw a kill, and over the whole day approximately 75 per cent of the hares got away and not one was torn to pieces. Several were held in a tug of war between two dogs, but in such a situation they died extremely quickly. In fact I ran my hand along the bodies of some of those that were killed: they were hardly marked, and were damaged far less than a shot hare. One hare was picked up by a dog, which proudly held it aloft; it briefly escaped and was caught again and just held as if the dog had no idea how to kill it. Briefly it cried out in a half-hearted scream before somebody ran up and killed it with two quick blows to the back of the neck.

Not only did the actual process of coursing surprise me, but so too did the crowd, for again there was a great variety of accents and types. Some wore wellington boots and donkey jackets and others sported tweeds and stiff upper lips. Some of the upper-class sporting ladies with their tweed skirts and jackets, their long woollen socks and flat shoes, looked most formidable, but they seemed to lavish love and affection on their dogs; even the dog food was special – honey, eggs, Bemax, baby food, and brandy in milk.

[11] Pronounced 'suff'.

Because my reaction had not been as expected, it occurred to me that the meeting might have been an exception, and that a smaller, less formal gathering would be more typical. And so, a few days later, I went to watch some whippet coursing in the Fens. It was bleak and cold out there, with about forty-five people and their dogs. There were tractor and lorry drivers, electricians, a mechanic, business men, and housewives, all waiting for the action. Even the judge seemed to demonstrate how coursing attracts people from different backgrounds, for his horse bore no resemblance to the fine hunter that had been at Huntingdon, it was almost as wide as it was high, and instead of a smart pair of leather riding boots the judge wore a pair of all purpose working clodhoppers.

The slipper had a great deal of trouble crouching down in gateways or on the banks of dykes, trying to keep out of sight. On the first course one whippet went plunging into the water after the hare, but the hare was quicker both over the land and through the water. Many of the dogs, waiting for their turn in the cold, shivered, and their small tailored coats seemed most inadequate. Some of the hares were driven towards the slipper, but for other courses the slipper, dogs, and spectators walked over the fields and the dogs were released once a hare had been put up. Only one hare was killed all day, yet those present appeared to have enjoyed their sport. One course was particularly memorable, for the small fawn whippet followed the hare for at least five minutes[12] around a large field until eventually it had to be called off by its owner. It was a game, persistent little bitch, that would have made a fine pet in any home and which, despite its long run, went on to win the meeting. Some people believe that names, places, and conditions have no influence over the behaviour and interests of intelligent, rational Man; the owner of the winning dog was a Mr Hare.

My visits to the coursing meetings came closely after attending a hare shoot, with a gun, and so my reactions might have been softened by the carnage caused by shotguns against driven hares. But even so, coursing to me was not so intolerable, or cruel, as I had anticipated. Since then I have attended another meeting where the ground over which the hares were driven was wet and heavy and 50 per cent of the courses ended with the death of the hare.

But although coursing is solely a sport and can claim little effect

[12] Most courses last between 45 seconds and one and a half minutes.

on the overall hare population, either for control or conservation, at least the hares killed are not wasted, but eaten. Abuses do occasionally occur and a beater explained to me that sometimes sheep or chicken wire is positioned to prevent hares running directly onto the coursing area. They are then released through a gateway one at a time; when waiting for their turn the hares often run in frightened circles between the wire and the beaters, so that by the time they are released they are exhausted and no match for the dogs. When this occurs there is no doubt that cruelty is involved. Normally, however, dogs chasing hares is not a sadistic activity or a horrifying sight, although it has to be admitted that if the actual death of the hare is as unimportant as coursing people claim, then it is odd that coursing with muzzled dogs was not introduced many years ago.

Although my reactions to coursing were unexpected, my feelings after the day at the hare shoot were completely predictable. I went with Arthur Sewell's youngest son, Brian, to a large East Anglian estate, where hare numbers are so great that each year, at the end of the pheasant shooting season, shoots have to be held to reduce the number of hares. Some locals think that the hares migrate to the lighter, drier land during the winter, and hares certainly seem to disappear from our cold and heavy clay during wet weather. Local farmers and shooting enthusiasts are invited to the shoots, as many game shooters do not consider hare shooting to be a sport, and invitations are always eagerly accepted and sought after. We both had guns and anticipated an interesting day. By the time we arrived, the starting point was already like a miniature military camp, with men swaggering about in camouflaged jackets, khaki anoraks, cartridge belts, boots, and waterproof trousers, and Brian had his gun in a leather case similar in appearance to the traditional violin case of the Mafia. A number of Poles were also there in military greatcoats and one man with a wooden leg was said to shoot almost as many guns and beaters in a season as he did game.

We piled into the back of a lorry with a makeshift roof supported by an insubstantial wooden frame that creaked and swayed. There were no special beaters, and the 'walking guns' had to drive the hares to the 'standing guns', shooting as they went. One man had no gun, just a game bag for carrying hares, and considering their weight and awkwardness he had a very strange idea of a day's sport.[13] As we lined up along a roadside two hares could be seen in premature March madness and at one stage it looked as if the buck was going to mount the doe. The drive started and hares began running ahead to a small strip of grass and young conifers. Their forms were quite large impressions in the light soil and I walked right past one which still contained a crouching hare. The next gun saw it and 'kicked it out' by shouting and stamping his feet; it bolted and fell dead with one shot, and a pool of blood was left on the soil where it fell. Some people claim to be able to attract hares to their guns by beating on the ground, or by blowing onto a piece of coarse grass held between their thumbs, but all the guns present were strictly orthodox.

As we approached the break, the number of hares increased and many ran through to the next field, and pheasants and partridges took off in large droves. We lined up beyond the grass and hares seemed to be loping and leaping about in all directions – it was hard to believe that so many hares could be living on such a comparatively small area. One ran directly at me and I raised my gun. My second shot left one of the back legs shattered and hanging on by a thin strand of skin, but the animal ran on, bleeding and screaming until it was shot again and killed by the next gun. There seemed to be hares everywhere, but fortunately no more came near me. The drive was a long one and at the end of it many hares were dead and a number of French partridges were walking about exhausted, unable to fly again.[14] The hares were put into a heap and the carrier commented on the fine 'lump of hares'.

Several drives followed, yet few hares seemed to escape and many were wounded, struggling on with shattered bones and broken limbs, screaming hideously, before they were finally killed. Some too seemed to run almost the entire length of the guns as if running the gauntlet, with the whole line of barrels blazing at them before they were eventually slowed and killed. Hares and pigeons, in range and out, were shot at and I was glad when the day was over. The final bag was 450 hares, twelve pigeons and

[13] Hares can vary in weight from 6 – 11 lbs.

[14] The French or Red-legged partridge was introduced as a sporting bird in the eighteenth century. It is hardier, and more easy to breed than the native English or European partridge, but it is a poor flier by comparison, and is thus not considered such good sport.

Coursing – two greyhounds stretch out after a hare. The winning animal is not that which kills the hare, but the one which follows most skilfully. (*Cambridge Evening News*)

The results of a driven hare shoot at Chilgrove in Dorset. Shooting can be a messy and painful method of control. (*John Tarlton*)

The Albany Basset Hounds following a hare's scent across plough. Slow but persistent, basset packs, like beagles, are followed on foot. (*Frank H. Meads/Shooting Times*)

The Portman Foxhounds close on a fox in the Stour Vale, Dorset. Notice the differences in dress of the riders. (*John Tarlton*)

ten rabbits; each gun was given a hare, and the rest were collected up by a game dealer. Over the three days of the hare shoot the tally was 1,622 hares, forty-four pigeons, and sixteen rabbits.

Because of the number of hares killed it is clear that they have to be controlled in some areas, for they can do considerable damage to cereal and root crops, as well as to young woodland. But again it is a tragedy that the most widely accepted method of killing hares is also the most cruel, and it is an unfortunate fact that there is no really humane way of controlling one of our commonest but strangest animals.

The other sport involving hares is to hunt them by scent with hounds, and this is done with packs of harriers, basset hounds, and beagles. The number of hares killed has little overall effect on the hare population; nevertheless, thirty packs of harriers, sixteen packs of basset hounds, and eighty-two packs of beagles in the British Isles are employed in the sport. The basset hounds and beagles are usually followed on foot and the harriers are followed by riders on horseback. To follow hares with a pack of hounds is an ancient sport but an extremely odd one, and it must rank in the eyes of many foreigners as yet another inexplicable British eccentricity. Those who participate, however, take their sport very seriously and usually claim that their main interest is 'to see the hounds work', that their main joy is 'to hear the music of the hounds', and that the death of the hare is irrelevant. They seem to adore the hounds and all things that are well-bred and of quality, which led one retired kennelman to tell me: 'At least my hounds were better-bred than the bloody gentry who used to hunt them. When they got drunk they would go to bed with anybody, they weren't fussy. When they developed a big gut that made bed impossible they'd get a butler. That's what butlers were used for; they were like stud stallions.'

Most people unversed in the language of hunting assume that harriers hunt foxes because of all the riders on horseback, but in fact they chase hares. My first hunt was with the Cambridgeshire Harriers, considered to be one of the best in the country, and putting on my hat and boots I was left in no doubt that dressing up plays an important part in blood sports. As Remo was too headstrong, and Jason was not fit, I had to visit some stables in Cambridge to hire a horse for the day, at a cost of £10. Three other immaculately rigged-out riders were already there; a man who during the week works for the IBA in London, and two well-dressed, affluent looking girls. Their horses were large and well groomed, fifteen or sixteen hands high, which made my disappointment acute when I was introduced to my mount; he or, more accurately, it[15] was short, round, and dumpy, closely clipped, with an ugly trimmed mane. It was so low that it was easy to mount, but sitting on it after Jason and Remo, it felt as if I was almost doing the splits. Although I was not pleased, at least the horse seemed to know that it was going hunting, for its ears pricked up, it looked eager, and it was said to respond to the name Bisto.

My immediate discomfort was not over, for as we filed out of the gate and into the wind I was last in line, just behind the enormous buttocks of a large horse. Every time its hind hooves hit the road the revolting beast passed wind loudly, freely, and disgustingly, in a series of long-drawn-out staccato farts. Being almost at the same level as the active vent, and with the wind blowing the second-hand oats, hay, and odious digestive juices into my face, it was most unpleasant and lasted for what seemed like several minutes. Even when the eruptions were over my comfort did not return, for at the trot, Bisto's short eager strides produced the same feeling as riding over cobblestones on solid rubber tyres.

Once out of the town things improved, the large horse's digestive system seemed to clear and we trotted the three and a half miles to the village. Conversation was polite, and when a car passed at speed, even the V-sign and the information 'You bastard', directed at the driver by one of the girls was done with control, dignity and decorum. The actual meet was in a small field opposite the house of the chairman of the local foxhounds and many riders had assembled; ladies with black coats and bowlers, men with jodhpurs and jackets, and girls with crash hats and chin straps; I was the only one with jeans and a donkey jacket. Everybody was very friendly, and soon the stirrup cup was handed round. Holding the reins in one hand and the crop and glass in the other proved too difficult and most of the sherry went down the horse's neck.

The lady Master and the whippers-in wore green jackets, and soon the hunt started along a sodden clay track from which muddy

[15] A 'gelding'.

water sprayed out as hooves splashed down, and coats were quickly dirtied. There were about fifty riders and fifteen couple of hounds (thirty dogs), all off to catch a hare; an absurd proposition. The Master Huntsman cast her hounds over heavy ploughed clay, and the 'field' trotted along behind. One horse with a red ribbon tied around its tail lashed out with its hind legs, but kicked only air, and I was advised to keep well away from it as it was dangerous. The clay was too wet and cold for hares, and the hounds moved on to a field of sugar beet; almost immediately they began to 'speak', and set off in full cry. My horse was watching the hounds eagerly and I too searched for my first sight of a hunted hare. I did not see it, for the hounds had put up a fox that had been lying out in the beet, and it ran off ahead of them with remarkable indifference, towards some council house gardens. The hounds were quickly called off and another hunt started in the direction of the Cambridge University radio telescope.

The hounds flushed some pheasants from a small piece of game cover, and suddenly a hare sped away. The dogs were off, and the horses followed, but almost as soon as we had started, the hunt was over. It was a small hare and it had headed straight for a wire netting fence. Finding its path blocked it had turned back and run into the hounds. The Master took the body before the pack could eat it and cut the hare's feet off while one of the whippers-in asked if any members of the Pony Club wanted a 'pad'.[16] 'Oh do go on, darling', one child was urged by her mother. Once the feet were off, the master flung the legless corpse to the hounds, and amid pulling, tearing, and growling, it disappeared or, in hunting parlance, it was 'broken up'.

The proud recipients of the pads were not 'blooded', but this practice does sometimes still take place. Shortly after Linda, my horse catcher, started hunting on a hired horse, she was blooded, at the age of eleven. Again the paws were cut off and dipped in the blood of the hare's ripped-open abdomen, and a smear of blood was put on each of her cheeks. She was so honoured that she kept them on for several hours, to show her parents, and she regarded the initiation as something of a status symbol. Now the whole incident seems senseless to her, but she does not regard it as a

[16] In keen hunting circles 'pads' and 'masks' (the paws and heads of foxes, otters or hares), are sometimes stuffed and mounted to remind the owners of outstanding hunts.

harmful experience, causing her to be cold and insensitive as some objectors suggest. In fact her enthusiasm for hunting has since waned, after she began to think of the hunted animals rather than the excitement of the actual chase. Even so she still regards hunting as being far less cruel than shooting or fishing, and she would still occasionally hunt if she had the time and had not sold her horse.

The next hunt started almost immediately and the hounds set off at a fast pace over winter wheat, running along the perimeter fence of the telescope. Because the land had been drilled the riders could not follow but had to trot carefully around the outside of the field. By the time the horses had travelled down one side, the hare and hounds had disappeared back along the other. After a short gallop over stubble the hounds were refound; there were no signs of the hare, for that had been caught and already eaten and another hunt was over.

Several more short, but fruitless hunts followed, over heavy clay, and with each stride Bisto seemed to get more tired and even shorter. As he flopped along and over a ditch, some young girls flew by on almost uncontrollable maniac ponies, which they rode with a skill and courage that bordered on folly. By early afternoon Bisto's breathing was so laboured that I left early to walk him back to the stables; he had hunted enough. Afterwards, I was as stiff as if I had played a hard game of football.

Those who follow hounds on foot seem to consider themselves to be the elite of hunting, the hardiest hunters and the most discerning. Yet whether this is a genuine enthusiasm for 'working hounds', or sour grapes at not having horses is difficult to ascertain, although it is obvious that far more can be seen from the back of a horse than on foot. Certainly the camaraderie amongst beaglers seems to be high and to the non-huntsman, books on beagling are almost unreadable because of the clichés, the perpetual praising of the 'jolly beaglers', and the constant exhortations to all masters of harehounds to study their quarry until they learn 'to think like a hare'. Of course with the supposed low intelligence of the hare the latter ideal should not be too difficult for most huntsmen, and if they do manage to think like hares then the homes, and especially the bedrooms, of masters of harehounds must be extremely entertaining places during the month of March.

On a clear, sunny January afternoon, I tasted the joys of being a 'jolly beagler', by travelling to the Hertfordshire borders to hunt with the De Burgh Basset Hounds, a private pack, owned and hunted by a businessman who was in the holiday villas industry. The meet took place in the early afternoon, and the Master, in his green corduroy jacket, white breeches, long socks, and shoes, stood holding his whip, his horn, and a glass of red wine, surrounded by ten and a half couple of basset hounds; long, low, flop-eared dogs which seemed far too near the ground to hunt hares. By the time the horn was blown and the hounds moved off, only seven followers had arrived and they all lined up along an old railway line to ensure that any disturbed hare would run in the required direction. I went with an enthusiastic fifty-nine year-old whipper-in with a wandering mind, who was armed with a handkerchief and a whistle to signal to the Master about the movements of the hare. He had been hunting hares on foot for many years and considered them to be extremely intelligent animals. He said they would sometimes run back over their scent to confuse hounds, occasionally they would disappear down rabbit holes, and he had once seen a hare perform the legendary 'hare jump'. The hare had been hunted for two hours and was running alongside a ditch when it stopped and suddenly leapt sideways and upwards over the ditch, travelling almost six feet into the air and a further six feet beyond the far bank of the ditch. It had then run off and squatted down in some scrub. The hounds 'checked' at the place where it had jumped and could not find the scent again. Although it had been 'viewed' by several followers it was decided that the hare should go free; 'she' had beaten the hounds 'and the Master raised his hat to her.'

The basset hounds were cast by their Master behind the kennels, and soon the hare came running by, over a field of half-harvested sugar beet, well ahead of the hounds. Slowly the pack 'got on the line' and began to follow, except for two young hounds who ran back to the kennels. By the time the main body of hounds arrived the hare had vanished and the scent had run out. Members of the field reported their observations to the Master, but it made no difference. The pack was then taken over ploughland and briefly set off in full cry towards a hedge; halfway there a hare got up behind them as if they had run straight over the top of it.

For the rest of the afternoon they hunted in fits and starts, with hares getting up and leaving the hounds far behind, and the scent quickly running out. They followed one to a hedge, by a copse and a small grass field where men had been ferreting that morning. As a result there were many rabbits lying out on the surface. Consequently the whole pack had several short bursts of coursing, with their heads up and scent forgotten. Rabbits were not the only animals in the neighbourhood for there were several sets of hoof prints[17] of fallow deer.

In a small field of tussocky grass the hounds again put up a hare and made off in full cry. The hare ran straight towards a single hound that had been hunting rabbits by itself, but on this occasion the hare must have been looking both in front and behind, for it beat the hound with a simple body swerve and was quickly lost. It was hard work following the hounds over the arable land and as the sun began to set I was looking forward to the end of the day. Just when it seemed that no more hares would be found, one got up and ran fast and straight along an open furrow. With the failing light the scent had evidently improved, for the pack took off at great speed, barking furiously, and disappeared from view. It was an hour before the whippers-in caught them and the exhausted Master up again; it had been the first and the last real hunt of the day, although darkness and distance had prevented the 'jolly beaglers' from seeing the hounds work, and all they had heard was the music of the hounds getting steadily fainter.

Back at the kennels the hounds were let into their spotless quarters and fed on a mixture of flaked maize, pork, and water, which was poured into troughs. They ate ravenously and soon the containers were licked clean. One dog had eaten at such a speed that within a minute he vomited the entire contents of his stomach up again, and then stood barking and growling, guarding his own vomit. As the doors of the sleeping accommodation were opened he began to eat it for the second time, and was helped out by a couple of friends. There were four doors to the various sleeping quarters; the first was opened and the Master called 'Young dogs', and all the young dogs waddled in. The next door was for 'old dogs', then 'old bitches', plus one wayward old dog, and the rest went through the final doorway. In front of a roaring log fire in the Master's old Tudor house, tea and mince pies were

17 'Slot marks'.

served as the huntsmen talked, laughed and exchanged stories about their day.

A meet of the Trinity Foot Beagles taught me no more about the 'jolly beaglers'. The pack was well turned out, though it seemed a matter of great sadness to the kennelman that he should have to hand over his dogs to students. In fact his whole life has been interspersed with sadness, from the age of seven when his mother rode her bicycle into a hole in the road and died as a result, with the council refusing to pay any compensation, arguing that she could not have been looking where she was going, to the recent past when he fell off a horse and broke a bone in his neck, forcing him to change from foxes to hares.

He does not dislike hare hunting and has hunted a hare with beagles for two and a half hours, but he does not consider that it is a sport to compare with fox-hunting. The normal length of a hunt is about forty minutes, depending on whether the students can handle the hounds properly. Unfortunately he is not greatly enamoured of many of the modern-day students: 'The students today are stupid, they learn so much until their brains come out of their ears and there's no room left for common sense. When told to exercise the hounds and to turn right, if I didn't go up and show some of them exactly where to turn they'd keep walking straight until they fell over.' One afternoon as the students were hunting the pack, they let the hounds wander too near a minor road; in his anger the kennelman loaded the dogs into the hound-van and took them back to the kennels, leaving the huntsmen a long walk through a village and back to their cars without the hounds.

In the first fen field of the afternoon hunt a hare was put up; it ran along the bank of a dyke and then in a large circle, before stopping in front of me and the rest of the field. In that situation I felt that I would 'see the hounds work' at last, because I could almost have caught the hare, so I was sure the pack would. Alas, where the hare turned from the bank, the hounds kept going straight on, and by the time shouts ('holloas') had attracted the huntsmen and hounds, the hare had run on and disappeared. The rest of the afternoon was spent in a fruitless search for hares. In one field of sugar beet there were plenty, seen by everybody except the hounds and huntsmen, and the only things that made the afternoon interesting were the antics of the followers. One girl, obviously extremely intelligent, had been hunting from the age of three, claiming that she did so in order 'to see the hounds work', although from the cynicism in her voice it was not clear whether she really believed her own affirmation. Buzzing at her side all afternoon was an excited young man with a refined accent who not only used the words 'super', 'frightfully', and 'awfully', but finished nearly every sentence with 'eh, what?': 'I went to the South of France for my holiday; frightfully nice, eh, what?'; 'Super day, eh, what?'; 'Where are you going this summer, eh, what?', and sometimes he just said 'eh, what?' for no reason at all. When coming to ditches most people walked down one side and up the other, but he always ran and jumped in a most manly manner, to turn from the far bank and grin a mouthful of teeth in triumph. After one such leap and a 'frightfully good, eh, what?' I realized what I was witnessing – the courtship display of the upper-class English male. As the sun cooled I decided to leave early; it was going to be a perfect dusk for watching deer.

Chapter Four

A Glimpse of Deer

Of all the animals living in the wild, none give more pleasure than free roaming deer. For deer have a delicacy of habit and a beauty of movement that no other animal can match; their senses and motions are welded together in a unity of visual perfection and physical harmony, and an encounter with deer leaves a lasting impression on the mind and a longing for quiet places. Their attraction is made greater by their habits, for those who wish to see them have to be out at dusk or dawn, long after the day-trippers and picnickers have returned to their homes, and before most people have fallen out of their beds and into their normal routines.

It is best to go out into the mists of an early summer morning, when the grass is still heavy with dew and the dawn chorus is at its fullest, for then deer can be seen, browsing or watching; playing or testing the air for scent and sound. But to see a deer, is also to see an animal haunted and dominated by fear. Each new noise, object, or smell, gives a conditioned reflex of anxiety, for over the centuries deer have been harassed ceaselessly by natural predators and men, and their large liquid eyes have learned not to trust. Now, in most countries the flesh eating animals that once preyed on them and limited their numbers have gone and so man is their only predator, and again in some places he has turned his predation into sport. Consequently deer hunting is one of the most ancient sporting pastimes in Europe, and in Britain it dates back to pre-Norman times, when harsh forest Game Laws protected deer for the pleasure of the nobility, and which meted out punishments and even death to those who transgressed. Then deer were common, but even after the agricultural revolution in which woodlands shrunk, arable fields grew, and deer numbers declined, deer hunting still took place, with hounds, horses, and carted deer.

When Jim married, shortly after the First World War, stag hounds met regularly in the courtyard of a local pub, and he would often watch them. There were no wild deer locally, and so one was brought into the pub yard by cattle lorry for every meet. Its hooves were then rubbed with a rag soaked in aniseed and it was released and allowed to run free. One morning the deer had become so used to human presence that it made no effort to leave, it merely sauntered across the road to graze on the grass verge and would not go. It stayed until the huntsman galloped up behind it cracking his whip, to make it take fright and run off.

Every effort was made to capture the deer alive, to save the expense of having to buy and transport another. The animal was run until it was exhausted and on the verge of collapse and the huntsmen would then try to whip the dogs away. Sometimes, however, they were too slow and the hounds would kill – as a small girl Jim's wife had been horrified when a deer was torn to pieces in front of her while she had been out for a walk along a bridleway. When death did occur the hounds were still whipped off as soon as possible, so that the carcass could be saved and cut up into joints of venison. One deer broke its back when it jumped over a wall into the sunken garden of an old manor house, and Jim received several tips of sixpence when he delivered the dressed meat to various hunt supporters. On another occasion his father caught the hunted deer after it had swum across the manor moat and was on the point of collapse; he shut it in a shed where the hounds could not get at it and waited there until the cattle truck arrived to take it away for another time.

Because deer are seldom seen it is assumed by most people that they are rare. Fortunately they are wrong, for it is estimated that there are now more deer in the British Isles than for over 400 years, and there are few counties in which no wild deer can be found.[1]

The first deer that I encountered at close quarters were the roe deer of the Thetford Forest, where as a boy I often acted as a beater for a shoot in which two uncles were members of the organizing syndicate. During pheasant drives deer were often disturbed, and those with guns shot at them indiscriminately. The Forestry Commission, on whose land the shoots were held, considered deer to be pests, in the same category as rabbits, to be exterminated in whatever way possible, and to most shooting men a deer was a trophy which demonstrated their high level of skill.

[1] Most of the deerless counties in the British Isles are to be found in Wales.

Little consideration was given to the deer themselves, to the damage they were said to cause, or to the suffering and cruelty that was inflicted upon them.

Since then attitudes have changed; the Forestry Commission regards deer as an asset, if properly managed; forest rangers are employed to study, control, and to conserve them; responsible shooting people will not attempt to kill them with shotguns, and legislation has also given them a measure of protection. But even so much more could be done, for all deer still suffer from the activities of greedy, ignorant people who behave like hooligans as soon as they pick up a gun. As a result deer continue to be found dead and dying from gunshot wounds. Many are also snared and coursed after dark by poachers and their dogs, and there are numerous hotels and restaurants that will pay good prices for the meat of freshly killed deer – proprietors and customers ask no questions, they just pay cash at the back door. Because of this trade horrific stories and photographs are available from all over England and Scotland, of deer dying tragically and slowly through wounds and illegally set snares. Such evidence of suffering and indifference completely destroys the myth of the British being an animal-loving nation, and by comparison, those who hunt deer with hounds appear to be almost saintly in their behaviour and attitudes.

The present East Anglian forests of the Breckland cover over 50,000 acres, broken up by sandy fields and areas of bracken and heather-covered heath, and in the woodland well over 1,000 roe deer live unseen by most of those who drive along the busy trunk roads that bisect it. But those who live and work in the forest see them, as do fishermen who go with rods and artificial flies to the Wissey, the Little Ouse, and the Lark, on quiet summer evenings, for as the sun sinks the deer leave the thickets and the blocks of pine and larch that hide them during the day.

The roe is our smallest and daintiest native deer,[2] standing only about two and a quarter feet at the shoulder, although movement gives it the appearance of being larger. It is elusive and graceful and once in thick woodland or undergrowth it is quickly lost. In the summer its coat is a rich russet, but in winter it changes to a dull grey-brown. Its ears and eyes seem larger in proportion to those

[2] The red deer is thought to be the only other native British deer.

of other deer, giving the appearance of great sadness and understanding, and the three-pronged antlers of the bucks are short and seldom exceed ten and a half inches in length.

I have had several dusk and dawn encounters with forest roe deer, accompanied by Rex Whitta, the Chief Ranger of the Breckland, who was one of the first rangers appointed by the Forestry Commission after its attitude towards deer changed. His feelings for them go very deep and he only controls deer with regret.

The first of my visits was early on a September morning. In the half light we drove into the forest along a rough track with plantations on one side and bracken on the other, and almost immediately three roe deer darted across our path with bounding grace. Their white rumps briefly allowed their movements to be followed, before they disappeared into undergrowth.[3] As daylight increased, so the nature and the variety of the forest could be seen; new plantations, open ridges, blocks of mature trees, late wild flowers, with the yellow heads of the great mullein standing tall and spear shaped, and areas of thicket. Rabbits were plentiful and a hare accelerated away from us erratically as if undecided about its gear and direction. Pheasants were numerous and a fiery golden cock was feeding among ordinary common pheasants with no sign of friction.[4] Rex then saw a broken branch with its bark scraped off as if a red deer stag had been fraying with its antlers,[5] and large slot marks appeared in the sandy track. As we approached an area of field beans adjoining the woodland we saw a small herd of red deer feeding; hinds, calves, and one stag with a large set of antlers. They slowly trotted off towards a belt of trees where they stood and watched us, and to the unfamiliar eye they merged into the shadows without movement. The red deer of the Breckland are the biggest in Britain and are thought to have been imported, or to have originated from escaped carted deer. Despite the work of the forest rangers their numbers are currently declining because of harassment by poachers, disturbance, and indiscriminate shooting by some of the land owners nearby. A few

[3] The white rump is also known as the 'target', and it is said to assist deer to stay together as they run away from danger.

[4] Some shooting people maintain that golden pheasants persecute ordinary pheasants although there is little evidence to support the view.

[5] New and growing antlers are covered with a sensitive skin, 'velvet'. When the antlers are fully developed, the skin dies and irritates. The deer then rubs it off against a branch or sapling. It is known as fraying.

weeks after my first visit a large stag was found at the roadside, crippled and dying from the work of car-carried poachers who had shot and then left their prey to die.

As the sun rose above a distant block of pines, the land began to steam, and a bouquet of pine wood and dew filled the redolent air. Several roe were browsing in a large area of newly-planted land, bucks, does, and half-grown kids. One buck stood motionless quite close, but he could hardly be seen with the naked eye as his red coat blended into the colours of scorched grass and dying undergrowth, and another also appeared, in good condition, but with only one antler. They were not eating the trees, but the grasses and brambles which grew profusely around them.

Soon the distant whine of car engines showed that others were up and that work and travel had started. The deer gradually faded into the forest, and we left to drive to a nearby market town for coffee. Halfway along the final ride Rex stopped: 'There's another, look', he said, pointing into a block of half grown pines. I saw nothing, until he directed my gaze to an avenue of dark trunks and fallen pine needles, where two rounded flickering ears and a pair of doleful eyes observed us a hundred yards inside the woodland; nothing could be seen but the fragile features of the deer's head, peering from behind a tree trunk, full of enquiry and concern. Yet Rex was so accustomed to deer that he had seen it immediately; the secret, he said, was that eyes generally focus on the vertical lines of planted trees and trunks, but to the experienced eye the presence of a deer forms a conspicuous horizontal intrusion.

Other visits since have also been memorable; fleeting glimpses of roe along the forest rides on an October night with the chill of the first winter frost in the air, and far away, in the stillness, the distant roar of red deer stags in rut – a noise resembling a moo, a bellow, and a groan, long drawn-out and full of frustration, passion, arrogance, and physical exhaustion.

In the late spring, with the frail fingers of bracken uncurling and the fresh green of new leaves on the beech saplings beneath the pines. As we stopped along a ride, a jay cried out harshly, as the other birds sang, and the forest felt as if it was throbbing with life, unseen, yet vibrant. Under tall pines a doe stood watching us, her beauty unaffected by her coat, which was ragged and patchy as it changed into its summer richness. A small buck browsed, half hidden by undergrowth, eagerly eating some needle-spined gorse. As we watched, a peculiar croaking noise seemed to indicate the presence of a frog, which was strange, for we were some distance from water. The call came again, only the second time it was above me, and a woodcock flew over on rapidly fluttering wings.[6]

A visit in the middle of the roe rut was also fascinating, for in the warm, sultry weather of July the bucks are often active in daylight as well as darkness. Then wild flowers lined the rides and beds of rosebay willowherb coloured the clearings with mauve. The rut of the roe is earlier than those of other deer[7] and the bucks can often be attracted by imitating the call of a doe on a small whistle.[8]

Twice, on hot humid days I went with Rex as he tried to 'call up a buck' at mid-morning, but on both occasions flies and mosquitoes were the only signs of life as we sat and waited deep in the forest. He tried again at five o'clock one morning, from the high seat overlooking a large clearing. He immediately attracted a fine looking buck, with small, well-developed antlers, but as it approached it obviously wandered into the territory of another, who quickly saw it off. The 'master buck' showed no interest in the calls, for several does were already feeding in the area, and he had no desire to investigate the presence of yet another.

From a different high seat, Rex was about to call again, when a doe and a buck emerged from a plantation of quarter-grown pines some 200 yards away. The buck was following her, sniffing her hind quarters, as she led him round in a number of small circles. She stopped briefly to allow him to stand up on his hind legs to mount her, but almost immediately the leading and following was resumed. In fifteen years of being closely involved with wild deer, it was only the fifth time that Rex had witnessed the actual act of mating, as it often occurs in thick cover. He blew one of his whistles to imitate a doe in a frenzy, to see what effect it would have on the courting couple; the doe seemed concerned and

[6] This display flight of the woodcock is known as 'roding'.

[7] The roe rut is early because of the phenomenon known as 'delayed implantation'. The egg is fertilized, but then stays in a state of suspended animation for several months. Sixteen to eighteen weeks before the kids are born the egg becomes implanted in the uterus wall and the development of the embryo then proceeds normally. Two kids are often born and triplets also occur.

[8] Bucks are usually called up for identification purposes and to be photographed.

started off towards us, but the buck was not interested and obstructed her path. He still had other things on his mind, and soon she led him off into the trees and out of sight. In the grass where they had been walking, a clear 'rutting ring' had been trampled down, showing that their walking and mating had been taking place for some time.

As early morning wore on and deer activity lessened, we decided to leave the forest, again without having called up a buck, when for the second time within a few minutes the unpredictable happened, for suddenly we saw a small buck with single pronged antlers browsing in some long undergrowth. Rex crouched low and tried again with his whistle. At the first few calls the young buck lifted his head, flicked his ears, looked, and listened, as if he couldn't believe his luck. Then, hearing further calls, he began walking erratically and cautiously towards us, clearly unsure of himself as he tried to locate the doe. In the past Rex has managed to attract amorous bucks to within a few feet of where he has been calling from, but a breeze had developed and thirty-five yards away the buck detected human presence, rather than that of a mate, and quickly turned and fled, bounding over small clumps of brambles as he went.

But despite its charm, its elegance, and its grace, the roe deer can do much damage, grazing as it does on grasses and herbs, as well as small seedling trees. It browses too on the buds and new shoots of freshly planted pines and the bucks batter and butt young trees with their small antlers during the rut. As a result the population has to be kept within certain limits and a knowledge of the individual animals has to be obtained. Troublesome and aggressive bucks have to be eliminated, whereas others which may dominate large areas can be in such control that rivals are kept away and there is little need to display or fray, and damage is negligible. In the Breckland most of the control is carried out by the rangers themselves, using high velocity rifles and soft-nosed bullets, and the deer are either shot by stalking, or from wooden towers, 'high seats', up which the rangers sit and wait for the deer to approach.

Only a limited number of sportsmen are allowed to shoot in the forest,[9] but elsewhere in the British Isles roe shooting and stalking

[9] In 1974 the Forestry Commission received £135,430 for shooting, fishing and stalking rights.

are becoming increasingly popular, and they are already well established as sports on the Continent. One evening during the buck shooting season, shortly before the rut, Rex installed a member of the Saint Hubert Club[10] in a high seat, and then he drove to another to try to shoot a buck himself. It was a perfect evening, with summer warmth, forest scents, and a placid blue sky. We climbed up a high seat on the edge of a cleared area of about twenty acres surrounded by pines and covered with dead and seeded grasses, clumps of bramble, and isolated saplings of birch, beech, and thorn. Perching on a bush in the centre was a small light bird which through my binoculars I could see was a red-backed shrike, a 'butcher bird', with chestnut wings, a grey head, and a slightly curved beak. Its nickname is derived from its habit of impaling its prey on a thorn or a barb of wire for later use; its main victims are beetles and small mammals and birds. When a cock yellowhammer approached the shrike flew at it, but although of a similar size the yellowhammer was less aggressive, and it gave ground. Both seemed to be worried by the presence of the other, as if each one had the task of protecting a nest and off-spring. They perched again and watched one another suspiciously, before the shrike flew off again; this time it ignored the yellow-hammer and pitched into an extravagantly coloured jay, searching for eggs, over twice its size. After a brief skirmish the jay flew off, completely confused by the ferocity of its small adversary, and the shrike returned to its bush, where it was soon joined by its mate.[11]

Two kestrels flew over in direct flight and a French partridge strutted along the roadway beneath us with her brood of eleven chicks, which were just getting their feathers. She hurried by, as if sensing our presence and then stopped, calling the stragglers that were chasing insects in the long grass. One ran towards her flapping its small wings vigorously to become briefly airborne, before crash-landing near its mother. When satisfied that all were with her, the whole family set off again down the ride.

A large roe buck appeared, having emerged from the pines or

[10] A club for those who hunt, shoot and fish. Its particular interest is deer.

[11] The pair successfully hatched off five young. With public access in the forest, illegal egg-collecting is becoming a problem and eggs of nightjars, shrikes, and other birds have been stolen over recent years. A clutch of shrike's eggs can make as much as £50 on the black market.

brambles; it had its full summer coat of rust-coloured red, with a black nose, dark eyes, and small antlers that seemed to match perfectly. Another buck and a young doe left the woodland for the clearing, looking sleek and fit; their coats were lighter and their elegant ears flickered and twitched constantly to keep away the flies. Several times they rubbed their heads along a heap of sawn timber to rid themselves of the constant buzzing irritation of the flies, and then they would scamper away almost playfully, before pausing to browse. As the light began to fade more deer appeared; one sat down in brambles quite close to the high seat, but it was not possible to see whether it was a doe or a very young buck, and so Rex did not shoot. Another richly coloured buck appeared some way off, grazing with a doe; Rex carefully loaded his rifle and several times he tensed up, causing his breathing rate to change, as he took aim through the telescopic sights, but on each occasion he decided that the range was too great and the shot too difficult, and he did not fire.

Beyond a wedge of pines a shot rang out, and echoes rumbled through the branches. Saint Hubert, the patron saint of huntsmen, had evidently provided one static hunter with a shot. When quietness returned a nightjar whirred into its bubbling song and another flew by the high seat with the loud 'yip' of its flight call. Rex had not managed to have a shot, and I had not seen a doe with her small kids, as I had hoped, but once again the forest had given me a glimpse of the life hidden within it, and there is no doubt that our forests have become important wildlife refuges of great beauty, quality, and variety.

We drove off to collect the hunter from his high seat. He climbed down in his dark coat, antlered tie, heavy dark green trousers, furred boots, a hat with camouflaged netting covering his face, gloves, and binoculars covered with green cloth. He had seen several deer, and so had we, dressed as we were in anoraks and with bare hands and faces. The hunter had shot a buck through the chest and so, to him at least, the process of dressing up had been worthwhile.

From a high seat shooting is comparatively easy, but there are times when stalking is the most practical, and that involves skill and a real knowledge of the deer. I went stalking roe early on a damp, cold, February morning, with a young ranger, Derek, who led me, with his rifle over his shoulder, into part of the forest where he felt that deer were sure to be plentiful. Walking along several rides we saw no deer, and then, far ahead, I saw what I assumed to be a hare. 'Muntjac', Derek said immediately and, sure enough, through my binoculars I could see that it was a tiny deer that quickly disappeared into a clump of dead and flattened bracken.[12]

One ride cut through a block of towering pines with the high vaulted branches spanning over into archways of a size that amplified the silence and gave an almost ecclesiastical quietness. The wind suddenly whistled in the tops of the smaller conifers, as if passing through telephone wires, and Derek sensed a change in the weather. When this happens the deer often alter their habits, and when there is a wind they become very wary and uneasy as hearing is hindered and they feel that their defences are incomplete.

It was decided that no deer would be seen and we returned to the van. On rounding a corner we suddenly saw three roe feeding at the edge of the ride ahead. Derek reversed the van carefully, climbed out slowly and loaded his rifle. The deer sensed the presence of intruders and sniffed the air and twitched their ears before wandering into the trees, browsing nonchalantly as they went. They approached a large severed branch where their winter coats merged so well that even with the aid of binoculars they were barely visible, and it was only the occasional movement of a white rump that betrayed their presence.

Derek quietly and steadily crossed the ride and approached them through the woodland – freezing, proceeding, and freezing again. When about forty yards away he raised his rifle cautiously and took careful aim. Suddenly something startled them for they bounded away, with their rumps flashing, before stopping to look at him through their puzzled eyes. He remained motionless and soon they resumed their browsing. Again he approached stealthily until he was close enough to fire. The sudden report rolled around the forest, hemmed in by the treetops, and two of the deer stampeded off; the other lay dead, three yards from where it had fallen. All was quiet and blood had settled in a fine spray on the evergreen leaves of a small laurel. The almost fully-grown female kid had died instantly, and its eyes were already dulling.

[12] A small Asiatic deer that now lives wild over a large area, having originated from escaped park stock.

Derek slit one of the thighs with his knife and threaded the other leg through, like ham-stringing a rabbit, and hung the deer on a tree. He then 'gralloched' it by splitting the animal open and removing the entrails. I asked to see whether the bullet had hit the heart as it had been a shot aimed at the body, but he searched for the organ without success. Astonishingly, I found it lying in the undergrowth. It had been completely ripped out of the body by the bullet's impact and torn through a hole in the rib-cage as big as my fist. He dug a hole and buried the head, hooves, and entrails, and the body was ready for the 'game larder'. Apart from a few ticks the animal was in excellent condition, and death had been instantaneous and without suffering.

Sometimes when a deer is shot from a high seat, others will continue to feed nearby, apparently quite unconcerned, as if fate has hidden from them the meaning of death. Occasionally, however, things go wrong and a deer is only wounded. When this happens the type of wound is assessed by the colour of the blood and a labrador or a German pointer is used to track the injured animal. Often the scent of deer and blood is so strong that the dog will kill when the creature is found, but the end is quick and it is better than leaving the deer to suffer and die in its own time. One afternoon Rex saw his pointer freeze and point as if he had located an injured or a sick deer; it held its position for several seconds and then leapt forward. Two naked figures screamed and ran off in alarm towards a car parked nearby, terrified by the cold nose on warm bare flesh.

Chapter Five

Fallow Deer in Forest and Woodland

It was only after I had made numerous journeys to the Breckland that I discovered the presence of deer within eight miles of my back door, for several herds of fallow deer, probably originating from old ornamental park deer, now live completely free in the district. Two herds inhabit small areas of woodland and copse surrounded by farmland, and more live in a large wood supervised and maintained by local naturalists.

The wood itself is ancient and made up mostly of oak, elm, ash, hawthorn, and hazel, and for generations it was coppiced by local people. Coppiced woodlands were of vital importance to many rural economies until the time of the First World War, for they were cut in rotation to provide wood for local agriculture and industry. Farm buildings, carts, fences, hurdles, the handles for hand-tools, and even thatchers' pegs came from coppiced woods, and farmers also used them as a source of cheap fodder for their livestock, when in the autumn their pigs rootled for acorns, and hazel- and beech-mast. The coppicing still goes on, but only to provide continuity and suitable conditions for the rich and varied flora of the wood, and the abundant cover and vegetation are also ideal for the fallow deer.

Fallow deer are larger than roe, standing over three foot at the shoulder, and they vary in colour from pure white to almost black. In summer the usual coat is chestnut, while some, particularly those in the New Forest, develop white spots, but in winter the colours fade to the hue of dormant bark. The buck is larger than the doe, and when fully mature it grows a set of large antlers that span outwards and upwards, and as they curve upwards they flatten and have a number of spikes protruding from the palmated main stem. It is thought that these deer are not natives of Britain, but were probably brought over by the Romans for sport or simply for decoration.

Now, wild fallow deer are probably the most common deer

living free in England, and although they are larger than roe they have all the beauty of movement and sharpness of features of the smaller deer. During the hours of daylight they will lie up in areas of thicket, while at dusk and during the night they will leave their cover for pasture land and will stay together in a herd.

My first visit to the wood was at sunrise in October, in the middle of the fallow rut. Light was dispersing the mist that hung over a large field of beans and the sky was clear, apart from gangs of rooks and jackdaws that flew noisily overhead. The bridlepath along the eastern boundary of the wood was cut up by the hooves of horses and there were also the slot marks of many deer that crossed a ditch in well-worn tracks. Through my binoculars I could see a doe feeding quietly in the distance, on stubble, and decided to get to her. As I moved through the trees, pigeons and pheasants periodically flew from their roosting places with a clatter of wings, and a pheasant suddenly called out in harsh warning.

Within 200 yards of the doe I cautiously peered around the trunk of an isolated but substantial tree. She still fed, but with her eyes and ears alert. Suddenly she held her head up and looked and listened intently, but she heard and saw nothing unusual and returned to her normal feeding. I decided to go deeper into the wood to approach her with less chance of being seen, but just ten yards in I was confronted by the sound of many running hooves and the sight of bobbing white rumps: as I had been watching, so I in turn had been watched.

I carefully advanced, but the doe had heard the commotion and had walked nervously into the wood. I froze, for she had caught me between trees, completely exposed. She knew something was wrong and looked directly at me as my breath drifted out in white clouds into the chilled air; I could do nothing and my muscles ached with the effort of remaining motionless. She advanced again, carefully and cautiously, picking each leg up slowly and deliberately until she was within twenty yards of where I stood. Suddenly she gave a short, sharp bark of warning, making me jump, and she bounded off on rigid legs for three or four strides, starting and stopping, and then she ran off normally into thick cover. Another darker deer wandered a few yards from me as I stood by a tree, and it moved on unknowing and unconcerned.

Walking along a small path I heard a woodpecker busily hammering at bark, hidden in some old ash trees and I followed the noise to see the bird at work. Standing by a small clump of hazel I could see nothing in the boughs high above, just dappled patches of bronze and copper from the rising sun, playing on the trunks and branches. Below, and forty yards away, the copper light caught and coloured the movement of a rich chestnut coat – I was downwind from a fox and it was weaving its way through brambles and dewberries straight towards me. It was in perfect condition, sleek, fit, and unhurried. Only four yards away it stopped and squatted down. Its brown eyes, clear and deep, looked up in relief, straight into my face. It looked, thought, and suddenly its brain processed my presence, for a look of panic flooded its expression and it fled with its ears turned back, to run in a large circle around me, studying me all the time, before hurrying away.

From a clearing in the centre of the wood I saw a large dark buck along the northern ride, quietly grazing and then carrying out its early morning wash. As I slowly approached, he wandered off through some brambles and into the trees. I hurried to follow but stopped almost immediately, for a large, lighter-coloured buck, with a formidable set of antlers jumped into the ride and disappeared in the undergrowth where the dark buck had gone before.

A few yards from where they disappeared hooves hit the ground and branches broke as antlers caught in conflict. The crashing and jousting grew louder and more intense, like the sound of fighting pirates in an old feature film, as antler hit against antler, but the foliage hid them from view. The fight ebbed and flowed for several minutes and then quiet returned. I crept into the trees and saw the victor, the large dark buck, standing arrogantly with his head aloft, only thirty yards from me. Some young bucks with small antlers were walking in single file around a tree, for no obvious reason, and he looked quite unconcerned about them.[1]

Slowly he moved away and when I showed myself the young bucks fled. Another fox passed by twenty yards away; I sucked the back of my hand (to imitate a young animal), it stopped, looked and listened, but I was upwind and it quickly trotted on with more urgency in its stride. Leaves swished above me as a grey squirrel jumped and a jay called out in alarm. The smell of smoke

[1] The circle in which the young bucks walked is called a 'play ring'. Its significance is not clear.

caught my nostrils and led me to an area where fresh woodland had been coppiced. The smoke hid my scent for there I surprised a doe still in her rich summer coat and her half grown fawn, a toy-like miniature of its mother with a coat of 'Bambi' spots. It was an unforgettable morning, and as I returned home for breakfast I felt that the day had already been well spent.

Other glimpses of the woodland fallow deer have been full of beauty, tension, and sadness; an April evening when thrushes, blackbirds, wrens, and robins sang as pigeons cooed, and then, with energy and clarity, the first cuckoo of the year heralded the start of summer. In the coppiced area, oxlips grew in profusion with their small flowers of primrose yellow, pools of bluebells hung in patches of blue mist, and darker early purple orchids flowered, as if sown by the random action of a benevolent hand. As my companion and I approached the central clearing we suddenly saw an albino doe browsing, just inside the woodland, and it was easy to understand why white fallow have been given the name Judas deer. We stopped immediately as casual movement gave away the perfect camouflage of more, darker deer, and fifteen of them walked into the open, their dish-like ears turned towards us and their deep, dark eyes looking enquiringly at us. We gradually moved into some brambles, but still the sad eyes watched us. They grazed and browsed for several minutes before moving off again into the trees, where even the white deer vanished from view. The song birds gradually grew silent as tawny owls began to hoot, the evanescent sun dropped away into a limpid mauve dusk and the wood fell into darkness.

It was approaching dusk when I had my most memorable encounter, at the end of a warm July day. I was sitting on a small wooden seat outside a shed at the edge of the central clearing. It was quiet and still as nesting had finished and the spring song of birds had died. It was a deep silence, and even the leaves had no movement. As the light slowly faded I heard branches swishing and twigs breaking as deer slowly approached. The sound of hooves through woodland got nearer and then stopped, to be replaced by the sound of grazing. It was obvious that the deer were actually in the clearing a few yards from me. A fringe of long grass by a small ditch gave me partial concealment but also interrupted my view; I was tense, straining to see, but could see nothing. Beyond the long grass I suddenly detected grey movement. It was a doe with something smaller bounding near her. A pigeon flew noisily from a nearby oak and both sprang away in alarm. I temporarily relaxed, but soon movement and sound returned. Gradually the noise of grass being plucked and eaten advanced, and just twelve yards away the deer moved into full view. There were three does in their summer coats, rich, and slightly spotted, and with them were three fawns, small, delicate, and no more than a month old. Two were spotted, sleek, and beautiful, straight from a childhood picture-book, and the other was lighter in colour, though with features just as fine. As they all grazed one of the fawns began to skip and dance around its mother, with movement so graceful that its small hooves hardly seemed to touch the ground. It ran, it jumped, and it kicked its back legs high with the sheer joy of protected woodland life. One of the does raised her head and looked straight at me, and as her eyes made out my presence, her ears and nose joined in enquiry. The other two does stopped feeding and they too stared at me. Then, without fuss the mothers and their young walked slowly by, their tails flicking at flies as they moved off into the wood. Quietness returned, and only the occasional hooting of an owl broke the silence. As I walked to the edge of the wood a mass of creamy meadowsweet lightened the coppiced area where oxlips had vanished, and the sweet smell of wild honeysuckle hung thickly in the warm, humid air.

My one sad sight of deer in the wood occurred in the early morning, when two bucks looked at me from behind a tree. They were both fit and well, but in the antlers of one was the tangled wire of a snare. The animal was in no danger or discomfort, but obviously poachers know of the presence of deer and are prepared to ignore suffering and to break the law to try and kill them.

Like roe deer, fallow can do much damage to trees and crops, but around the wood they are fortunate, for most of the farmers enjoy seeing them on their land. To prevent them from becoming too tame and to reduce the amount of damage that would otherwise become intolerable, a professional stalker kills some, from a high seat, but the aim is to control, not to exterminate. Even so problems still exist and new trees to improve the look of the land cannot be planted, for the deer quickly kill them by stripping the bark, often chewing any protective polythene as well. They can be particularly troublesome as harvest time approaches because of their habit of lying down in high corn, for not only do they lie down but they also circle round like a dog before finally descending to their resting place. One farmer likens the situation to 'having a herd of bullocks living loose on your land', and feels anger when he sees them in ripening corn, but he too would be reluctant to lose them.

Strangely, it is the naturalists who are more concerned about the deer than the farmers, for in the wood they eat large quantities of shoots and plants with long Latin names, as well as the oxlips, and there is talk of the need for control and references to 'these pests'. Most seem to favour the use of high-velocity stalking rifles to reduce the number of deer, as the cost of deer fencing is too high. It seems that as always the long Latin names are going to win and sooner or later the deer in the wood will be 'managed'; their refuge will also be an abattoir, and logically and realistically there can be no other solution.

Although the most common method of controlling fallow deer is by stalking, in the New Forest the New Forest Buckhounds still hunt with horses and hounds and hunt over the same land where Norman noblemen experienced the exhilaration of the chase. Each year about a third of the forest deer are culled by stalking and the use of high seats, while the number killed by the buckhounds is extremely small. In one recent year only a single buck was hunted to water and shot, and the number seldom exceeds four or five.

Despite its name the New Forest is England's oldest existing forest and it still retains much of its ancient appearance as well as many of its medieval customs. It is a microcosm of wild places, domestication, and rural habitation, with areas of inhospitable moorland – heather, heath, black bog – and dark pine forest, intermingled with leaf shaded glades in woods of oak, beech, and ash, patches of fertile farmland, and straggling villages and hamlets as old as the forest itself. Few village streets have kerb stones or harsh concrete street lights, for the roadsides are of grass and the night is lit by stars. Ponies and cattle wander at will and many of the people who live in the forest are still 'commoners' who retain their 'commoners' rights'. There is a Verderers' Court; old men can be seen collecting horse manure from the roads for their gardens; pigs are released into the forest for acorns and beechmast, and the buckhounds meet regularly to chase deer.

I was fortunate enough to get a ride with the Buckhounds, borrowing Josh, a horse belonging to an Australian nurse who has lived and hunted in the New Forest for many years. Again her situation shows some of the inexplicable contradictions of hunting, for she is a remarkable woman; several nights each week she works in an old people's hospital, a job demanding great compassion and dedication, and one of the reasons why she works is to enable her to hunt. During the day she looks after her few grass fields, a small herd of beef cattle, and her horse. When any of her stock becomes ill or causes her concern, neighbouring farmers call in to give her advice and a dairy farmer further along the road is always on hand to help out. On his small farm he has 250 cows that have to be milked night and morning and during the day he is able to turn many of them out onto common land. His one workman milks in the morning, starting at 6.00 am and the farmer himself milks in the evening. His working day starts at 9.00 am and he finishes at 11.00 pm, seven days a week, a total of over ninety hours. Such a situation in agriculture is not uncommon, yet the legend of the farmer's feather bed persists.

The day before the hunt I took Josh out for a ride; a dark stocky cob of 14.1 hands. As soon as he moved into a canter I was nearly off for he did a sudden jump and a buck. 'It's sheer *joie de vivre*' my hostess informed me; it was sheer devilment, it seemed to me. After a long ride through forest and over heather-covered moor I took him into a wide shallow stream to drink; he then began to paw the water with one of his front hooves showering water over me, and then he curled his tail around his flanks and began to lie down. I kicked him and hit him, wondering whether to jump off before he rolled over, but fortunately he changed his mind and I quickly rode him to the bank.

The meet was held close to the small grass fields of Josh's home, on an area of common land overlooking an old inn. When I arrived most of the horses, hounds, and huntsmen were already there, including the huntsman with his whip and green coat, and women with black coats and green collars on which the antlers of the fallow buck were embroidered. Several of those present were almost living caricatures of the hunting fraternity, with overbearing manners and piercing voices which sent the 'supers', 'awfullies', and 'frightfullies' an exceptional distance, but there were others too who appeared to be quite normal and well-adjusted. One woman thought it wrong to hunt and to like hunting, but she admitted to being guilty of both sins and she was sure that she would be punished for it in any after life; she considered herself to be addicted, however, and could not give it up.

Old locals looked on knowingly and enviously at proceedings as more riders arrived; men with bowlers and others with riding hats, and one eighty-year-old lady on her pony. A Forestry Commission keeper on a small sweating horse also turned up, in a tweed jacket, trousers, and hat, and wearing wellington boots with a hazel twig stuck down one leg to act as a crop. The setting was perfect with the serried ranks of tall pines on one side and the wild heathland, clusters of wind whipped birches, and a far off line of ragged pines stretching away into the distance on the other.

Most of the hounds were loaded up into a horse box and ten tufters[2] moved with the huntsman and whippers-in into the trees. One group of riders went along a muddy ride while the others followed the hounds into the woodland. It was then that I travelled at a speed that I did not match again during the next three and a half hours, for Josh decided that he did not like holly leaves against his closely clipped body and made off in top gear, backwards. Despite having the strap under my chin my hat went flying and the horse only stopped when he reversed into another holly tree, where he spun round in a number of tight circles with the holly leaves driving him frantic and scratching my face and penetrating my trousers. Finally the tangle of horse, holly, and reins became so great that he stopped and I dismounted as gracefully as the needle sharp leaves would allow. A rider had stopped to see if help was needed: 'I've never seen a horse travel at such speed backwards before' he said in amazement.

After that events were slow and the sound of the distant huntsman calling to his hounds gradually faded deep into the woodland. We waited in a ride, surrounded by tall trees, before walking over a bridge and a small moorland stream. All was quiet apart from the snorting of horses and the tread of hooves, and a light drizzle intruded on the stillness. Someone galloped off to try and find the hounds, and a small group of riders approached us; they too were lost. Tiring of waiting and listening we moved

[2] Tufters are the few hounds used to 'rouse' a deer before the hunt actually starts. Once a deer has been 'roused' and the tufters can keep its scent, the rest of the pack joins in.

on, away from the trees and over a road where the woodland changed to moor, an expanse of heather and heath, birch and bogs, rolling ridges, and gentle valleys, all in the soothing shades of winter. The New Forest only covers 145 square miles, yet distance seemed limitless. I followed several riders along the rim of a wide basin of bog where at its base ooze turned into a stream of liquid peat. It was surrounded by treacherous black mud beneath moss and straw-coloured clumps of dead grass.

Movement stirred as something hurried towards me, moving round and under the high tufts of heather. It was a New Forest fox in its thick winter coat. It was the lightest fox I had seen, the same colour as sand and the lifeless fronds of withered bracken. It was moving with urgency, its ears pricked forward; when it saw me it stopped, turned, and fled towards a small group of trees. Somewhere the hounds had disturbed it and I had upset its line of retreat.

Faintly the horn sounded from beyond the lowest lip of land and some riders rode on to higher ground to gain a better view. I made off in a straight line towards the sound over the bog, and though it was running with water and ooze Josh walked through it with ease. Another fox, running fast and leaping over the heather, passed close by, a green woodpecker laughed in the distance, and a December blackbird sang.

Two hours after the start of the hunt I saw the hounds again, moving through heather. The keeper and two other riders went away from the action as if anticipating the movement of the hounds and I went with them. The other riders moved after the small pack. The land was wet, with high heather and clumps of gorse, and as we moved up one side of the valley, the horses, hounds, and the rest of the field moved up the other. The tufters were on the scent of something and began to speak as a small group of deer moved off hurriedly in front. They ran in a half circle and paused silhouetted against the skyline, but as there were no antlers among them, the hounds were called back, and the does trotted off. Almost immediately another doe got up within a few yards of us, jumping, jerking, and bouncing in uncertainty. Lying in the heather her dark coat had provided perfect camouflage, but standing and running her white rump acted almost as a beacon.

The keeper had been right, for the hounds came towards us,

followed by nearly all the horsemen who had refound the hunt. We again crossed the road and moved towards pine forest. Car followers with their windows wound down stopped to admire the horses and two women with headscarves, long raincoats, and old bikes, told of a pricket[3] they had seen move into the trees. The huntsman cast again in the woodland and I followed the keeper, who was acting as a flanker to see if any deer crossed the forest rides. We trotted and galloped to keep ahead and Josh responded enthusiastically, as if relieved to be off. Several gallops followed, one along a waterlogged ride of heavy clay, at the end of which Josh suddenly stopped. I momentarily kept going and my groin crashed into the saddle's pommel, leaving me in excruciating pain, probably explaining why so many people who hunt seem to have funny voices.

The woodland was empty of deer, as was more heathland. An area of old forest with massive and mature oaks and beeches looked promising, but again the hounds found no scent. As we plodded over a wide, gravel-bottomed stream into heather, bracken, and gorse, a feeling of frustration could be detected in the riders. Again the huntsman moved off to cast his hounds in woodland but the keeper did not follow, as he decided to do the hunting himself for he was sure that the bracken and gorse must hold bucks. I followed him, as did two other riders. Shortly after the hounds and the rest of the field had disappeared we moved towards a dense patch of seemingly impenetrable gorse. Almost immediately two of the bushes started to shake inexplicably. The reason became obvious straight away, for well-developed antlers were tangled up in the branches as five fallow bucks hurriedly rose to their feet. Those caught up quickly broke free and they all ran off towards an area where it was said that the hounds did not hunt. A brief conversation followed; one of the other riders felt that it was not right to call for the hounds, or to hunt in that direction. The keeper thought nothing of hunting etiquette, however: 'Sod that', he said as he stood up in his stirrups and cupped his hands over his mouth to 'holloa' for the hounds (huntsmen do not shout, bawl, or bellow, they 'holloa'). There was no response, and so he holloaed even louder: 'Holloa', 'hollOOOOOOA', 'HOLLOOOO-OOOOA'.

[3] A two-year-old buck with spiky horns instead of branching antlers.

Eventually the huntsman trotted up with the hounds, which he cast into the gorse, noses down and 'sterns' working, and they immediately began to speak in high-pitched, excited yelps. We followed through the gorse, down a small, steep-sided valley, over a stream and onto heather, where the five bucks were cantering just ahead, their antlers giving them the appearance of being top heavy; there was a white one, a pale one with white spots, and three in their normal winter coats. Excitement seemed to fill the riders and horses as the deer ran off. Some lost riders, hearing the hounds baying, found themselves up with the bucks and Josh galloped hard as we wheeled away from the open country and went again towards woodland. The huntsman was close behind his hounds and it was everyone for his or her self as we careered into the trees. Just inside, a woman with a refined accent who earlier in the day had been telling me about the joys of 'watching the hounds work', had stopped, and she too tried a ladylike holloa. She sat looking at a buck which was watching her discreetly, half hidden by trees. One of the whippers-in rode up:

'What's the matter?' he asked abruptly.

'There's a buck in there by itself.'

'Well, madam?'

'It's by itself. Why don't we hunt it? Where are the hounds?'

The whipper-in was not pleased.

'Madam, the bloody hounds *are* hunting.'

'But the deer . . .'

'That's what they are bloody well hunting, madam.' He turned in exasperation and galloped off into the trees. The woman flushed and looked indignant; her enthusiasm for 'watching the hounds work' had evidently waned.

As the brief altercation ended, the horn sounded and the hounds spoke again. We were all off together, riding hard, with Josh near the front and overtaking horses much larger and sleeker than himself. The sun came out and we were hunting at last in hot blood, with hooves pounding and spray flying. I felt a great surge of excitement as we left the ride and galloped into woodland – wind and mud flew in my face, holly dragged over skin as I crouched low by the horse's neck, and small branches thudded against my protected head. There was a short pause as we listened for the hounds and then we started once more through trees, fallen leaves deadening the sound of hooves and spurting upwards. Josh was almost at the front and as we ploughed through the wide gravelly stream at full gallop we were showered by a cloud of sunlit spray.

We stopped again. The hounds had lost the scent, and riders sat sweating, mopping their brows and stretching their legs, and a man with a branch-bloodied nose sniffed loudly. The muddied horses stamped, steamed, and rested. It had been a time of hectic chase, hard and hot, and it made the earlier watching and waiting seem worthwhile. The hounds moved out of the trees again and we followed after a short wait. I had briefly felt the exhilaration of being the hunter and almost immediately I saw the deer once more. The hounds spoke far off as we walked slowly along a narrow road through the gorse, when the light buck came cantering towards us. It saw the riders and veered off to the right; it was hot, saliva frothed around its mouth, and its long pink tongue briefly flopped out. My mood immediately changed from one of enjoyment and satisfaction to one of regret, and my feelings went out to the buck and away from wanting a long, hard hunt. It seemed a tragedy that such a dignified animal should be pursued, with the possibility of death as the conclusion. Two Belgian riders next to me spoke excitedly in French; they were businessmen who had flown in the day before especially for the hunt, and at the end of the day they were due to drive immediately to Heathrow to fly back to Brussels.

It was the last we saw of the buck and the hounds scented it no more. The main pack remained shut in their horsebox as the deer had emerged too late in the day. The setting sun sent shafts of light through heavy drizzle, and a rainbow formed as clouds blackened. I turned Josh's head in the direction of his stable. My knees, calves, thighs, and back ached; I had been almost seven hours in the saddle and was soon enjoying the bliss of a hot bath.

Chapter Six

Stags, Moors and Mountains

Red deer, although less widespread than fallow or roe, are the deer most often featured in art, literature, and poetry. Pictures of them even appear in some travel brochures, to lure tourists and their money into wild and remote places. There is no doubt that the mature red deer stag, finely featured and elegant, yet lordly and powerful, is one of the world's most magnificent creatures. A good animal will stand over four feet at the shoulder and weigh in the region of 300 pounds, and when it has a set of fully developed antlers it has a look of beauty, majesty, and arrogance.

Scotland is the country normally thought of as the home of the red deer, and the sight of a stag silhouetted on a highland skyline surrounded by heather, wild skies, and an expanse of open and natural desolation, sums up the attraction of Scotland and symbolizes the freedom of the deer. Yet the red deer is a woodland animal which, as the Scottish forests were gradually cleared, had to adapt to mountain living for survival; and up to 200,000 deer now live in the Highlands and Islands.

Despite this, red deer can be seen in many other parts of the British Isles: in the Lake District, the Breckland, and the New Forest, but their main English stronghold is in the West Country. There red deer thrive, on Exmoor, the Quantock hills, and in the countryside surrounding them.

The Exmoor deer are true natives of the area, and on the moor they are as much a part of the normal scene as the cattle, sheep, and wild ponies that share their grazing. With the presence of deer, so traditions concerning hunting, stags, horses, and hounds, have grown up, and to many of the old Exmoor inhabitants, stag-hunting is as important as football and mass-entertainment to those who live in our large industrial cities. Many holiday-makers and affluent townspeople who buy retirement or second homes on the moor, find stag-hunting barbaric and distasteful, but to those who live and work there, the hunt often provides the only real break from

The kennel huntsman leading the Culmstock Otterhounds across the River Exe. Note the wading staffs, the terriers among the pack, and the woolly coats of the pure-bred otter hounds. (*Frank H. Meads/Shooting Times*)

The East Sussex and Romney Marsh Foxhounds running to the first draw. (*John Tarlton*)

A coarse fishing competition in the Fens. Such a river will yield catches mainly of roach, chub and bream, with occasional eels and pike. (*Cambridge Evening News*)

Game fishing – a fisherman, with gillie close at hand, tailing a medium-sized salmon he has caught on a spinning rod in the Scottish Dee. (*Arthur Oglesby*)

the rigours of exacting a living from the hard and often alien land.

Farming life really is hard on the moor, and the 265 square miles of purple heather, spectacular coastal cliffs, stone walls, moorland, wooded combes, small farm fields, quaint villages, and wandering livestock, do not provide a comfortable, or an easy livelihood. For Exmoor is a place of poor soil, high rainfall, and bad weather, offering those who live by working on the land little but never-ending toil. Yet the locals are tied to the moor by loyalty and tradition, and to them it is a place where they see beauty and find fulfilment.

Most of the farms are owned by the families that work on them, and range in size from between fifty and 300 acres. An indication of the bare living that some of them make is the amount they pay each year to enable them to hunt with the Devon and Somerset Staghounds. For although the printed minimum subscription is £60 per annum, many pay only £10, £20, or whatever they can afford. Again, although stag-hunting is often associated with the upper-class and privilege, many different types and classes hunt. A lady relation of the original Duke of Wellington regularly follows the hounds, still riding side-saddle, and a High Court judge and an ex-Lord Mayor of London are also associated with the pack. But the hunt also includes working farmers, small businessmen, and even a number of postmen. Indeed, when I went to meet the Master of the neighbouring Tiverton Staghounds,[1] himself a working farmer, I asked to see the 'boss', for when he came to the door, wearing dirty trousers and speaking with a broad country accent, I thought he was the cowman.

All over the moor, in private homes, exclusive hotels, and public houses, sets of antlers, and complete stuffed stags' heads are as common to see as rubber plants in suburban sitting rooms. The signs of living deer are also widespread, but they are usually missed by the holiday-makers who pass through; they assume that the roadside tracks are made by children, and that the numerous slot marks are the footprints of sheep. To those who know the habits of deer, however, the wild deer of Exmoor can be easily seen. There are at least nine herds, with a total population of between 700 and 900, and the way to observe them is to be out at dusk or in the early morning.

[1] There are only three packs of staghounds, all in the West country: the Devon and Somerset, the Tiverton, and the Quantock.

The deer are now said to be as healthy and secure as they have ever been and their management is left to the hunt, which usually kills between eighty and a hundred deer every year. Although many farmers suffer deer damage, most are tolerant; if damage does occur, they know that they can get compensation, and if a deer that has been living on their land is hunted and killed, they know that they will receive joints of venison. But they also tolerate the deer because they enjoy seeing, or taking part in, the hunt. It is suggested locally that if hunting was banned, each farmer would take deer control into his own hands, deer damage would not be accepted, and the future of the red deer on Exmoor would be extremely bleak. For confirmation of this it is said that when for two short periods in the past hunting was stopped, poaching and uncontrolled killing followed, and deer numbers declined rapidly. On the first occasion it was caused by Oliver Cromwell, when he outlawed hunting, and in the early nineteenth century it happened again when the pack was sold, and the deer population fell to just fifty animals.

The centre of the moor, and of stag-hunting, is the village of Exford, a small village tucked away in the hills, where talk of hunting and horses lacks the social pretension found in the high-class fox-hunting shires. It is an attractive village of brick and white-washed cottages, and front doors that open in two halves, like those normally found leading into stables. Because of its peace and charm, newcomers have been attracted to the village and over twenty of the houses are now the second homes of those who live and work elsewhere. Many of the villagers resent this, for their children have to move away from the village when they marry, simply because there are no village houses left for them.

The kennels of the Devon and Somerset Staghounds are just outside the village, a black block of buildings and wire runs, spotless and smelling of disinfectant. The staghounds themselves are larger than foxhounds; big, beautiful, and affectionate dogs with sad eyes, and as they clamber against the wire for a pat on the head or a friendly word, they seem incapable of aggression or ferocity. The huntsman has a deep attachment to his hounds, and one of the great sadnesses of all hunting is that after six or seven seasons, when age slows the dogs down, the huntsman takes the old hounds out of the pack and shoots them.

When a deer is hunted, it is usually pursued to water, where it stands at bay, until it is shot at close range. The carcass is then bled, by slitting the deer's throat, as would be the procedure in an abattoir, and taken to the 'larder' at the kennels, where it is cut up into joints. As I talked with the huntsman, standing in the larder, two stags' heads minus their antlers were on the floor. He was telling me how hunting had changed, how roads and great streams of car followers created problems of control and scent and how they, and wire fences, made the deer turn more than in the old days. Consequently the tasks of both the huntsman and the hounds have become steadily more difficult.

He regrets that many other aspects of Exmoor life have also altered. A few years ago stags' heads would not have been wasted, or fed to hounds; the tongues would have been rolled and pressed and the brains would have been fried for breakfast. The boundary hedges of the small fields were once cut and laid by hand and the spare wood was used on house fires during the winter. Between the jobs of sheep-shearing and harvest, men would go and cut peat, to be dried and stored, and in case of severe weather many families would buy a sack of flour to be made into bread. Housewives made their own preserves and jams and often a pig would be killed in the autumn to be cured and smoked. The villagers and people were almost self-sufficient and little was wasted – 'even the dog muck at the kennels was collected up to be used in tanning'. Today the hedges are cut by machines and life is dependent on coal, electricity, and the visiting baker. 'Now, as soon as everywhere is snowed up, a pylon falls down, or the miners go on strike, the people have no fires, no food, no electricity for their deep freezes and they are starving.' He hoped that hunting would not change any more, or have to stop.

The biggest change in hunting is the advent of car followers. On an average day the Devon and Somerset Staghounds attract seventy horses and riders, with as many as 200 riders on a big day, but they are usually outnumbered by cars and sometimes there are as many as 300 or even 400 car followers, with drivers and occupants all anxious to see the meet and the course of the hunt. As a result the roads become jammed with cars, long queues form, and motorists who want to continue their journeys become frustrated and irate, hounds get lost, horses shy, and some people predict that because of the chaos created, cars may well end stag-hunting before any prohibitive parliamentary legislation.

The objectors to stag-hunting are highly vociferous and organized, and some often suggest that the deer are actually killed by the hounds. If this was so the sheer size of the red deer would make the sport intolerable, but in fact the hounds rarely get at the deer, and death is delivered by gun. It is also likely that a stag could severely injure any hound venturing too close, as antlers make formidable weapons. Confirmation of this can be found in a quiet Exmoor wood where the inscription carved on a block of oak, simply reads 'September 10th 1882. Stag hound Recorder killed here'. Local legend has it that Recorder, a particularly faithful and courageous old hound, was killed at that spot by the antlers of a stag.

Some opponents of hunting also maintain that stalking could be attempted; such a proposition is only partially realistic, for the use of high-velocity rifles in a comparatively small area, frequented by tourists and campers, could be extremely dangerous. In the summer and early autumn, stalking would probably be safe, if carried out at dawn, but once the days shortened, then real risks would exist. On the other hand many hunters maintain that no stalking is possible and that hunting is the only way to control the deer. Yet even some stag-hunters participate in 'deer drives' to reduce numbers, in which hinds are driven towards men with guns.

Throughout the hunting area the League Against Cruel Sports has purchased blocks of land which it uses as deer sanctuaries and into which the hunt is forbidden to enter. Many of the objectors are new to the area, but even some local people with lengthy Exmoor roots dislike the hunt. One old man was put off when young. He was fishing in a small boat off-shore with some friends, when a hunted stag took to the sea and swam past the boat. The hunters rowed after it, put a rope around its neck and slit its throat as it swam, they then got the fishermen to tow the carcass to the shore. The old man saw cruelty and arrogance and did not like either, and his dislike has remained constant ever since. Knives are no longer used and some hunting people say that once a stag has taken to the sea, they accept that it has defeated them and they let it regain the shore and get away.

Most of the local people who do not hunt seem to have no interest in it, and have no strong feelings about hunting. They know that deer numbers have to be controlled and they prefer the work of the hounds to the activities of night poachers with their lamps and guns. Some poaching still goes on, but the appropriately named Exford policeman, PC Speed, is seldom troubled. When poaching does take place deer are often wounded and left, and the hunt then has to be contacted to take a few hounds into the woods to find the injured animal and put it out of its misery.

But the Exmoor people's attachment to deer is not limited to a liking of hunting, poaching, or venison, for the deer are also enjoyed simply for the beauty and character that they give to the area. Not far from the busy tourist town of Minehead, with its holiday camp and candy floss, a main road cuts along the edge of the moor giving an impressive view of heather, trees, and rugged coastline. Standing back from it, on a hillside, is a small brick and slate cottage, with dense mixed woodland behind and a well cultivated vegetable garden in the front.

Mr and Mrs Stark, a farmworker and his wife, live there, and each day he goes down to a nearby farm to work, while she busies herself around the home and garden. Four years ago as she worked, she noticed that a half grown deer, still with some of its infant spots, stood watching her in the wood. Several days she noticed it, and as she went from job to job in the garden, she would sing, or speak to it: 'What are you doing then?' 'Are you all on your own my dear?' 'Have you lost your mother, poor thing?' She thinks that it was an orphaned calf that wanted company, and as she spoke to it, so the young deer seemed to become more settled. As time passed, she started to go regularly into the wood, to leave potato peelings and kitchen scraps as food, and the young calf would watch her, hidden by trees. After she had returned to the garden, the deer would come down and feed. Mrs Stark always used a blue bucket, and gradually, as soon as the bucket appeared, the deer would walk down to meet her.

As familiarity grew, fear decreased, and the deer learned to trust the friendly woman with her blue bucket. Mrs Stark called the young hind Topsy, and whenever she went into the wood she would call: 'Are you about Topsy?' and the deer would quickly appear. One day she called but there was no response, and Topsy stayed away for several days. It was thought that she must have died, or that she had been killed by poachers, then suddenly, one morning, she reappeared. At first she was reluctant to approach the garden and her food and kept returning to some bracken up the slope by the trees. 'I wonder what's wrong', Mrs Stark thought, 'but then out popped this tiny deer; it was so pretty with its lovely spots, and Topsy had given birth to a calf of her own.'

Other deer live in the wood around the house, and in the garden a forsythia bush that overhangs the fence is a particular favourite for night-time browsing. Because of the deer, the hunt also passes through the wood each year, but so far Topsy has been missed by the hounds. On one occasion as the hounds and riders moved through the trees at the top of the hill the huntsman shouted down, 'Any about?' Topsy was standing by the garden fence. 'No-oh', Mrs Stark shouted back, and her old Border collie barked at the commotion. Poachers have not discovered Topsy either, although they have been active in the wood. One day Mr and Mrs Stark found a hind with her bottom jaw shot away, and all they could do was make her as comfortable as possible as she died. They found another that could not walk properly and they carried her into their old stable where they tended her all night, but despite all their care and attention, she too died, in the early morning. They buried her beneath an old apple tree, and as they set about the depressing task, Topsy stood on a bank and watched them.

The day I visited the cottage Mrs Stark was gardening. She took me through the garden gate and into the wood. 'Are you about Topsy?' she called. The hind was there, thirty yards away, her fine features showing through the dappled light and moving leaves, her dark eyes watching, and her moving ears showing unease at the presence of a stranger. She retreated and stood half in birch shadow and half in bright sunlight, with low branches and green bracken around her, fitting in so perfectly that to look away, just for a second, was to lose her in her surroundings. As we returned to the garden, Topsy advanced to the food that Mrs Stark had left from her blue bucket, and once I had passed through the gate and returned to the garden her concern ceased. The trust between the wild deer and the understanding countrywoman was touching to see, and as I left I hoped that they would continue in peace and that their relationship would not end in tragedy.

To see the moor and the hunt at first hand I had hoped to ride, but with the visitor's 'cap' being £8 per meet and the hire of a horse £22 a day, it was out of the question. Instead I arranged to go out in the early morning with the harbourer and then to follow the progress of the hunt in the van of a regular follower.

Even for five-thirty in the morning at the beginning of September, conditions were cold and wet, with the wind gusting to gale force and the rain teeming down. As light came I drove over the top of the moor. It was barren and bleak and even the wild ponies were sheltering, with their tails into the wind, behind the roadside beech-hedgebanks.[2] By the time I joined the harbourer in his car, the rain had ceased. Before acting as a harbourer he had been the huntsman of the Devon and Somerset hounds for several years, but on retiring he had found that he could not give up hunting altogether. Each evening and morning before a meet his task is to 'harbour' the deer, to search for a 'warrantable' stag, a stag that can be hunted.

We waited for several minutes in his car by the main road, as he said that deer could usually be seen grazing in the nearby fields at dawn, and that as daylight improved they would slowly wander off into the woods or lie down in the bracken. The wind and rain had made them change their normal habits, however, and no deer could be seen. Because of the lack of deer we moved along a side-road and stopped just beyond a cattle grid; from that position we could see across a small combe, on the far side of which was a field of felled woodland, where bracken grew and where a large stag stood feeding nonchalantly. It had a fine set of antlers, with one slightly palmated at the top. We got out of the car and cautiously moved along the leeward side of a stone wall; moss and grass covered its ledges, and the willows and beeches which grew from the top had their leaves seared brown by the unseasonal cold. The wind blew harder and my hands throbbed as if it was mid-winter; my cheeks tingled and my eyes watered, but still we watched as the stag grazed some 300 yards away. A squally shower passed overhead, and when the rain stopped shafts of misty light burst over an eastern hill-top, illuminating the stag's golden-red summer coat and making one antler shine almost white. Beyond the small field a tightly-packed wood of birch, beech, oak, and ash fell away towards the grey and uninviting sea, and spirals of mist rose from parts of the forest, as if it was on fire. We returned to the car and moved lower down into the valley and from there we could see another stag sitting in the wind-flattened bracken. Its head and antlers merged perfectly with its surround-

[2] A traditional Exmoor field boundary – a stone wall partially covered with earth, and with small beech trees growing from the top.

ings and if left undisturbed it would have remained unseen by most of the road-users later in the day. It was a big stag, and the harbourer was pleased with his morning's work; he had found two large deer, either of which promised to make a good hunt.

The meet was held at the top of an open stretch of wet moorland. Cars, horseboxes, and riders arrived, the wind still blew, and occasional icy showers made it uncomfortable. As the riders prepared to move off they looked cold and many wore large, windproof riding coats. The red-coated huntsman and his whippers-in rode off with nine tufters (four and a half couple), 'to rouse' the deer. As they walked towards the small combe and the field of bracken, the army of cars left to park near our early morning vantage point.

The huntsman walked through the wood and into the bracken with his hounds. Looking across the small valley three stags could be seen clearly, each one sitting, and unseen by the huntsman. The stags sat tight, until the hounds were almost on to the largest animal. Instead of running for safety, it trotted over to one of the other deer, and moved it out of its bed by digging its antlers into the smaller animal's side. The large stag went down in the vacated bed, and the young stag ambled off towards the trees and the sea, with four hounds in lazy pursuit. The stag with the palmated antlers was the next one to be roused and three hounds followed him off. The largest stag again did not move until the huntsman and his remaining hounds were almost on to him, and despite the shouts of the whippers-in he too ran towards the sea, and away from the open moor, easily clearing a five-barred gate as he went and taking the last two hounds with him. The horses and their riders moved away, as did the cars, and I joined my driver, a shopkeeper who follows the hunt in his van at every opportunity.

Several times along the road we stopped to listen. On either side were steep, rocky, and densely-wooded slopes, and we could see no signs of life. Other car followers went in our direction, but some accelerated off elsewhere. All were trying to anticipate the movements of the deer and the hounds and nearly all seemed to think differently. My chauffeur decided that one of the stags was being hunted and that the rest of the pack had been taken to the wood. We followed the road upwards, out of the trees, until we stopped on the side of a high, wide valley overlooking blocks of pines, open grass, and areas of bracken. Below us, two hinds trotted out of some trees with their half-grown and slightly spotted calves; they did not seem unduly concerned at the distant baying of hounds, and after a brief stop they moved slowly into a larger block of regimented conifers. On the opposite side, a distant stag appeared, moving towards more woodland, and several minutes later a solitary hound picked up the scent and disappeared in pursuit. More movement appeared below us, and a fox, with the white tip to its tail clearly visible, trotted across a narrow ride.

For the rest of the day we saw little life or action, although we spent our time looking for the hunters and hounds. It was rather like a hectic car rally with no specific route; we drove along isolated stony tracks, through woodland, by boulder-strewn streams, full of churning brown water; we travelled down into deep combes, and up onto moor; we saw glimpses of bog, heather, small fields of grass, and oats cut by binders, but we saw no deer, and nothing of the hunt. As the day wore on so the search became more frantic; up and down, here and there, looking and searching, but never finding. At one stage we met one of the whippers-in with a single hound, but he was little help, for he too had lost the riders and the rest of the pack. Most of the other car followers were faring no better; some passed us in one direction, others sped past in another. There were old ladies in large cars, a bearded Water Board official on a small motorbike, and knowledgeable men of the moor who seemed to know everything about the hunt except the whereabouts of the hounds.

As one last attempt to find the action, my driver turned down a small winding road that ran along the coast. As we descended and approached a number of small cottages, several riders appeared and we were waved down by a man who had a holster for a folding gun on his saddle. The rider dismounted and took out his shotgun and the shopkeeper took a twelve-bore from the back of his van. As he follows regularly he often arrives where the hounds have a stag at bay before any of the riders with guns, and when that happens he has the task of shooting the deer. He was told that the stag with the palmated antlers had been hunted, but had led the riders and hounds round in circles through the woodland before running down to the beach and swimming out to sea. Despite what I had been told earlier by some people who support the hunt, it was decided to walk along the beach in the hope that the stag had returned to the shore, in a state of exhaustion, so that it could be shot. The tide was out and we walked in a line over pebbles and around large boulders. There were two riders, walking in their large leather boots, black jackets, stocks and bowlers, and the shopkeeper with his gun. It was like a scene from an old Victorian country drama. There were no signs of the deer along the foreshore, and when the cliffs became too steep for the escape of the stag, the search finished. The rider and the shopkeeper put their buck-shot cartridges back in their pockets, disappointed that the stag had somehow escaped.

As we returned and the cliffs grew less steep, a youth shouted to us excitedly that he had found the tracks of the deer. 'Us slotted he up the cliff', he informed us, and it was clear from the tracks that the stag had crossed the beach and climbed the cliffs to life and freedom. The sun came out and a flock of mallard circled round and settled on the heavy swelling sea, their blue wing flashes glinting in the sun. The sea was pastel blue, and beyond the foaming surf and rolling water the Welsh coast could be seen clearly. The day was ending in warmth and beauty.

The traditions and sport of Scotland involving red deer are completely different from those of the West Country. The seven million-acre area is far larger than Exmoor, and because of the harsher conditions the deer are smaller. Despite this, they too have to be controlled, for in the winter the cold forces them down into the valleys from the high ground, and they can do much damage in woodland and farm fields. A herd of deer in a field of turnips or swedes can ruin the crop and it is said that two deer can eat as much as four sheep or one bullock. Like cattle, deer have no front teeth at the top and they pluck rather than bite; consequently in obtaining one mouthful of turnip, the plucking action uproots the whole plant. The deer then moves on to the next turnip, and the process can be continued along a whole row. Also, if winter conditions become severe and deer numbers are large, starvation sets in and there is much suffering. In order to try and reduce the problems of marauding deer and starvation, an annual cull of one sixth is attempted, which, when added to the natural mortality rate among the very young and old, keeps the deer population within bounds. The normal method of control is by stalking with high-velocity rifles, a sport that is usually associated with the wealthy and the landed gentry. It is a comparatively young sport, having taken place as we know it for only 200 years. Most of the sportsmen go to the Highlands in the early autumn before the red deer rut, to shoot stags, and it is the employed stalkers and gillies who are left with the more difficult and less spectacular task of stalking hinds when the winter is at its worst.

The Highland estate in the Grampians where I went stalking is over 60,000 acres in extent and consists of a wooded valley and barren mountains. It was originally owned by one man, but has since been turned into a family company to make the taxes more bearable, and now, in addition to the laird, there are a number of other men associated with it, most with long hyphenated names or grand military titles. The road leading to the estate runs through a rugged glen, with ridges, crags, towering corries, and bare rock faces, while the low ground is divided into woodland and fields for grazing sheep and cattle.

The entrance to the estate is over an iron bridge which crosses a small stream; a private road then runs two miles through mature pine forest, overlooking a long loch that fills the valley floor. As I drove by one end, white wind-blown sand lay in dunes and the beach curved round like a wide half moon lapped by breaking waves. White horses broke the surface of the deeper water as the wind gusted down the narrow glen, which continued into the distance and out of sight. The large house was made of granite with a number of ornamental slated turrets giving it a slightly absurd look, and to one side of a small courtyard were several outbuildings, including the gun room, where the two stalkers and the gillies were already assembled. Nearly all wore tweeds and plus-fours, modified to reduce bagginess. The stalkers were the ones who would be responsible for finding the deer and carrying the rifles, and the gillies would have the task of bringing back the shot stags.

They were a cheerful group, with broad Scots accents and genuine 'Och ayes'. A few years ago they would have been short-haired, addressed by their surnames without the prefix 'Mister', and aware of their station in life; now some of them wear their hair over their ears, the laird calls them by their Christian names, and they are allowed a point of view. In a locked glass-doored cupboard were a number of stalking rifles in a rack, and sets of antlers, most dating from the nineteen-thirties, adorned the walls. In the centre of the room was a large table, on which a new gun-case rested, and benches and seats were along the walls.

Two children ran from the house to release some kennelled beagles and then a tall, arrogant, adolescent youth strolled in, wearing newly-acquired camouflaged trousers, ill-fitting and gaudy. He had all the self-confidence and precocious conceit that wealth and privilege can give to those who know no better. His voice was public school, and his accent was so affected that he made even BBC newsreaders sound coarse. Inevitably, he was called Clarence, and was the son of a well-to-do family. He walked to the table and took out his new stalking rifle, together with telescopic sight, 'the most expensive in the shop', and then he launched into a lengthy oration about deer, rifles, and stalking. He was not addressing anyone in particular, but everybody in general: 'When I was coming up on the train it stawped at about two-thutty, and I could see a switch[3] from the carriage window. I nearly gawt my rifle down and shawt it where it stood.' When the laird came over, wearing a woollen jumper, baggy plus fours, and long woollen socks, Clarence's attitude changed to one of almost grovelling, obsequious respect, and he even addressed him as 'Sir'.

The laird and his family are generally liked by those who work on the estate and live in the surrounding villages and he was said to be a good and generous employer. 'We'll go and have breakfast now and be ready at nine-thirty', the laird said, and left, taking the objectionable Clarence with him. 'Och man, wha' d'you make o' that', the long-haired stalker commented as the others laughed. He then discarded most of his Scots accent: 'I saw a switch from the carriage window', he mimicked.

'Don't worry, he's not coming with us', the chief stalker informed me with relief. Later, one of them told me: 'When we get young toffs like him out on the hill,[4] we take them the longest and wettest way round; that brings them down a bit.' As the party in the house sat down to breakfast, the gillies and stalkers sat around the gun room and opened their sandwich boxes.

There were to be two stalking parties, and two Land Rovers pulled up outside the gun room, one towing a horse box; the

[3] A stag with four points on its antlers is known as a switch. A twelve-point stag's head is known as a 'royal'.

[4] The mountain on which the stalk takes place is always referred to as 'the hill' in ordinary conversation.

horsebox would take two ponies for the second group, to carry back the shot stags. At 9.15 am the two who were to stalk with the chief stalker arrived. They were not wealthy businessmen, or rich clients wanting a day's sport, but the laird's fourteen year-old grandson and his lean, lanky, and bespectacled friend; both looked too delicate, sensitive, and intellectual to shoot deer. The grandson was completely different from Clarence; under five feet tall, quiet, reserved, and with a brace over his teeth. He was wearing a complete stalker's outfit – miniature plus-fours, a tweed jacket, and a deerstalker hat – and was evidently already being groomed to join the ranks of the next generation of high-class country sportsmen.

The chief stalker collected a rifle from the cupboard and ushered us, together with Hamish, a gillie, into the Land Rover. Hamish was not going to take a pony, instead he would collect any shot deer on a Sno-Cat, a small tracked vehicle which masters areas of peat hags and bogs better than ponies, and which can cope with all but the steepest of slopes.

We drove through the woodland and a gate, and out into open deer forest, an area of desolate moorland, mountain streams, and high summits shrouded in mist. The dun greens and browns of the summer upland pasture showed the poor quality of the grazing, and over the whole estate, 700 stags and 2,000 hinds are the only animals to wander in search of food.

'Oh look, there are some beasts', the young boy observed, pointing over to a distant hillside where a number of specks could be vaguely seen. Through binoculars the herd of stags showed up clearly, moving in a long line away from us. It is one of the peculiarities of red deer that for most of the year there is strict segregation of the sexes, and the hinds and their calves move about in herds separate from those of the stags.

At a 'wee burn' the Land Rover was parked next to the Sno-Cat, where Hamish was to wait and switch on his walkie-talkie set when and if he heard a shot. Before the stalk actually started, the stalker looked carefully at the herd, lying on his back and steadying his large telescope against his knee, and he too referred to them as 'beasts'. When he had decided the best way to approach them, we moved along the bed of the stream to avoid the raw wind and to keep out of sight.

The water ran over rocks and around boulders and into a series of small pools, where Hamish had seen an otter working its way upstream the day before. It flowed at the bottom of a winding, steep-sided cleft, carved deep into the solid granite by the action of water and time, where ragged outcrops of rock and smooth grassy slopes covered the sides, and ancient alders and birches, with moss and lichen covering their trunks, clung by their roots to a precarious hold. Heather replaced grass at the top of the steep gorge-like sides, and several times we cautiously peered over the brow to view the deer. As we drew nearer we could see that it was a large herd of about 100 stags, with their coats ranging from dark red to the colour of fine sand. Most of the antlers were still in velvet, with the heads varying from those of fully mature beasts with many points, to young stags with small antlers and little hope of success in the approaching rut.

We worked our way upstream again, sometimes walking half way up one of the sides, with an almost sheer drop of twenty or thirty feet onto boulders below us, and occasionally we descended to walk along the bed of the stream itself. A smaller herd then came into view away on the far side, but they were too distant to take any interest in us. As we drew nearer to the main herd we briefly had to rise to the top of the bank, when jutting rock and deep water made it impossible to pass, and there we had to crawl through flowering heather until we were able to get down to the stream's bed once more.

The movement of the stags slowed; some browsed and others sat down in the grass and heather to chew the cud. The stalker and the young boy went on, bent double, the stalker leading, still with the rifle over his shoulder. When they reached a small, peaty sidestream they crawled in and disappeared from view. No movement followed, and I stayed peering through the heather at the deer some 250 yards away. The wind was just right and they were completely unaware of our presence.

Still nothing happened along the sidestream, and after ten minutes the stalker and the boy reappeared. They moved further away and crawled into some heather, sliding slowly through it on their stomachs. They stopped, the rifle was taken from its canvas bag, and before proceeding further they took their hats off. 150 yards away from the stags they stopped again and the boy moved alongside the stalker, who took careful aim at one of the stags to make sure that a shot was possible. He then pushed the rifle over to the boy who, resting the barrel on a tussock of grass, lined up his sights on the chosen stag.[5] Despite our tension, the stags still did not move, but chewed contentedly. The stalker wanted his stag to rise, to make an easier shot, and he waved his hand, but the movement was not seen. At the third attempt the stag's head whipped round in surprise, and slowly it rose to its feet, majestic, but troubled. A shot rang out and in an instant all the deer were on their feet, galloping over a nearby ridge and out of sight. The boy and the stalker walked slowly after them, not unduly concerned, and with the stalker again carrying the rifle, but there was no body and no signs of blood. It seemed to me that the bullet must have missed; but then three hundred yards away we came across the stag, it was dead, having collapsed in a small peat hag. The bullet had entered near the heart, and the animal could have felt little pain in its short and final flight. The rest of the herd had gone and were already just small specks moving up into mist.

Hamish was contacted on the radio as cold rain began to fall in white, wind driven sheets. Wildness and emptiness were all around us, and somehow it seemed the right place for the death of a deer; it had known little fear, it had not fled from hounds, or suffered the indignity of an abattoir. It had died where it had lived, on the wild mountainside. The stalker cut a hole in the animal's neck, just above its breast bone, and dark red blood gushed out. As the torrent eased he pumped one of the front legs backwards and forwards to briefly increase the flow, and then he proceeded to gralloch the carcass. He cut off its genitals and slit open its belly, before rolling the body over and sending the entrails spilling out in a heap, to be left as carrion for crows, foxes, and the pair of golden eagles that live around that particular 'hill'. Its large stomach was full of grass which to a farmer would have represented much damage to fields. At one time the stalkers were allowed to keep the kidneys, heart, and liver, as a perk for their work, but efficiency and control have reached the Highlands, and in the interests of hygiene and bureaucracy they now have to be left in the carcass until after sale.

From its teeth it was estimated that it was an old stag, nine or ten years of age and just beginning to 'go back'. Its antlers were

[5] The stag to be shot is picked out for a particular reason; old age, injury, a good head, etc.

quite large and well formed, and still covered in velvet. The stalker peeled the velvet off, leaving the main stem and tines of the antlers slimy and shining white, like newly exposed bone. The velvet has no use, except in the Far East where it is said to be an aphrodisiac, so he threw it away. Peat was then rubbed onto the antlers to make them look more natural; by so doing the carcass would also fetch a better price, although the amount and quality of the venison would not be affected.

Slowly the Sno-Cat advanced, crossing boggy hags and undulations that would have caused numerous difficulties for a horse or pony. The body of the stag was tied onto the bonnet and it was estimated that it weighed between 140 and 180 pounds. The estate would get 22p a pound; in southern England at the same time venison could be obtained from 'high-class butchers and game dealers' for 135p per pound. It is said that the British market is small (at exorbitant prices it is hardly surprising), and most of the Scottish venison is exported to Germany.

The stalker gave the gillie instructions where to take the Sno-Cat and we moved off again, walking up to higher ground but keeping below the mist. It was still cold and overcast – hind stalking in frost and snow must be extremely uncomfortable. We stopped for lunch overlooking a wide valley where more stags were grazing on the far side, and beyond them was woodland, the finger-like loch, and then high land and distant mountain tops. From the droppings and slot marks it was clear that we were again very close to deer. After going on a brief reconnaissance the stalker led us down the steep-sided slope and through an old birch wood, where we began to climb. From a plantation of pines a small party of hinds watched us intently, their heads and ears jerking with concern, but as we moved higher we passed onto open grass, while the pines continued on our right and the signs of deer got even fresher.

Above us, all we could see was a grassy slope and an overcast sky. Then we stopped, and as it was the turn of the tall youth to shoot he and the stalker cautiously advanced. I followed, and as we approached the brow, we flattened ourselves into the grass and advanced slowly by pushing forwards with our legs. The land levelled off and then began to rise steeply again, and through a fringe of varied grasses we could see the stags clearly. They too were sitting down and some of the fine, aristocratic heads seemed to be looking straight at us, from a distance of only 100 yards. The peace, the quiet, and the beauty, viewed through waving grass, gave the scene an almost dreamlike quality.

Inching through the herbage close to a herd of furtive wild animals, I was conscious of the basic and ancient feelings of the hunter, a combination of taut nerves, concentration, caution, and uncertainty. The deer had a commanding view of the area and any hurried movement would have led to disaster. Carefully the stalker and the youth stopped behind a small outcrop of rock and the gun was taken out of its cover. Two stags saw movement and stood up, looking anxiously towards us. The rifle fired, loudly and suddenly, and at 100 yards it seemed almost impossible to miss. The deer were puzzled, unsure of the sound or its direction, so they got to their feet slowly and trotted to the edge of the pines before moving away, out of vision. A solitary stag remained and he only walked ten yards. He stopped, his back legs collapsed beneath him and he rolled over backwards, his limbs kicking out violently and flailing air. The stag was dead and again the bullet had passed close to the heart.

Not all stags die that quickly, for some 'sportsmen' buy a day's stalking and shoot without practice, while others refuse to use telescopic sights as they prefer a more 'sporting shot'. Such 'sport' often leads to the difficult task of tracking a wounded animal miles over the mountains to put it out of its agony. Sometimes the wounded and crippled deer, in pain, fear, and trailing blood, is driven across mountainsides, until a road is reached and only then is the final bullet delivered. The whole aim of such a callous exercise is simply to save the task of humping the carcase over rough ground. When deer numbers get too large and stalking cannot cope, they are also driven towards hidden men with guns who then open fire. When the bullets begin to fly the deer panic and much carnage and unwarranted suffering is often the result.

The stalking that I saw was well conducted, and both stags died almost instantly. The position of the second stag was too difficult for even the Sno-Cat to reach, and so after gralloching the carcass, the stalker seized it by the antlers and dragged it behind him. Despite its bulk the deer flopped easily behind, leaving a thin red trail of blood on the grass. The stalker was a dedicated, conscientious man, with a wide knowledge of his deer, and to him it had been a typical day on the 'hill'. Two young gentlemen had tasted sport and two carcasses were ready for inspection. The remainder of the deer were high up on their summer pastures, safe from all predators except Man.

Chapter Seven

The Empty Holt

Despite the fact that I have walked for miles by running water, and spent hours just looking and listening to life in the rushes and reeds of the nearby brook, the one animal that I have always hoped to see, yet never have, is the otter. In my early teens, my hopes were increased by reading Henry Williamson's *Tarka the Otter*, a book which influenced me and affected me considerably, and which I have re-read several times.

The otter has not always been absent from the brook, for there are stories of these sleek, soft-furred, bright-eyed animals being seen along the whole of its meandering length. During the First World War some children in a small village close to the source trapped a large dog otter in a deep pool; one of them ran off to fetch a local farmer, who returned with his shotgun and killed it as it came up for air. Another otter, again a dog, was killed by hounds in the Fifties, close to where the brook feeds the River Cam, where the water is still and deep. It was around the same time that an old fisherman saw otters several times as he fished from the brook bank in one of our meadows. In the stillness and warmth of several summer evenings he saw a bitch otter and her cubs emerge from their holt among the tangled and water-covered roots of an old hawthorn tree, and there they would swim and slide down the mud bank into the water in play.

One afternoon I found a large roach floating dead, with a gaping hole in its side, but whether an otter or a large pike had caused its death I could not tell. Since then I have searched for other signs, but have found none. Otters may have been present or passing through, for with hollow willows, thorn thickets, twisted and submerged roots, as well as beds of sedges and rushes to give cover, they could have remained well concealed.

Since then much of the wildness has been removed and the tree which gave shelter among its roots has been ripped out and burnt by those whose business is land drainage. In the course of their work the engineers lowered the bed of the brook so much that beneath one of the road bridges the foundations of an earlier bridge were uncovered, forming a small island during dry weather, and surrounded by ledges and islets of stone, brick, and mud. Any otters passing through would have to travel that way, leaving as they went strategically placed droppings, or the prints of well-webbed pads, but the bricks remain clean and only water voles, wagtails, the occasional heron, and children, leave their footprints in the mud.

Throughout much of East Anglia the story is similar, of rivers and marshes where otters were once seen, now almost empty. Yet despite this, otter hounds still hunt, and on most Saturdays during the summer the hounds and the call of the hunting horn can be heard as the Eastern Counties Otterhounds search for the scent of a creature that is seldom found.

From many other parts of the British Isles reports are the same, of rivers and streams that once attracted otters now being largely deserted, and where the piping whistle of an otter is rarely heard. Several times I have stayed on a small farm in South Devon in the village of Otterton, where otters were once plentiful, and where the River Otter flows through water meadows and then salt marsh down to the sea. There, in the past, locals regularly saw signs of the animal that gave the river and the village its name, but now the most common animal to hunt its waters for fish, eels, and wild birds, is the mink; a carnivorous, water-loving, polecat like creature that lives wild in several parts of the country after escaping from fur farms.[1]

Although otters are seldom seen along the river, many of the locals do not object to the hounds meeting and working along the banks, for it is an event that has taken place at least once a year for as far back as most of them can remember. Several still watch them pass through and recall how they once played truant to follow the hounds and huntsmen when they met on the river bridge. Occasionally, at Sidmouth or Budleigh Salterton, where many monied people not acquainted with country life choose to retire in comfort, there will be complaints about cruelty and blood sports, and even factory farming. After one such outburst many

[1] From 1965 to 1970, the Ministry of Agriculture undertook a special campaign in an attempt to eradicate mink. Over 3,000 were killed, but complete eradication is not now thought practical or possible.

of the local shopkeepers put up notices in their shops proclaiming: 'Free range eggs', 'Free range pork', and 'Free range beef', and in the Otterton Post Office there is still a sign saying: 'We guarantee each egg individually layed'.

Otter-hunting itself is among the oldest forms of hunting with hounds, dating back to the time of Henry II, yet even to some of those who follow other country sports, the otter hunters have a reputation for unbridled blood lust. At one time a man who is still an extremely keen follower of beagles, also hunted otters, but he stopped after seeing the fate of an otter that had beaten the hounds. The master found it in a hole, exhausted, after a long hunt. He pulled it out with his hands and threw it while still alive to the pack, as the followers shouted in triumph and encouragement.

After my most recent visit to the Otter I decided to go further into Devon to go out with the Dartmoor Otterhounds, an old-established pack dating back to 1825. I hoped that by so doing I would catch a glimpse of an otter and also see if the methods of hunting were the same as those used to hunt Tarka. A night of torrential rain preceded the Saturday of the hunt, and as I drove over the River Dart a few miles from the sea I was doubtful whether hunting would take place. An old water-wheel churned round, as its mill race spewed a mud-heavy torrent over it, and the river itself was far wider than its normal summer size; it was in full spate, a frothing swirling waste of red-brown water.

Several hunters had arrived hopefully at the meet, but they were soon informed that hunting had been cancelled. They did not leave, but drank and talked steadily in the nearby pub. They were a mixture of 'posh' and country people – a woman teacher from the Isle of Wight, a long-haired youth who trained dogs for the blind, a Roman Catholic priest, another teacher, a part-time roadman, and a rabbit-catcher with his blonde-haired, blue-eyed girl from the Home Counties who spoke as if she was fresh out of public school.

The talk was of otters and otter-hunting; how the otter's best friend was the otter hunter and how hunting was better than shooting or trapping. From their own hunting, and from information gained from other hunts, they were convinced that the otter is far more widespread than is generally believed, although the density is much lower than it has been in the past. The big reduction came in the freezing winter of 1962–63, when otters died in large numbers. This is thought to have been caused by a combination of the extreme and prolonged cold, and the accumulation of harmful chemicals in the water, particularly dieldrin.

Since then otter numbers have increased, but in normal circumstances the hunters no longer kill otters, an arrangement, they said, which they had agreed with the British Mammal Society. The washed-out hunt was in early September and the season was almost at an end.[2] It had been quite a successful one; they had hunted approximately forty days, they had followed twenty-three drags[3] and they had found eleven otters. Only one had been killed and that had been an accident. At the end of the day the otter had suddenly got up between the master and his hounds as they were heading for home. One of the terriers seized it and the hounds quickly killed. During the same period the hunt had found twenty-nine mink and killed eight. They considered that they were doing farmers and the Ministry of Agriculture a favour by killing mink as they cause much damage in fisheries and hen-houses, and some farmers were said to ask the otter hounds to hunt along their streams.

From the hunters' talk it seemed that otter conservation was important to them, but whether the concern was out of conviction or a regard for their public image was not clear. They claimed that otter hunters knew more about the distribution and density of the otter population than most naturalists, 'for we are the only ones to go out looking specifically for otters, and hounds are the only reliable way of finding them'. Over the last ten years they have only killed twice, whereas in the 'old days' about sixty would be found in the course of a season and up to twenty killed. Then too, a line of men with ash poles, 'stickles', would stand across the shallows to prevent the hunted otter from moving freely along the river; this practice has since been abandoned, except when hunting mink. It was said that dog otters are usually the ones to be hunted and killed, as the bitches carry little scent. 'A bitch with cubs has virtually no scent and can more or less swim away in front of the hounds, and if they don't see it they can't kill it. Otters breed throughout the year and small cubs have been found

[2] The otterhunting season usually lasts from April until September.
[3] 'A drag' is the overnight scent of an otter.

in every month. Since the widespread use of chemicals, several sterile bitch otters have been found; they have scent as nature has no reason to keep it down.'

They admitted that in their present density otters do little damage, and that few fishermen now kill them. In fact, it was generally agreed that the heron, which is protected by law, does far more damage than the otter, which enjoys no protection. Most of those present took part in other field sports; the road sweeper shot pigeons, bringing them into range with decoys on poles, a woman regularly rode with harriers, the dog trainer followed stag hounds by Land Rover, and another still went badger digging and claimed that only the week before he had taken an order for a badger ham, a meat that is said to taste like pork and is good for filling sandwiches.

By the following Wednesday the weather had eased and the water level had fallen sufficiently to allow the River Lydd to be hunted. Being a week-day fewer followers were at the Fox and Grapes pub by the appointed time. At 10.45 the sprightly seventy year-old Master arrived, driving the hound van, which appeared to be of almost equal vintage, and at 10.50 the Master, two women, and the Roman Catholic priest retreated into the pub. The priest was one of the whippers-in and in his broad Irish accent he ordered a round of whiskies – doubles, ordered by brand names according to taste and experience. The hunt was supposed to start at 11.00 am, but at 12.10 they were still drinking whiskies, and I had lost count of the number of rounds. A few more followers arrived, including the rabbit-catcher and his girl, and a fifty year-old woman with an upper-crust accent who kept telling anecdotes about 'Mummy and Daddy'. They quickly installed themselves in the public bar and followed the examples of the others.

The Master eventually drained his final glass and blew his horn and we moved out into fresh air. He wore a patched up navy jacket and darned socks and looked far removed from my idea of a Master of a hunt. Most of those in cars must have been well over the breathalyser limit, but they all managed to arrive safely at the river, close to a large, secluded country house, built of local stone, where the hounds were released from the hound van. They were a motley collection of woolly-looking otter hounds, half-bred hounds, foxhounds and two terriers. To the untrained eye otter hounds look far from pure bred, having a distinctly mongrel look, with brown and grey curly coats, tails held close to their back legs almost guiltily, and flopears and sad eyes that give them a friendly, yet querulous expression. As the hunt started the hounds seemed quite uninterested, rolling in the grass and cocking their legs and squatting over thistles. A middle-aged woman follower joined me and pointed out what was happening. After 200 yards the Master sounded his horn and all the hounds went to him. I thought that he must have already found an otters' holt. 'Why has he stopped?' I asked.

'Oh, he's only relieving himself as usual', came the reply. Shortly afterwards, as the Master tried to get round an obstacle on the bank, he stumbled and, slowly and elegantly, sat down in the muddy water until it was well above his waist. For some reason, as we continued, my companion proceeded to tell me the details of her past sex life. It had certainly been more varied than that of the average registered hound, but taught me little about otter-hunting.

The small river was still far above its normal level and the summer shallows only showed themselves as waves and patches of white topped water. Sheep were in the meadows to the side and the scene was peaceful, uncomplicated by the presence of scent, otters, or mink. It was so peaceful in fact that at 1.15 we returned to the cars for dinner.

On resumption of hunting, the air still held the odour of consumed alcohol. 'It's a good thing', the Master informed me, 'the smell has the same effect on huntsmen as dangling a carrot in front of a donkey.' We moved up a small side stream with dense bushes and fallen trees along one bank, to look for mink. The priest poked his pole into some piles of dead wood as the hounds milled around him, but nothing bolted. 'He's a bloodthirsty devil', the woman told me, the history of her sexual affiliations finally exhausted. No mink were found and we returned to move up the river where the water was still high, fast flowing, and muddy. Two hounds located scent, and vigorously dug – after a mouse.

At a bend, the bed of the river turned to sand and gravel, and we waded across the shallow water. It was surprisingly warm, but treacherous as it tugged at shins and shoes, and the pole of the otter-hunter was shown to be of extreme importance in staying upright. Those who hunted regularly wore shoes with holes in the sides and soles to allow the water to drain quickly away, but my shoes continued to squelch for some distance. Alders and willows lined the banks and occasionally a hound spoke as if gaining a fragment of scent. The two terriers struggled on, well to the rear, finding the high water and full ditches difficult to negotiate; it was surprising that they did not get washed away and drowned. They were not the only members of the pack to face difficulties, for at fences of tightly drawn wire the newly entered hounds,[4] who had not yet mastered the art of squeezing through the strands, sat whimpering dejectedly until offered assistance. Gradually the river bed changed to boulders again and depth increased. One hound splashed through the water, looking and smelling under ledges and banks, and as he spoke others leapt in and swam against the current into deeper water. They streamed onto the far bank and sped away with deep-throated baying. By a shingle bar near an ancient stone bridge they got keener, faster, and noisier, but then the 'music' faded as the drag disappeared. It was at a point where two branches of the river met and the hounds were well out of their depth as the brown water pulled and churned around them while they searched for scent.

After some discussion the right fork was taken; stinking lilies grew on the banks and elders, thorns, and nettles grew under tall trees of ash and oak. Through a field of maize other scents were found and the hounds went away from the river as if after a fox. The Master called them back, all except one old bitch who sat down moodily and who wanted to go elsewhere. With the scent gone it was decided that we had been following the drag in the wrong direction and we returned to the bridge and the point of turmoil where the waters met. On a small brick ledge one of the followers found an otter's 'spraint', which proved, he said, that an otter had passed that way recently. The hounds again took to the water but, swimming with the current, they had no control and a young hound disappeared as it was sucked under. Ignoring the treacherous bed, the rabbit catcher plunged into the water (which was well above his waist) and, despite the strength of the torrent, managed to grab the helpless animal and pull it to safety. The other hounds were called back as it was considered too bad to continue and we returned to the cars. The hounds were ordered into their van, the priest got changed, the dripping rabbit catcher started up his car and switched on his heater and the fifty year-old

[4] Puppies in their first season of hunting.

lady substituted a skirt for her wet trousers and told another story about 'Mummy and Daddy'.

As the conditions in Devon had been unfavourable and no otter had been either seen or really hunted, I waited until the weather had cleared and the rivers had dropped to their normal summer levels, before going out with the Eastern Counties Otterhounds to see if they were any more successful. The meet was due to be held close to the sea at Snape, a small Suffolk village. The day was bright with a warm September sun that filled the roads with the last of the season's holiday motorists. The countryside was typically East Anglian, slightly undulating arable land, and many of the hedges that had been left bordering the fields and roadsides were already heavily tinted with the deep red of haws and the orange of ripe rose hips. Combine harvesters were cutting the last of the weather-flattened wheat and barley and burning stubble poured smoke into the eastern sky.

The followers were already at the bar of the pub when I arrived and whisky was again the main drink. The Master, an antique dealer, wore a smart red coat, blue cap and blue stockings and he explained why drink was important: 'Otter-hunting is always a matter of right water levels', he said, 'on both the inside and the outside'. Three other older men were also in hunt uniforms of blue jackets with red collars and brass buttons, and red ties and red socks. One was a retired farmer, and another a journalist. Other followers were in ordinary clothes, including two gamekeepers with broad Norfolk accents and pint mugs. The largest was big, beery, and happy, despite having a stiff right leg which had only been out of plaster two days, following a road accident in which he had lost a knee cap. But instead of staying at home, resting in front of the television set, he thought that the exercise of the hunt would do him good. Another man waited outside the bar with his small son. He was on the management side of Quaker Oats, and enjoyed the glimpses of the countryside that otter-hunting gave and which he would not otherwise get.

The morning's hunt started on the River Alde, where it runs through a sluice into salt water. On the way we passed the Maltings, a famous concert hall, causing one of the keepers to comment: 'That's where they do all that drama stuff, you wouldn't get me going in a place like that'. The few days of hot, dry weather had made the Alde far different from the Devon rivers which rose in moorland and flowed over stone. The water was sluggish, having oozed from deep clay, with black mud at its edges and marshland and reed beds further on. The hounds moved and hunted well together, putting several ducks and moorhens to flight, and when hunting takes place along lowland waterways during the breeding season, much damage and disturbance must result. After a short time the pack left the river and crossed the high protective bank to make off into the marshland beyond and below – all the pack, that is, except one pure-bred otter hound, Paleface, who stayed with the foot-followers. She was three years old with a light coloured woolly coat and large mournful eyes. As the others hunted she would sit down, or wag her tail, completely uninterested.

Small ditches and dykes dissected the reeds, rushes and sedges, and were crossed by bridges made from single planks of wood, and soon the Master and his pack were lost from view. The hounds began barking and baying enthusiastically and some of the field crossed one of the bridges over a ditch of black water to see what was happening. After a time the Master and the mud-coated hounds reappeared; they had caught and killed a twenty-pound coypu.

There are many coypus in the East Anglian marshes, despite the efforts that have been made to exterminate them. Imported from South America and now running wild, they are giant, rat-like rodents, with large appetites, and their excavations undermine river banks and drainage channels and cause considerable damage. Like the mink, they too were farmed originally for their fur, but some escaped and breeding colonies quickly became established. I saw my first coypu as a boy, at the fair, when a notice outside a small tent lured me in: 'Come inside and see the world's largest rat, caught in England', it read. I paid my sixpence, and inside was a coypu, tame, well-fed, and content, nibbling quietly in a large cage.

In another ditch the hounds began to speak again, and they dived in, stirring up the black stinking mud, but they found nothing. The Master sounded his horn and called them out and returned to the river. They eagerly followed, pushing past those walking behind and muddying trousers. Again they were a mixed bunch of pure bred otter hounds, foxhounds and even beagles; they worked eagerly with the first to speak usually being a large old foxhound, almost as wide as he was high. Paleface still quietly padded along behind the footfollowers, wagging her tail and looking as if she wanted to find a more intellectual pursuit.

The river became shallower as we moved upstream, and where part of the bank had caved in, the collapse was attributed to the work of coypus. In some rushes two hounds dived simultaneously and caught a young hen pheasant. It was killed and rapidly devoured. Two others caught a skulking rabbit, and again its end was short as the hungry hounds gulped it down. At a small thicket of willow the pack started once more, running through the wood and along a ditch; the Master thought that they were after another coypu and called them back. 'You wait until we find the real thing', one of the regular followers informed me, 'when we find the drag of an otter the music of the hounds is altogether different.' At a small bridge where the water was shallow and ran over gravel the Master called his pack together and held them with the help of his two young children who were acting as whippers-in, in place of the regulars who had been delayed elsewhere. His son soon got tired of waiting for the hound van and asked for more peas for his peashooter.

We had left the pub at ten to twelve. At ten to two we were back inside for dinner, and there we stayed for another hour. When we emerged the hounds looked hopeful; they were in the hound van, with the sliding door at the back slightly up to allow a row of hounds' heads to look out. The afternoon's hunt was to be in an area of salt marsh close to the estuary of the Alde, reached by a drive along narrow and deserted country roads, which led to a farm and a well-worn farm track. The hounds were eager to resume hunting as we descended from good arable land to rough fields of grazing, rushes, and ditches, which stretched out behind the estuary wall. Beyond, the estuary spread out in sky-matching blue water to the distant shore where woodland spread down almost to the water's edge. The boats of summer sailors ploughed widening furrows through the rippling water and flapping sails joined the intermittent speaking of the hounds and the cries of encouragement from the huntsman. The hounds spoke almost immediately they arrived at the sea wall, speeding inland, allegedly on a fresh line, and following scent by the side of a ditch. A marsh hare ran off at high speed and disappeared into the distance, and the hounds followed, spreading out in a long loping line. The whippers-in had become bored, even with their peashooters, and the Master had to retrieve his hounds almost single-handed. At hunt functions he wins awards for the quality of his horn blowing, and with more hares attracting the attention of the hounds he gained plenty of practice. Eventually he collected them and returned them to a ditch that gradually widened, running close to the sea wall, and by it they found the carcass of a dead coypu with long red teeth. Some hounds also found several dried out and long dead rabbits, which they ate with relish. As the dyke widened, rushes grew thickly on both sides from gleaming soot-black slime, and the hounds eagerly searched for animal scent. Some went into the deep water and swam from side to side with their tails stretching out behind like rudders. As the hounds worked on one side of the sea wall, three herons stood on black mud on the other as the tide slowly receded, allowing them to advance over an old oyster bed that seemed to be decaying and desolate. A short-eared owl flew from a bank, flushed out by a straying hound, gulls wheeled, soared, and glided in the sun-filled air, and Paleface came up to me, wagged her tail and sat down, as clean and as bored as she had been at the start of the hunt. More rabbits and marsh hares got up, and as a warm breeze came off the water, the tang of salt dried our mouths.

As we made our way back to the farm at a leisurely pace I was again regretting that I had not seen a real hunt and there had certainly been no trace of an otter. A farmer, encased in a cloud of dust, was busy baling some straw, and several of those hunting loitered to pick ripening blackberries that lined a steep-sided drainage channel of stagnant water and odious mud. It was then that the hounds began to speak again and they plunged into the ditch and worked among the nettles and briars of the banks. They ploughed backwards and forwards and the black water frothed with the movement of anxious, working limbs. A coypu jumped from one bank across the water into the undergrowth of the other, and as the hounds swirled excitedly in the black cauldron, the baying reached a crescendo at the rich, fresh scent. Paleface moved away from the unedifying sight to lie down in some long dry grass – she just could not get interested.

The square old hound suddenly dived half way up the bank and others followed an instant later. The coypu was immediately dead; death was too rapid to be cruel and the mud was too black to show blood. The corpse was torn apart by powerful jaws and as its entrails were gulped down and its bones crunched, champing hounds growled to safeguard their own tasty morsels. The dogs climbed out, gleaming with a sheen of black filth from head to foot; Paleface stood up and looked aghast as a dripping foxhound bumped into her, blackening half her head. A tall, well-dressed man with two children at his side, a long way from the city pavements to which his clothes seemed more suited, looked down his nose with obvious disapproval as the hounds began again on a 'roaring scent'. One of the old uniformed followers looked at me knowingly; this was the real thing, the genuine music of otter hounds and not merely the baying of coypu killers. Nods, winks, and whispers were exchanged; should they go on, despite it being late in the day? The scent ran out. 'It must have been a heel line, of the otter coming in and going up that ditch over there, to that small wood', one of the followers said with the assurance of an expert. The hounds came back towards us and suddenly they roared again. They were in hot pursuit; suddenly they dived into reeds and another animal was dead. 'Has it got long ears?' one asked, 'they really need an otter to sharpen them up. They haven't killed one properly for two seasons.' Despite the 'roaring scent', the knowing looks, and the data given to the British Mammal Society, the hounds had killed another coypu, making the day's tally three rabbits, three coypus, and a pheasant. The followers and the hounds had enjoyed their day and even Paleface got into the hound van with an air of relief and contentment. I was content too, for although I had not seen an otter, I had not seen one killed either.

Chapter Eight

The Return of the Rabbit

Although for many years foxes, hares, deer, and otters were the animals that provided sport for those with money, land, or social connections, there were cheaper pastimes which provided entertainment just as enjoyable for ordinary working people. The quarry was not so noble, or considered by the gentry to be at all 'sporting', but to ordinary countrymen, with snares, dogs, nets, guns, or ferrets, rabbits gave good sport and cheap food.

Then, the rabbit population was free from myxomatosis, its breeding grounds and habits had not been restricted by the modernization of agricultural techniques and the mechanization of farming, and rabbits bred and multiplied throughout the country. Rabbit warrens were common in fields of pasture land, pitting the surface with countless burrows, and the rabbits themselves would graze on the grass so heavily that sheep and cattle were not able to enter some fields until mid-summer. In the same way root and cereal crops suffered, with rabbits living in the hedgerows and grazing and nibbling the crops around the perimeter of the fields in a wide strip.

When myxomatosis struck, rabbit numbers plummeted. The disease was introduced into this country from France in 1953 and over the following two years its advance was swift and deadly, and rabbits became rare. Not satisfied with the rapid advance some farmers carted infected rabbits about their land and introduced them into populations that had remained healthy. Soon the hedgerows were devoid of familiar life and the warrens were deserted. The rabbits died slowly, as their eyes became swollen and filled with pus, obscuring all vision. They wandered about lethargically, in fear, unable to find the safety of their burrows. It seemed that the disease must be final in its consequences; rabbits died in thousands, above ground and below, and the smell of death poisoned many country walks. The work of the weather and subsidence in the soil gradually obliterated the abandoned burrows from view, and it seemed as if the rabbit had never been introduced into the British countryside.[1]

Those who simply saw their farms and holdings as economic assets and who had welcomed the cruel and contrived slaughter viewed the results with satisfaction. In 1955 there was a bumper harvest and crops of all kinds grew on land which in earlier years had produced rabbits, light yields, and nothing more. In some areas the production on the land increased by between 15 and 20 per cent. They considered that the end had justified the means and economic efficiency had triumphed yet again over humanity and morality.

Astonishingly, the rabbit did not disappear completely. After a few years of apparent extinction, suddenly the occasional rabbit was seen running again into wide hedgerows. Numbers remained low for several years, but then a population explosion took place. The rabbits' resilience and their ability to survive is surprising, for in addition to men and myxomatosis they have numerous enemies. Badgers and foxes dig up many litters of young rabbits from the shallow 'stops' where they are born, and foxes take many adults. Stoats and weasels are also very fond of rabbits and will track them down relentlessly. Often a rabbit, sensing that it is being pursued, will freeze and scream out in fear. One old rabbit catcher (who at the age of eighty still plays cricket, and could be the oldest active cricketer in England) has seen stoats take rabbits several times: 'The stoat is so persistent that he follows the rabbit wherever he goes. Finally the rabbit seems to become mesmerised and the stoat rushes and grabs him at the back of the neck. You usually hear a horrible scream for about half a minute and then silence. The stoat has bitten through the neck and on their teeth is some substance which keeps the wound open and the blood comes out and the stoat will have a feed on the blood straight away. I have seen a doe stoat weighing perhaps a pound, dragging a rabbit yard after yard to her young ones in a burrow. She pulled it through bushes and long grass and her strength was extraordinary. I have often been surprised at the strength of these little creatures when it comes to providing food for their young. But they are not just killers; four or five stoats will play together, playing, dancing, and jumping about. They are full of play.'

[1] It is thought that rabbits were introduced into this country by the Normans, and were known as coneys.

Now the rabbit has returned, but it is with mixed feelings that country people have welcomed it back. The sight of new burrows and bobbing tails brings back memories of 'the good old days', and at harvest-time something of the old harvest feeling briefly returns. As the combine harvesters eat their way to the end of a field, the rabbits again run for cover, and men with twelve-bores try to shoot them. But most countrymen also remember the amount of damage that was once caused by rabbits. They know that damage to crops cannot be allowed to pass unchecked and that rabbits must be controlled. Strangely, almost the only people, apart from those connected with the land, who dislike rabbits are Cornish fishermen, who are extremely superstitious. Quite why they hate the rabbit nobody seems to know, but it is probably connected with the sighting of rabbits during daylight being associated with bad weather. One morning shortly after nine o'clock, as I went with a Devon gamekeeper to feed his young pheasants, we saw a rabbit running unconcernedly along an open bank. 'To see them run or play at this time of the morning is a sure sign of bad weather', he informed me. The day continued to be fine with an open sky and a hot sun and I assumed that I had just learnt a piece of unreliable weatherlore. That night, clouds rolled in, the wind got up, and for two days the rain lashed down. There was widespread flooding, boats sank (including Edward Heath's *Morning Cloud*), and at my overnight accommodation the garden was flooded and a raging torrent flowed down the garden path and washed away the gravel. Crashing thunderclaps shook the house and the landlady put the cutlery away wet. 'I'd better stop doing this bright steel', she said, 'else it'll attract the lightning inside.' With the crashing and rumbling almost directly overhead, I thought that it would be unwise to doubt that piece of old country wisdom as well.

Every so often myxomatosis recurs, striking down the rabbit colonies, but it appears to be less virulent than the original strain and more rabbits survive. The reason for this is thought to be due to their greater resistance and to a weakening of the original strain of the disease. It is also a fact, in many areas, that more rabbits now live almost entirely on the surface, 'bush', 'scrub', or 'stub' rabbits, and so they come into less contact with the fleas which carry the disease. Occasionally a whole colony appears to be wiped out, with no survivors, and there are rumours and suspicions that 'the Ministry' has introduced a new and more lethal strain, but this is denied, as the deliberate spreading of myxomatosis was made illegal in 1954.

Perhaps the chief reason for the rabbit's survival is its adaptability and its ability to reproduce itself rapidly. A young female rabbit can become pregnant at four to six months and, with a gestation period of between twenty-eight and thirty days, they can have up to five or six litters a year. Some experts consider that the breeding season of the rabbit lasts from February to September, but it is likely that during mild winters it is even longer and pregnant does have been found in most months of the year. Indeed, I have seen clear signs of territorial behaviour at the end of October.

But although rabbits are back in large numbers, the overall population is unlikely to reach pre-myxomatosis levels, for the landscape that they once found so favourable has changed, as methods of agriculture have altered. Arable fields have grown in size, reducing the number of hedgerows and ditches, and the amount of pastureland has shrunk, leaving fewer places where the rabbit can find cover to live, burrow, and breed. Even so, it is now common to find crops badly grazed, and many areas of young forest are threatened. In consequence snares, guns, rifles, gas, whippets, and ferrets are being used in forests and on many farms, as rabbits have to be controlled once more. The overall cost of rabbit damage is many millions of pounds in the course of a year and there is no doubt that they cannot be allowed to eat and breed unchecked. Occasionally, when numbers climb and damage to our crops becomes obvious, I will go out with the dogs and a gun, and shoot at whatever is flushed. In the company of the dogs, when a rabbit is wounded it is quickly caught and killed, and again the use of dogs, far from being cruel, saves a great deal of suffering. Since myxomatosis, many people will not eat wild rabbit, yet the meat is good, white, and tastes something like chicken, and even at 50p per rabbit it is good value for both the eater and the shooter.

After 'mexy' had swept the country, many ferreters got rid of their ferrets as they could foresee no further use for them, and long nets were left in the corners of sheds to rot. Now both are in great demand. New ferreters are learning the arts and frustrations of working ferrets, and dogs too, are seeing ferrets for the first time. One farmer, forgetting that his dog had never seen a ferret, was watching two ferreters at work on his land when a ferret emerged from a hole; his dog rushed in, shook it, and killed it, and left the ferreters without any means of flushing the rabbits.

With the return of ferrets, another alarming and entertaining sport has been resumed; the sport of ferret-legging. This involves releasing ferrets down a volunteer's trousers, usually to win a few shillings or a pint of beer in the local pub. Some also release them in their shirts and one old countryman is said to have let a ferret and a rat loose simultaneously in his shirt. Another claims to have had as many as seventeen ferrets down his trousers at the same time. A slight variation is to let a ferret down a pair of trousers and keep it there for as long as possible. The *Guinness Book of Records* states: 'Record durations for keeping a ferret down a pair of trousers with ankle ties are unsatisfactory owing to reports of the ferrets being tranquillized. The competitors are abusing the National Health services in applications for free anti-tetanus injections.'

The battle against the rabbit has also been aided by the introduction of one or two innovations. Those who enjoy ferreting but dislike digging can buy ferret collars containing a built-in radio transmitter so that when the ferret 'lies up', the receiver is switched on and the exact location of the ferret can be found, and digging is kept to a minimum. Another form of rabbit control, which has developed into a highly dangerous sport, is night shooting from a moving vehicle; a practice which in most cases is illegal but which takes place on quite a large scale. When I first tried to shoot from the back of a moving van, I found it virtually impossible. I could see the rabbits, but not my sights, and the rabbits fled away from the headlights suffering little more than fright. It was not the driver's fault, as he normally drives a twenty-three-and-a-half-ton tanker and handled the small pick-up easily enough. Yet neither I, nor the other gun could hit anything except fresh air and stubble. In fact all we managed to achieve was to bring a number of concerned people to the illuminated doors and windows of their houses along a nearby road, where they viewed with alarm the headlights and crashing guns.

To see night shooting as it is normally carried out, I visited a neighbouring farm on a warm June evening, when a foray into rabbit country was planned. Reg and Philip, two young farmers, and Arthur Sewell's two youngest sons, Brian and Bernie, had guns, and they were joined by two youths, a 'picker-up' and a spotlight operator. With combat jackets, cartridge belts, and guns, it was like a meeting place for armed guerrillas, rather than an organized shoot. Two of the guns and the two youths climbed into the open back and crouched down and Philip drove off along a country road. 'You'll enjoy this', Bernie told me, 'Reg always thinks he's John Wayne once we start.'

At the first field the manual spotlight was connected up, and Reg and Bernie stood with their guns pointing over the driver's cab, ready for action. The powerful spotlight joined the headlights in the search for rabbits, and the picker-up prepared to jump from the moving vehicle whenever required. After the first fusillade the guns decided to change positions, as shooting was far too difficult from the bumpy back. Bernie was eager to change, for on an earlier expedition he had been bounced right over the driver's cab and onto the bonnet, a trip that had cost him three days off work to recover. In fact the new position seemed even more dangerous than the first, for they both sat on the bonnet, each straddling a wing mirror, with one foot hooked around the front bumper. Then we were off again over spring barley, the lights searching for rabbits, and the two on the bonnet with their guns pointing upwards, resting on their thighs; John Wayne never looked better, not even when riding shotgun.

Pink eyes reflected back and the guns took unsteady aim; rabbits ran, shots rang out, and the picker-up leapt into action. One rabbit was wounded and scrambled on, dragging two broken legs behind it; Bernie was going to shoot again at close range but the picker-up ran towards it as if he could catch it. He could not, for the wounded rabbit twisted and turned and, on reaching long grass, it disappeared down a burrow, probably to die of shock and in agony. More rabbits could be seen in the field and the Land Rover stopped to allow the guns to jump down and take steadier aim. Back on the bonnet for another drive along the edge of a field the two guns bounced as the Land Rover accelerated. Suddenly Reg's legs shot into the air and momentarily his back rolled flat over the engine, but he managed to regain his position and balance before any damage was done. A hare got up and sped away, turning and twisting in front of a trail of flying dust as it tried to evade the spotlight. A brief rest followed as the guns climbed warily over the wing mirrors to walk painfully for a few strides to get the stiffness out of their shaken bodies.

The next field was on the far boundary of the village with houses on two sides. Because of this it was decided that it should be shot at high speed in the hope that doors would not open and the usual telephone calls to the police telling of strange lights and shooting would be avoided. The ride was bumpier than ever and the guns and the two boys were tossed about even more violently. Suddenly, by a large hedge, eyes again reflected light, they had no pink tinge, and were clear and bright, brighter even than cats' eyes along the middle of main roads. It was a vixen and her three-quarters-grown cubs. Three vanished into the hedge and the fourth made off across the open field. 'She's the vixen leading us away from the cubs', Bernie shouted, and Reg urged 'Go on, go on', as he had never shot a fox. As Philip tried to get the groaning Land Rover to accelerate up the hill, the fox sped away with its ears pointing back towards us. As the headlights bounced it was seen in broken illumination, getting well out of range, until after one jolting bump the fox had vanished into the opposite hedge. Another hare got up and darted away and in the turmoil and fury of the chase, Reg thought that it was a rabbit and at twenty-five miles an hour on a bouncing bonnet he shot it stone dead, a reflex action of aiming and shooting. There were no rabbits elsewhere on the hill as the hunting foxes and the motorized fox hunt had caused them to retreat underground.

Brian changed with Bernie, and Bernie joined me in the cab to explain in greater detail the finer points of this hazardous exercise. Bernie likes his shooting – once, after sawing himself out of a tree with a chain saw, he went out walking with his twelve-bore, and a broken ankle, while still on crutches.

In another field, well away from the houses, the rabbits were further from the hedges and ditches that would have given them shelter, and instead of running for cover they skulked near the ground and flattened themselves away from the spotlight's beam. The Land Rover stopped and the guns approached by foot. A rabbit ran and Brian fired both barrels, yet it ran on, directly at him, until he swung his boot and the rabbit cartwheeled into the air and landed dead. The others cheered as if a goal had been scored at Wembley, and all the rabbits still out feeding in the next field were frightened back to their burrows. As the guns returned to the Land Rover a near accident occurred as both Reg and Brian were thought to have climbed into the back and we again moved off.

Unfortunately Reg was not aboard, and as he went to jump onto the already moving vehicle he shouted 'Go on'; Philip thought he shouted 'Whoa' and slammed on the brakes. As a result Reg tumbled into the back among the dead rabbits, chipping a piece off his gun as he fell. In fact, it was surprising that nothing worse happened throughout the evening, for the main words of command to the driver were 'Whoa' and 'Go' which both, through the roar of the engine, sounded identical.

As we moved off again towards the farm, there were no rabbits. A tawny owl flew across the field on silent wings and a lapwing dive-bombed the Land Rover, calling out angrily as its ungainly half-grown chick ran clumsily out of the light. At the end of the evening seventeen rabbits had been killed, slightly fewer than had been expected, and all the occupants of the Land Rover were still in one piece, a fact that I found most surprising. From the chasing and shooting, and the danger to both the rabbits and the participants, I could well understand the appeal of night shooting to those who take part. Shortly before midnight, as we refreshed ourselves in the farmhouse with coffee, Bernie gave me his final piece of advice: 'If you write anything on this you'll have to call us the midnight cowboys'. There is no other possible description.

Chapter Nine

Pheasants and Foul Play

Away from the Land Rover, rabbits, searchlights, and night-time firing, shooting in more orthodox forms has expanded beyond simple recreation, the control of pests, or the filling of the cooking pot, for it has developed into an industry with an annual turnover of thirty-five million pounds. It involves over three-quarters of a million gun licence holders and many more who retain old shotguns outside the law. Once more, a complete cross-section of the community takes part, from lorry drivers and labourers, to stockbrokers and company directors, and from people who live in council houses to others who inhabit large stately homes.

To those who enjoy shooting, birds are the main attraction, and shooting airborne game gives them far more satisfaction than firing at running rabbits or driven hares. Yet despite its current popularity, it was not until the autumn of 1726 that a Mr George Markham first shot a flying pheasant, in Berkshire, and in so doing he heralded a change in shooting habits and attitudes that has continued until the present time.

In the early days the use of flintlock and percussion cap muzzle-loaders made shooting a fine art and, sometimes, a dangerous one. Today members of the Muzzle-Loaders' Association still go out with their powder, shot, and eccentricity. One elderly man, (who now shoots with a modern gun) remembers how, as a boy, he learned to shoot with a muzzle-loader, when he and a friend would take it into the fields, together with lead shot and home-made gunpowder manufactured from saltpetre, charcoal, and sulphur, in the hope of shooting a dinner. As the gun's hammer was missing it took both of them to fire; one would aim and, when he was on target, he would raise a finger and the other would strike the cap with a small hammer. Now shotguns have become far more sophisticated, being hammerless and firing cartridges that can be automatically ejected. Much of the skill has also gone, replaced by quick-firing repeaters, show, and sheer firepower, and consequently shooting appears to some people to have become a substitute for warfare.

Like the people who participate, shooting itself varies considerably, from the farmer who occasionally walks over his fields with his gun and dog, to highly organized and extremely expensive shoots, when landowners in syndicates, or wealthy men who have no countryside connections shoot driven pheasants, partridges, or highland grouse, using beaters, loaders, gun dogs, fine talk and fat wallets, and where the fee to shoot can be well into four figures for the season.

The most expensive shooting, and the type that many people consider to be the best, involves driven grouse, and in Scotland over three million acres of heather-covered hills are given over to grouse, with a further one million acres in northern England. It is a costly sport, in the more exclusive areas, and a thousand pounds can be asked and obtained for a few days shooting. With the grouse flying fast and low over the butts it requires much skill and because of the cost, grouse shooting has become associated with the upper-class, with tweeds, money, and public schools, and as a result it is a sport which is subjected to much ridicule as well as envy.

Because the grouse is unique to Britain, many monied continental sportsmen buy or hire grouse-shooting, and it is said that to see a party of excitable Belgians, Frenchmen, or Italians, shooting in neighbouring butts can be very entertaining. Often they break all the rules and follow the birds round with their guns and fire off to the side, spraying their neighbours with shot. Their reflexes also explain why so many continental gunmen are rushed off to hospitals every year and why posts are hammered into the grouse butts when foreign guns are due; then, if they swing round the only things damaged are the gun barrels.

At the other end of the shooting scale the cheapest sport is obtained from pigeons, when ordinary village men and youths take out their prized guns, handed down or bought from savings, to shoot flighting pigeons once work has finished. All it costs them is the price of their cartridges and sometimes a pint of beer at the pub afterwards, where they talk about their sport and give away some of their bag. Pigeon pie makes a good dinner (better than grouse, many think) and so there is always a sale for pigeons, which enables the good shot to shoot at a profit. When pigeons are flying well, bags of over 100 are not uncommon and the shooting can last all day.[1] Decoys are often used to attract the pigeons and are placed in stubble, or on poles up trees, and many sportsmen who have tried all types of shooting consider pigeon shooting to be as skilful and as satisfying as any.

Before he retired, Jim would shoot pigeons, or any bird or animal that could be eaten, but he was not interested in convention, or a 'good sporting shot', his main concern was to get something for the pot. One of the shots he remembers with the most satisfaction he took while standing behind a large old willow tree on the edge of the spinney. Over the fields he could see a small flock of pigeons working their way across the furrows towards him. As soon as they were within range and feeding quietly he fired. They were so close together that when he went to see what he had hit, nine lay dead, all from the one shot. They were tame pigeons too, but Jim did not worry, he put them in a sack and when covered by gravy and crust they tasted every bit as good as wild woodpigeons.

But although shooting at a variety of birds and animals takes place in most areas, the birds most usually linked with shotguns are pheasants and partridges, which form part of the real essence of the British countryside. The sight of a long-tailed cock pheasant strutting in the spring, with its plumage the colour of bronzed autumn leaves and wild sunsets, or a covey of partridges bursting into flight and gliding over a hedgetop, gives a sense of continuity and security to the rural scene.

Jim was like most old countrymen of his generation and enjoyed a strange love-hate relationship with 'those bloody ol' long tails'. To him a cock pheasant represented both a good dinner and a challenge, and if he saw one he would endeavour to take it by fair means or foul, whether it was flying, walking, perching, or sleeping, in season or out. If he saw a shootable cock pheasant when he hadn't got a gun, then he would angrily take off his cap to scratch his head, and call it various names, none of which sounded remotely like 'pheasant'. Yet despite this, if he saw a hen pheasant, his attitude changed; even in season he would sometimes put down his gun, and nothing gave him more pleasure than the sight of a hen pheasant feeding with her brood among the wild grasses and flowers of a dusty cart track, or flying fast over a field of ripening corn. Pheasants also helped him to forecast the weather, for if they

[1] The largest number of woodpigeons shot by one man in a single day was 550 by Major Archie Coats, near Winchester on 10 January 1962.

were suddenly early going up to roost in the evening, or were late down in the morning, it was sure sign of rain or bad weather. Pheasants still call out 'cock-up, cock-up' on winter evenings as their wings clatter among the branches as they go up to roost in the trees of the spinney. And somehow, each year, a number manage to escape the guns and the foxes, and their evening calls are almost the only sounds of the countryside that remain unchanging.

There is no doubt that rearing pheasants artificially maintains their numbers in many areas, but partridges have not been so fortunate. Before the Second World War most of the large shoots, especially in East Anglia, relied on wild partridges for their sport. After the war, however, the English partridge had virtually vanished, and in the years since they have remained so scarce that their very survival as a breeding bird has been tenuous.

One old retired gamekeeper looks back with nostalgia to the days when partridges were plentiful, for he was headkeeper of a large estate where royalty and noblemen shot as guests, and where coveys of partridges ensured large bags. He started work on the estate at the age of twelve as a woodman, cutting spits for thatching and making sheep hurdles. Often he would accompany his father, who was head gamekeeper, on his early morning and evening rounds to inspect the line of vermin traps, and he decided that he too would become a keeper. He went to train at Windsor Great Park, where he was one of fifteen keepers and three deer keepers, and where 20,000 pheasants were reared each year. When his father died he moved back to the estate to replace him. He spent the rest of his working life there and still acts as a beater when shoots are held.

Eight keepers were then employed on the estate, and between 200 and 300 brace of partridges were shot once or twice each season on every keeper's beat. 'There was a four year shift of farming then; horses and ploughs, and barley and wheat stubbles an' that, and some of 'em never got ploughed up 'til after Christmas. Then there were four or five flocks of sheep on the estate; kale, turnips, swedes, mustard, kohlrabi; there was seed layers, grass, sanfoin, clover, and all that. There was enough natural food all winter; for the winter was the chief trouble to the partridges.

'Now you get thousands of acres of just ploughed land; then the sprays came along and killed all the insect life and that was the end of partridges. We started up again after the war, but there wasn't much stock about, for during the war when there was no keepering, we were getting a dozen to fifteen cars a day stopping at the roadside, Sundays especially, with rifles, four-tens, and twelve-bores. Things got so low and the partridges didn't seem to come back, that we decided to rear some pheasants.' Before the war, in a good year, they shot between 400 and 500 pheasants on the 8,000 acres of the estate as well as 7,000 to 8,000 partridges, and 25,000 rabbits. 'We used gin traps for the rabbits in those days, until 1958. One feller used to come and collect 'em. He used to collect them all round here; he used to take five thousand a week to Luton and five thousand a week to Liverpool. He used to give us sixpence each and sell 'em for eightpence; he made enough money so that one of his sons could take on a big farm.' Now pheasants are the main bag and only a handful of wild partridges are shot; some French partridges are reared for shooting, but English partridges tend to be too difficult and temperamental to rear in artificial conditions. On one keeper's beat, map records were kept for many years showing the position of each nest; one year there were 177 nests, but now, 'if they've got seventeen nests that would be about all.'

Farming methods have changed and much of the habitat on which the partridge once depended has been destroyed. Over most of lowland Britain the story is the same, hedges and trees have been cleared and intensive arable agriculture has replaced mixed farming. In many areas it is only the shooting farmers who have retained woods, hedges, and copses, and their land appears as wooded islands in tracts of treeless prairie. Fortunately there is still some hope, for agricultural techniques and landscape are continually changing. Some farmers are beginning to appreciate the benefits that hedgerows and trees give to people as well as to wildlife and the habit of growing successive crops of winter wheat is again providing shelter and insect life for partridges. Recently, the grating calls of wild partridges have again been heard on warm spring evenings and the population seems to be slowly on the increase; as a result some partridge shooting on a limited scale is again taking place. Even so, partridge numbers are never likely to recover to pre-war levels, and so the preservation and breeding of pheasants now occupies much of the time and money of those who want to shoot.

The pheasant is an attractive bird, both in the fields and on a dinner plate, and a properly cooked pheasant has a taste far superior to that of domestic poultry. This partially explains why there is still a strong tradition of pheasant poaching in many areas, and stories abound of evenings spent snaring pheasants at roost, getting them drunk on raisins soaked in whisky, and of 'bird-napping expeditions', when men with a long net, and lights tied to their chests, went one side of a hedge while beaters went to the other. The birds would then fly away from the noise and into the net. Gin traps were also used to get pheasants; they were covered lightly with chaff or straw and pieces of potato were placed over the plate of the trap. When a pheasant went to feed the jaws of metal would snap shut around its head and death would be immediate. It was a common practice, too, for ploughmen to set snares in the corners of the fields when ploughing stubble. The snares would be of wire or horse-hair and corn would be sprinkled around them to attract those pheasants driven out of the field by the activity of the horses and ploughs. At the end of the day a dinner would often have been caught and a pheasant would fill the empty 'docky' bag.

The old West Country fox-breeder poached pheasants legally until quite recently, as he had some land that adjoined an estate where large numbers of birds were reared every year. A few weeks before the shooting season began he would start putting corn down near his boundary, to lure his neighbour's pheasants to feed. He sprinkled the corn around a number of pheasant traps made from wire mesh, which he propped up so that the pheasants could walk into them and away, without getting caught. The day before the shooting season commenced he would put the corn down as usual and remove the props so that the pheasants had to walk into the traps. Once in, they were unable to get out and the following morning he would always have the first pheasants for sale while the price was at its highest.

With changing habits and greater affluence, poaching has altered and there are few poachers who use the old skills on bright moonlit nights. Now, most use lamps and air-guns to get the roosting birds, when the weather is at its worst. One would-be poacher not far from the farm asked a friend to help him poach a cock pheasant that roosted every night in the overgrown garden of the local greengrocer. One shone the light, the other fired the gun and collected the bird, and then they both ran. When they got home they discovered that they had shot a bantam cockerel.

In some areas very little poaching goes on, causing a Devon gamekeeper to conclude that now 'people are too lazy and well off to poach'. When he does his early morning rounds he sees very little activity before 8.00 am and then there is a great rush along the country lanes to get to work in the nearby city by 8.30 or 9.00 am. When he first started work as a gamekeeper poachers created constant problems, especially for a neighbouring keeper; he was a keen flower grower and every time he went to a horticultural committee meeting some of his pheasants went missing. But where poaching does take place regularly, both methods and motives have changed. Once it was done by one or two locals, for the pot, or to make small additions to their low incomes, but now poaching is often a hit-and-run job, carried out by people who live many miles away. They raid release pens and roosting coverts with wholesale slaughter in mind for a quick and sizeable profit, and gamekeepers who try to intervene expose themselves to violence and possible injury.

The forms of pheasant shooting range from the small rough shoot, to the large estate or syndicate where the shooting rights are as important as the farming interests, and where there is a large financial stake. Many farmers still enjoy walking over their fields occasionally with their guns and dogs in the hope of an odd shot, and even if they get nothing they are seldom disappointed, for they see and feel the state of their land, and they share in the communion and companionship that has existed between man and dog for hundreds of years. Several times each winter, brother John and two or three friends walk over the farm; they breed no pheasants and control no 'vermin', and if after an afternoon's 'walk round' they have shot a pheasant, two pigeons, and three or four rabbits they consider that they have been successful. By comparison, large shoots employ gamekeepers to trap and kill anything thought to be harmful to gamebirds, they breed large numbers of pheasants and the bag for a day's sport is sometimes measured in hundreds.[2]

[2] The largest British bags recorded are:

Snipe	1,108	five guns	Isle of Tiree, Inner Hebrides 25 October – 3 November, 1906
Hares	1,215	eleven guns	Holkham, Norfolk 19 December, 1877
Woodcock	228	six guns	Ashford, County Galway 28 January, 1910

It has been estimated that the pheasant population after a good summer is approaching twenty million birds; half being truly wild, and the rest having been reared and released.[3] To supervise their welfare, about 4,000 gamekeepers are employed in England and Wales, with a further 2,000 in Scotland, many of whom are responsible for grouse. About a third of the reared pheasants die before the shooting season begins, due to disease, natural predation, and also because, on release, some continue to search for manufactured pheasant food instead of seeds and beetles. To help reduce this number, studies are being made of the movements of wild pheasants and their young, and a number of hen pheasants have been fitted with radio transmitters so that their whereabouts can be tracked. Among reared pheasants the mortality rate is highest immediately after release, while the danger period for wild chicks is when they are still small – about a third die because of rain and cold.

It is the shooting involving reared pheasants which causes the most controversy – there is even a true story of a woman who asked if it was right that pheasants reared for shooting had their wings cut off and were fired into the air by a spring. Reared pheasants are in fact released into the fields and are entirely free, and each year between 10 and 15 per cent survive the shooting season to live on as truly wild birds. My two shooting uncles rear about 250 birds every year and do the keepering themselves, while in another nearby village an artist rears pheasants in seventy overgrown acres of disused gravel diggings, where he holds small shoots for invited guests. There the beaters fight their way through dense

---

Grouse	2,929	eight guns	Littledale and Abbeystead, Lancashire 12 August, 1915
Grouse	1,070	one gun	Lord Walsingham in Yorkshire 30 August, 1888
Rabbits	6,943	five guns	Blenheim, Oxfordshire 17 October, 1898
Partridges	2,015 (plus 104 picked up later)	six guns	Rothwell, Lincolnshire, 12 October 1952
Pheasants	3,937	seven guns	Hall Barn, Beaconsfield, Buckinghamshire 18 December, 1913

The greatest recorded lifetime bag is 556,000 birds, including 241,000 pheasants, by the second Marquess of Ripon (1867–1923). He dropped dead on a grouse moor after shooting his fifty-second bird of the day on the morning of 22 September, 1923.

Guinness Book of Records, 1973

[3] On a hired shoot with a keeper the cost of each shot bird is about £7.

brambles, willow thickets, and water, and at the end of four or five drives, a handful of pheasants, a few pigeons, a hare, and an occasional snipe or woodcock make up the entire bag. The part-time gamekeeper fills his time by feeding the pheasants and organizing lorries tipping or collecting gravel. He dislikes killing and will not watch or take part in a shoot, and he even leaves his employer to set the traps for 'vermin'. Nevertheless, he is always on hand at the end of a shoot for the traditional tipping of the keeper, when each gun gives him about three pounds. Collecting his money, he seems most unlike any normal gamekeeper, never wearing tweeds and with no touch of his cap; instead he sports a dark beret, a long raincoat, and wellington boots which seem to exaggerate the way his feet splay out to the side. When he was called up into the army, at the time of the Korean War, he saw no shooting there either, for when told to walk along a straight white line, his feet failed him and he was discharged back to the gravel pit.

Over the nearby ridge of chalk in the next village, several farmers and a professional golfer have joined together to form a more typical shoot over 1,400 acres. About 1,000 pheasants are reared every year, but because the shoot is long and narrow, enabling birds to get out at the sides, less than 40 per cent of the pheasants are shot. The management of the shoot is undertaken by one of the farmers, an excellent self-taught naturalist, and a young gamekeeper who is employed to look after the pheasants and to combat trespassing predators, both animal and human. From time to time poachers cause problems. They are thought to be local people using air-guns, who find out the whereabouts of the pheasants by getting one of the regular beaters 'tanked up' in a local club. Once several pints of beer have been drained one of them says: 'There aren't many pheasants about this year, Sid.'

'I know there are I've seen plenty.'

'Don't give us that. I'd have thought you'd have known your pheasants by now, there's just none about.'

'That's not bloody right, you should have seen 'em today.'

'Come off, Sid, it's a bad year.'

'No it's not, Field Spinney's full of the buggers,' and it will be Field Spinney that is the next pheasant covert to be visited.

Last year an uneasy situation developed when Bernie the 'midnight cowboy' planted two acres of mustard, a crop much favoured by pheasants, in his employer's small field on one of the boundaries of the shoot. It attracted local fowl as well as pheasants, and during one Sunday afternoon shoot, the only thing shot was a straying red cockerel. Then, one night some carbide mysteriously appeared in the field, contaminating the mustard so much that the pheasants all left.

For some time too a local gypsy took an uncharacteristic interest in country walks, particularly along a footpath that bisects part of the shoot and where hares can always be found. He would walk along the footpath with his lurcher at heel, while his two sons would walk either side of the path, fifty yards into the field. He insisted that all he was doing was enjoying the fresh air, although at the same time the number of hares seemed to decline. Later, another gypsy made an offer for the dog and he sold it for fifteen pounds. Since then his interest in walking along the hill seems to have waned, although it may well be only a temporary phase, for there is already another lurcher puppy growing up in the smokey atmosphere around the horse-drawn gypsy caravan.

To try and combat poachers the gamekeeper, the farmer, and the local policeman go on regular patrols around the coverts after dark, but so far the poachers have avoided capture. To make life more difficult for them, tight wires at various heights have been strung through some of the woods and there are twenty alarm guns attached to trip wires. They are loaded with blank cartridges and point downwards; some gamekeepers load them with live cartridges and place them above old ploughshares. When an intruder trips over the wire, lead shot then ricochets in all directions.

Several nearby farmers have experienced trouble of a different kind, from Cypriots hiring land and shooting across their boundaries. In true continental tradition they blast off mainly on Sundays and shoot at skylarks, thrushes, and sparrows. Some Cypriots have even started driving into the area from London at weekends, and they fire from the roadsides at anything with feathers. To try and catch them a stuffed pheasant was placed in a roadside field, and one Sunday afternoon that too was filled with lead pellets.

I went as a beater on the farmers' shoot, an occupation enjoyed by many country people; it was a cold and blustery morning, with banks of heavy black cloud, showers, and small patches of brilliant blue sky. There were thirteen beaters assembled including the night rabbit shooters, Bernie and Brian, with the latter's dog, and the two young shooting farmers, and they were joined by a computer programmer on a week's holiday, the village policeman, who was head-beater, the young tweed-clad gamekeeper, two old men, and two young boys. Bernie was immediately in good form: 'I hope you've got your bullet proof vest on', he said, 'they've got some terrible shots here today. Last time somebody shouted "duck", we all ducked, but it was a partridge.'

The eight guns and an assortment of dogs got into the Land Rovers, and a 'picker-up', a retired gamekeeper with his dogs, drove off with them, to pick-up any wounded game. We piled onto a canvas-covered trailer with planks as seats around the sides, and a tractor pulled us out of the farmyard. The first drive was to be for partridges over a large ploughed field, bordered on one side by a small meandering river. We moved into position in a long line across the cold, wet ploughland, with a 'flanker' on each end to wave a white flag, to try and prevent birds flying out at the sides and away from the guns. Ducks flew up from the muddy, rain-swelled water, quacking in alarm. They circled high and fast in the strong wind, planing on air and careering along precariously in the strong eddies and currents and using their wings as air brakes to control speed. As they moved over the guns, firing made them fly off in a ragged wind-driven line, but none were hit.

The policeman blew his large horn and we started to walk towards the guns half a mile ahead; few birds were seen and the guns hidden behind butts made of straw bales had little sport. The drive ended with several unflown partridges running through the guns and into sugar beet, like rugby players crossing the line to score a try.

Another tractor ride took us onto the hill for the next drive, also over plough. It was hard work in the cold wind with mud clinging to our boots. Several hares got up, their ears rising and falling in uncertainty; they stopped and looked, and then ran off, some to be shot and others to run to safety. Two large coveys of partridges flew forwards over the guns, high and fast; several flew on with the wind behind them and others fell like stones. A guest gun had been successful; with his boots, green coat, hat, cartridge belt, and dark glasses, he looked like some prohibition gangster. The next drive was in a narrow strip of kale, dripping with water, and as all the beaters crowded in, banging their sticks against the stems the leaf-held water showered down even more. Some pheasants flew, but as it was early in the season many were missed. I caught a glimpse of a hare among the stems, but it failed to emerge, and somehow it managed to slip through the net of beaters. At the end of the drive several pheasants were collected up, and Brian's spaniel picked up a crouching pheasant, alive, out of a hedge.

A field of sugar beet followed and a number of pheasants flew hard and low away from us. The guns fired and birds were hit and missed, and one cock, flying high over the guns, suddenly crumpled in mid-air, feathers flew, and it plunged to the ground. Because of the distance, only after the bird was dead and nearly down did the report of the shot reach us. The action then stopped for dinner, and as the guns went into the farmhouse, we retired to a barn and sat on tin cans and implements, until the keeper brought us our food; beer or tea, cheese rolls, ham sandwiches, pork pies, and cake. One of the old beaters passed the time by telling us how to smoke a fox out of an earth, and a farmworker who joined us gave a lecture on the new generation of college trained farmworkers, ending with 'You don't need bloody qualifications to clean out ditches, do you?'

The afternoon drives were along the side of the hill, over fields and through woodland. The walking was forever up and down, the wind blew, and at times heavy rain fell in sheets, but all the beaters kept going, including an old man who was well over eighty. In one field hares ran from the beaters in all directions and two of them, obviously looking backwards, ran straight at each other. One stopped at the last minute and the other leapt three feet into the air to avoid collision. Brian's spaniel then started off in pursuit, ignoring all shouts of command. As the hares ran up the hill the dog was soon left far behind, for with their long back legs hares find it far easier to run up hill than down.

One of the belts of trees was full of rabbit holes and the population was so high that an acrid smell permeated the air around them. Many pheasants flew from the trees, except one young cock which had evidently never seen guns or beaters before, and simply flew to the top of a small ash tree. Bernie tried to shake it into flight, and then he threw lumps of wood, but still it just perched, watching him with interest. If it had been perching near his mustard, he would have shot it as it sat. A lot of pheasants were shot and several times the old beater next to me allowed tightly skulking hens to go undisturbed. He justified his action by saying in a whisper, 'You've got to leave some for seed, haven't you?' As we approached the end of the wood, tapping the trees with our sticks, we could see many pheasants running before us, yet at the end of the drive far fewer seemed to fly out into the open and over the guns. The rest seemed to have disappeared. As I looked back a hen pheasant emerged from a rabbit hole and disappeared back into the trees. I wondered how many others had used that method of escape. The drive had improved the bag and it was said to have frightened the pheasants: 'They'll fly better next time.'

The final drive was a long one, over fields of potatoes and sugar beet. Several coveys of partridges went forward, including a large family of 'Frenchmen',[4] who only flew half way. We came across them again later, crouching in the beet, exhausted and unable to fly again. Guns and dogs had enjoyed their day, as had the beaters, who each received three pounds for their labours. The guns each took a brace of pheasants and the rest were sold to a game dealer. Between forty and fifty pounds is usually obtained for the pheasants, a sum which normally covers the cost of the beaters.

Most shoots involve a number of farmers or members of a syndicate, pooling money and resources to hire, buy, or run their shoot, but there are still a few large estates where shooting is organized entirely for the sport of invited guests.

The estate where the old gamekeeper once preserved partridges is one such shoot, a shoot whose name is synonymous throughout the shooting world with 'quality' and 'tall pheasants', and to get an invitation to shoot there is an honour which, to most shooting men, cannot be bettered. Approaching the village and the estate it is immediately obvious to the knowing eye that it is a shooting area, for there are belts of trees, woods, hedges, and small coverts, coniferous and deciduous. It is the sort of countryside that has been both preserved and created, and through which week-end trippers dawdle in their cars during the summer.

At one time the estate was owned by a solitary Lord, but now it is a family trust. I did not wish to shoot, but I wanted to see

[4] Red-legged or French partridge.

the shooting from the position of the guns, to have birds driven over me and to see the famous 'tall pheasants'. The butler-cum-driver greeted me at the house, thinking that I was going to shoot, where the other guns were already assembled. They were in good spirits and sported tweeds, woollen socks, caps and hats (including a deerstalker), and one even had tufts of hair on his cheekbones in the authorized upper-class manner. My host, Nigel, greeted me warmly. He was wearing a fawn shooting outfit seemingly weighed down with cartridges; he is a friendly, pleasant man, with a reputation for being one of the best game shots in the country.

We clambered into an old twelve-seater ex-RAF bus, together with two dogs. Everyone was talking happily, a mixture of anecdote and anticipation. Nigel called out 'Drive on, Dickerson', to the driver, and Dickerson drove on. The first drive was over sugar beet where two beet-harvesters were working, but they pulled off the field as soon as the beaters and guns took up position. Nigel's brother, Robert, dressed in a jumper and an open-necked shirt, had no gun.

'Aren't you shooting?' I asked him.

'Oh yes, my loader's got my gun', he replied. Medlock, a gamekeeper from a neighbouring estate, carried his twelve-bore. On some of the really big shoots each man has a loader and a pair of guns, and a pair of top-class Purdey or Holland and Holland guns can cost as much as £14,000. Robert was in England on holiday from Kenya where he owns and runs the Lake Nivasha Hotel. He had decided to have a day's shooting as his wife had delayed their return, having arranged to fly to New York for four or five days' modelling. 'I told her that she was a bit long in the tooth for that, but she would go.' Like his brother, he too was a good shot, and throughout the day he smoked long Havana cigars which he lit from a cigar lighter hanging from a cord around his neck.

The beaters and four of the seven guns lined up to drive the game across the beet to the others. The soil was wet, but unlike our heavy land it did not stick to boots. The sun shone from a lambent blue sky and with the gently rolling landscape, the unseasonal winter warmth, and the field boundaries marked by hedges and woodland, it was a pleasant place to start the day.

All the keepers took part in the beating, including the head-keeper; a genial, quietly spoken man, with a ruddy complexion, who for many years worked in an office, until he could stand it no longer. Gamekeeping suited him perfectly as he had always liked the countryside and the wildlife in it, and he says that he will never go back to working at an office desk to be hemmed in by four walls, repetition and pedantry. Because of his dedication to his job and his concern for his pheasants he has not been away for a holiday since 1954. The old keeper was also there, as well as many old locals 'making a few shillings on the side'. As the beating started, pheasants were soon flying forwards and to the sides, and hares ran in all directions. It was near the area where I had seen the hare shoot, and I was amazed how their numbers had recovered after just one summer.

Nigel was on the left flank and, as a pheasant flew over him he aimed his gun and fired. There was a tremendous bang, he appeared to stagger, and the bird flew on unharmed; his single-trigger twelve-bore had managed to fire both barrels simultaneously, while he was using extra powerful cartridges.[5] His gun then began to function properly and he started hitting birds at an almost impossible height. The birds would fly past him at a distance that would have been considered out of range by most shooting farmers, and then in silence the hit bird's wingbeats and flight would falter and it would plummet to the ground. Because of our distance from the action the gun's report followed several seconds after the bird had folded and fallen towards the ground. Twice, high birds flew over him and both times they were hit so hard that they literally stopped stone dead, as the impact jolted them upwards amidst a cloud of feathers. Each time, the bird seemed to hang in the air for a second or two and then drop straight and hard, as if life was already a far-off experience; only an expanding cloud of feathers drifting slowly downwards showed where flight had ended. After the first such bird Robert observed: 'I wouldn't fancy being the housewife who gets that. Although it's ready plucked you'd break your teeth on that lot.'

Half way over the field the beaters stopped and walked round to the other guns and then started towards us. More pheasants flew and more long shots struck home; some fell dead and others fell flapping down with body wounds or broken wings, to land

[5] He was using a twelve-bore 32-inch barrelled Winchester full choke single selective trigger magnum gun and Gythorp $1\frac{1}{4}$ oz nickel plated No 5 shot. The 32-inch barrel is extra long. The barrels of most twelve-bores are 28 or 29 inches.

clumsily, cartwheeling over the uneven surface of the field. Some of these 'runners' ran for cover on a railway embankment where they evaded capture as sniffing dogs hunted excitedly, while others were run down and retrieved, to join the day's tally. Even in this company one black labrador, not satisfied with dead or dying birds, began to course fit and fast hares. The hares were almost impossible to see as they ran, with their ears pressed down, between the rows of beet. They were in no danger from the dog as their speed was far greater, and the dog was in no danger from its master as it was always much too far away.

Another drive over beet was less successful, but back at the bus all were satisfied. Then came a shoot in woodland and I went with a Cornishman, a top class clay-pigeon shot, who looked the part in his tweeds and deerstalker. We went through some planted pines and a belt of scrub and into a grass field, while some beaters drove pheasants into the area of the main drive. Pigeons flew over and several of the guns, hidden by trees, fired. Two pigeons flew towards us, and with an automatic reaction the Cornishman swung his gun upwards and fired both barrels in quick succession. The two pigeons crashed to the ground, showing that with clay or feathered birds he was a superb shot. One of the birds was dead, the other was winged; I went to break its neck to bring it relief, but I pulled too hard and its head came off in my hand. I felt disgusted with myself. 'You should have known better than that,' the Cornishman observed, but whether clean or dirty, death is the only end product.

As the pheasants began to fly he told me to stand close behind him to act as loader. A hen bird flew over; he swung up and over and the arc was completed by the line of the falling bird, which crashed like a stone into the top of a hawthorn tree, where it became wedged in the prickly fork of two branches. I was so absorbed by the shot and the tumbling death that he had to load the gun himself for the next shot. A solitary partridge flew in low and fast, but he only winged it and it flapped into the belt of scrub. No dogs were in the area and it was not recovered. At that stand he shot and killed five pheasants as well as the two pigeons.

The final drive of the morning was close by, with the beaters going through a wood on a small hilltop. The guns stood well back in a large semi-circle and I stood at one end with Dickerson, to wave our handkerchiefs to try and prevent the birds flying to the side. Nigel had changed guns to a small twenty-eight-bore, but it seemed to make no difference and even with less powerful cartridges he fetched birds down from a great height. Several thudded down near me and were retrieved by his golden labrador, as well as by the dog of a picker-up. As the tapping of the beaters in the wood got nearer, all the guns had good sport with plenty of high birds. Suddenly the cry of 'A fox, shoot it', turned all eyes to the base of the wood. A fox had broken cover and ran towards one of the guns. He let it get close and then fired; the animal stumbled, but regained its feet and ran back along the front of the wood, its brush straight out behind. It was clear, as it stumbled again, that it had been hit hard in the front shoulder. As it approached Nigel it seemed that it would surely die, but suddenly it changed direction and went back into the wood towards the beaters. The beaters continued to advance, pheasants still flew, and then the line of men with sticks emerged. There was no sign of the fox, either dead or alive. There had been two in the wood and the other had slipped quietly out and moved silently along a hedgerow, evading both beaters and guns.

The beaters went off for their dinner, and we rode in the bus to an old country pub, where some of the guns were met by their wives. It was to be a sit down lunch in the saloon bar, but as I had forgotten my shoes and jacket I went into the public bar with my anorak and wellington boots. Nigel sent the barman in for my order, a sandwich and a pint of beer, and this was met with blank disbelief by a man in dirty overalls and a cap who sat at a table with his mate, eating his dinner and drinking beer.

'Cor, bugger me', he said, 'you missed a chance there. Only a pint of beer.'

'Yeh, you should have had half a bottle of brandy', interjected a smarter individual propping up the bar.

'Half a bottle? A whole bottle. They can afford it', the man in the overalls observed. 'Cor, bugger me, you missed a good chance there'. He said 'Cor, bugger me', several more times as he ate, and occasionally he glanced through the window to make sure that his sludge tanker was still parked outside.

From next door the sounds of dinner being served and drinks being ordered came through in refined tones: 'Come on, sit down for dinner'; 'Get me a vodka, old boy'; 'A gin and tonic please, darling.'

The orders made the sludge tanker driver shake his head even more. 'Cor, bugger me, you missed a good chance there. Still, we did all right one day, didn't we, Bert? We was parked by the road in a little lay-by when suddenly this lot was firing off all round. Like the bloody war all over again. When the drive was over we cleared off and when we stopped there were four pheasants lodged on the back. Did we take 'em back? I should think not, we whipped the bloody feathers off and I had roast pheasant four days running. Cor, bugger, what a chance you missed.' After more thought and muttering he returned the wrapping paper to his empty sandwich box and left with his mate. As he drove away his head was still shaking sadly and I could imagine what he was saying.

After my dinner I joined the loader and the driver in the bus. They had finished their tea and sandwiches and were guarding the guns and the dogs. The loader, Medlock, was the head gamekeeper for a nearby duke and the driver was a general odd-job man. Neither of them objected to being addressed by their surnames: 'It's the way they've been brought up. You don't expect anything different; if they called me something else I would be worried.' The only time they objected to being addressed without the 'Mister' was when spoken to by estate agents or commercial travellers, ' 'cause they are no different from us and should know better'. Medlock the keeper had once worked for a local agricultural contractor, but had been sickened by forever having to bulldoze hedges and uproot trees, even when the birds were nesting. He decided to do something different, and now he finds the job of gamekeeper extremely satisfying.

The dinner party in the pub finished and the guns and two wives brought the smell of spirits and cigar smoke into the bus. Talk and laughter levels had increased, and it was obvious that they had dined well on the pub-served shepherd's pie and trifle. The first drive of the afternoon was over more sugar beet. The guns again stood in a semi-circle on ploughland, with a small country road dividing them from the beet and beaters. The beaters were in a long line in the distance, and soon they began moving slowly towards us. A London stockbroker was the nearest gun to me, a man who shoots because it provides almost his only chance of getting away from the city and into the country.

The day ended with yet more beet, bordered by a newly-planted belt of pines, and the guns stood halfway down a long depression, again in a half-circle on ploughland. Several birds zoomed in, and their approach could be seen a long way off. Some lived, some died, and one flew on for several seconds before crashing dead, in front of a hedge. The sun's rays burned bronze as it fell away to the west; a partridge dropped, lifeless through lead, and two hares ran into the distance and disappeared over the horizon as two dark specks. As the beaters approached the young trees a short-eared owl flew up in jerking, lazy flight; it flew over their heads and over a gun, but it was left unshot.

The beaters' work was finished and the head-keeper looked well pleased with the day's sport that he had provided. The guns clambered into the bus to return to the house and their cars, and another day's shooting was over. The final bag was made up of 135 pheasants (fifty-three cocks and eighty-two hens), two partridges (both English), eleven hares, four rabbits, and four pigeons.

Both the estate shoot and the farmers' shoot were well organized, with the emphasis being on quality rather than quantity, and with a sufficient number of beaters and pickers-up to ensure that the suffering of wounded birds was kept to minimum. There are shoots, however, that do cause concern, where the main stress is not on the sport or the overall welfare of the pheasant, but on the size of the bag at the end of the day. Bad shots with no real interest in their quarries, or knowledge of the countryside, buy themselves into a shoot, and anything that moves in front of them is blasted, regardless of species, distance, or sex. Pickers-up are too few or non-existent and many birds and animals are left to crawl away to die, while the owners of such shoots seem only interested in their financial returns. It is on these shoots, or with similar shooters, that roe and fallow deer are still maimed and wounded by inadequate shotgun cartridges and where the successful gun boasts of having 'shot a deer'.

It is also unfortunate that most gunmen regard the shooting of a snipe or a woodcock as something of a shooting status symbol. Yet both birds are extremely delicate and beautiful, and the woodlands and wetlands where they breed are shrinking in size each year. In addition, once shot they are rarely eaten and their deaths seem to be a pointless waste of life.

Another regrettable aspect of shooting is the fixation of many shooting men on 'vermin control'; for all animals or birds which prey on, or compete with the almost sacred pheasant are immediately classified as 'vermin'; consequently policies of extermination are attempted where some tolerance or selective management could be permitted. In the past excuses for excessive pest control could be made, for management and conservation techniques had not been studied or developed. Also, in days gone by, the sale of vermin helped to supplement the low wages of the keepers, and wings, feathers, furs, tails, and skins, were all sold. Forty years ago the old partridge keeper sold his fox skins for 8 shillings each, and jays' wings, crows' wings, and pheasants' tails were all sent away. While still at school he remembers going mole-trapping; he killed 150 moles and sold the skins at 8d each.[6] Now, however, few keepers send off their victims as they are reasonably well paid and in any case there is no need to be so harsh on predators, as reared birds can be protected more easily than in the past.

Over half the damage to gamebirds is caused by foxes and members of the crow family, and both are persecuted without mercy on most shoots.[7] Yet with creosote, tar, or electric fences around release pens, some foxes could be tolerated. During a recent season on the farmers' shoot, a sudden influx of foxes was experienced and twenty-seven were snared in four months. There were obviously too many for the good of either domestic fowl or pheasants, and consequently keepers should aim at balance, and not at extermination.

Because of the conflict of interests between shooting and hunting, much public relations propaganda is preached concerning the harmony in which foxhunters and pheasant shooters are supposed to live, but in reality the relationship between the two groups is more of an uneasy tolerance, which occasionally breaks down into open confrontation. During one shoot adjoining fox-hunting country, 146 pheasants had been shot by dinner, and the guns were well on the way to obtaining a 'record bag'. During the first drive in the afternoon, the hounds and horses of the local hunt charged through the lines of beaters and guns in pursuit of a fox. After the disturbance only twelve more pheasants were shot; the

[6] Current prices are: mole skins 4p each, weasel skins 11p, stoat tails 3p, rabbit skins 6p, water-vole skins 10p and complete coot skins with wings 10p.

[7] Research has shown that over 50 per cent of nest losses are caused by corvids and foxes with the remainder being divided almost equally between badgers, rats, stoats, cats, hedgehogs, and another equal group made up of damage done by dogs, grey squirrels, and unidentified predators.

hunt was banned from the land for the rest of the season, and the language was far from brotherly.

Carrion crows, magpies, and jays, are considered to be some of the worst pheasant nest wreckers, and in many areas the carrion crow has become a rarity because of persecution. Before a crow can be shot it first has to be identified as a crow and not as a rook or jackdaw, which do less damage. One way is to follow the guidance of an old country saying: 'If you see one rook, it's a crow, and if you see three crows they are rooks', for crows are generally solitary birds, whereas rooks fly about in large flocks or small gangs.

Crow shooting is said to be a highly skilled task, for crows are cautious birds and quickly take to the wing. One keeper always approaches a pair at a nest by getting his wife to wear something bright and conspicuous to attract their attention, while he creeps up on them from another direction. They are also said to be intelligent and can count up to two; consequently another way to shoot them is for three people to approach a nest, and one to remain beneath it until the birds return. If two people try the same technique, the crows will not fly back until both the intruders are seen to leave.

Regrettably, magpies are given the same harsh treatment, and although there is no doubt that they steal many eggs, it seems unreasonable that one or two pairs cannot be tolerated by gamekeepers, for they add both colour and character to the hedgerows. It is also a pleasure to see jays flying into the tree tops, and they have a reputation far worse than they deserve. Fortunately many gamekeepers are good naturalists and realize that jays are wrongly maligned and permit them to live on their land; the wise keeper also realizes the positive advantages of having jays, for with their harsh cries that greet any intruder, they make excellent watchdogs, and many poachers have been caught because of the torrent of treetop abuse that has followed their progress.

Mammals too, are shot and trapped because of the damage they are said to cause. The damage done by rats and stray cats can be readily seen, but the evidence against hedgehogs, stoats, and weasels is less clear. Some keepers have an almost pathological hatred of hedgehogs and will trap them relentlessly, while others say that the mouth of the animal is too small to break pheasants eggs and that it will leave nests alone. It is likely that the distrust of hedgehogs stems from old stories of how they are supposed to suck hens eggs, steal milk from the teats of resting cows, and one old story that attributes the disappearance of whole clutches of eggs to hedgehogs rolling over them and carrying them off on their spines. For once, all the folklore and stories about them hold little truth. If a hedgehog visits a hen-house and finds an egg with a weak shell, or already cracked, then the egg will go. Similarly, if a recently calved cow has an udder so full of milk that it dribbles onto the grass, a passing hedgehog would not ignore the opportunity of lapping up the milk, for wild hedgehogs are partial to milk, and can often be attracted into gardens by saucers of milk being left out at dusk. The blame for whole clutches of eggs disappearing without trace is also unjustified, with foxes being the most likely culprits.

There is no doubt that stoats and weasels take eggs, from all birds, and a weasel has even been seen to climb a post and enter the hole of a nest box at the top, to clear up a brood of young blue-tits. The number of gamebird chicks and eggs taken, however, is more than compensated for by the mice, rats, and rabbits, that they kill, and their wholesale destruction is unfortunate and unreasonable. Because of their knowledge of the habits of wild creatures, gamekeepers find it easy to catch stoats and weasels, in a variety of traps. They catch far more dog stoats than bitches, about twelve to one, because the males are less careful and more inquisitive than the females, but it is possible to catch a whole family of weasels one at a time. One old keeper reckons that as he goes on his round he can tell the whereabouts and the type of vermin in his area from the alarm cries of blackbirds, for he believes that the warning notes vary for stoats, foxes, cats, and people.

The most worrying aspect of all predator control is the continued illegal killing of birds of prey, a practice that is carried out on a large scale wherever gamebirds are preserved for shooting. After talking to keepers in many parts of Britain it seems likely that a sizeable majority break the law regularly by shooting owls, hawks, and falcons. It is inevitable that birds of prey take some gamebirds, but when thousands of pheasants are being reared, the odd poult taken by a tawny owl, or the few chicks taken by a kestrel, make little difference to the overall numbers available for shooting. At one time kestrels were a nuisance when pheasants were raised in rearing fields, but that was more a fault of the system rather than an indictment against the kestrel, and now there are more efficient ways of raising pheasants that keep them safe. It is true that an occasional tawny owl causes panic and fear near release pens, killing a few birds and preventing the others from going up to roost, but the habits of an occasional owl do not warrant the indiscriminate killing of all birds with talons and hooked beaks.

Part of the dislike of owls extends back into the past when the sight of an owl, particularly in daylight, was said to be a portent of death. It was also believed that owls were witches in disguise, and the evil associated with them stemmed from the eerie quality of their flying and calling at night. In the days of smoke and steam on the railways, a local signalman started to have an owl perch on the signal next to his box. It made him feel so uneasy that one night he suddenly raised the signal and shot the bird several feet into the air, afterwards it never used that perching site again.

The attitude of the old Devon fox-breeder towards birds of prey is typical. As I spoke with him about his pheasants and foxes, a hawk flew over and I asked him what it was and whether he killed them. 'That's a bloody sparrow hawk; them are restricted see, you can't kill none of 'em by law; they've been restricted for two years, an' you aren't got to kill 'em 'ave ee.' Disregarding his knowledge of the law I asked him how he killed them. 'I shoot 'em as a rule. They'll knock down an ol' partridge won't 'em. The ol' buzzarrrd 'e's a rogue; he won't take a full size pheasant but 'e'll take one arrf grown.'

A few years ago the most common and simple ways of killing birds of prey were by using poisoned baits or pole traps. On one occasion a gamekeeper left a pigeon injected with strychnine in a small clearing. When, later in the day, he visited the site the pigeon had gone but there was no dead hawk. In a panic he eventually found the poisoned carcase; it had been picked up by the estate cowman and taken home to be cooked for his dinner. He had a large family of ten daughters (all with names such as Marina, Daisy, Primrose, and Buttercup, like his cows), and he had taken the pigeon to help with the family budget. After his fright the gamekeeper set no more poisoned carcases. Poison is still sometimes used illegally, as are pole traps, which are similar to gin traps and which are fixed to the top of poles where birds of prey are likely to perch. Once caught the birds are often left fluttering upside down until they die or are killed. The traps are found particularly on large and isolated estates where visitors are rare and where public roads and footpaths are few and far between. They are usually set by gamekeepers, with the landowners' knowledge and approval and there are reliable stories of several owners also being prominent public figures and members of conservation bodies. The lawlessness will not be reduced until the employers responsible, as well as their keepers, are prosecuted and fined heavily. Until the less responsible shooters cease their destruction, they should be seen as the real 'vermin', running loose and uncontrolled through the countryside.

Chapter Ten

Water and Wildfowl

A large number of shooting men also prize wild ducks and geese, yet in wildfowling too, indifference and lawlessness among some wildfowlers give much cause for concern. Wildfowling itself, like other country pursuits, has a long tradition, dating back to a time when shotguns were unknown and waterfowl were taken with snares, nets, and traps. Many fowlers made their entire livings from killing and selling birds, while others went out into the marshes and wetlands in the early mornings and late evenings to supplement their wages and to obtain cheap meat.

When gunpowder and shotguns made killing easier, so wildfowlers used guns fired from the shoulder, as well as larger punt guns that were discharged from small boats or from the top of dyke banks. They resembled miniature cannons, and when shot into compact rafts of floating ducks, large bags could be obtained with single shots.[1] The punt-gunners were tough, hardy individuals, and for winter warmth they would often cover their chests with goose fat and brown paper. One old wildfowler remembers his punt-gunning father wearing such an under garment; he would wear it under his shirt and vest for at least a week, and as time wore on, so the smell became ever more rancid.

Necessity no longer forces men out into remote, wild, and wet places, yet wildfowling has never been more popular and the handed-down skills of the past are now used for sport. Most rough shooters enjoy getting the occasional mallard as they walk by their local stream or marsh, but wildfowlers concentrate their shooting on ducks and geese. They build hides to shoot at flighting ducks as they drift down onto autumn stubbles or winter-sown wheat, and wherever wildfowl are present, on marshes, estuaries, or open water, wildfowlers will follow with their guns and dogs.

[1] The record in a day using punt guns is 704 brent geese, plus 250 picked up later, on the River Blackwater in Essex in 1860 with thirty-two punt guns.

Unlike those who shoot grouse or pheasants on well organized drives, wildfowlers often shoot alone or in twos and threes, and tweeds and shooting sticks are never seen. They wear clothes suitable for the harsh conditions which often confront them, designed to give them warmth and waterproofing. During the course of a season the keen wildfowler will encounter deep water, wet mud, cutting winds, and turning tides, and he will face physical challenge and even danger. Although the sport is often looked down upon by upper-class game shooters as being a low-class exercise and scarcely worthy of the name sport, wildfowlers themselves often feel slightly superior to those who shoot in more formal surroundings. To them wildfowling creates a challenge and demands a level of skill that no other form of shooting can match, and they will travel many miles for the opportunity of a morning or evening flight at one of the areas renowned for its wildfowling. Consequently, to mention the Solway, Loch Leven, the Severn, or the Ouse Washes to a wildfowler, is to see his eyes light up and his trigger finger twitch.

The Ouse Washes are situated in the heart of the Fens and make up one of the most important areas for wildfowl and wading birds in Europe. In the summer rare and common birds breed, closely watched and protected by various conservation bodies, and in winter large numbers of ducks and swans flock in from their northern breeding grounds. At its peak, the wildfowl population rises to over 60,000, with up to 42,000 wigeon, 7,500 teal, 7,000 mallard, 5,500 pochard, 3,650 pintail, 1,000 shoveler, 700 tufted, 100 gadwall, 1,200 Bewick's swans, 400 mute swans and fifty whooper swans. These figures[2] mean that at times a quarter of the entire British wintering population of wigeon is on the Washes, as well as 14 per cent of North-West Europe's Bewick's swans.

Before the Fens were drained, wildfowl were present in even greater numbers, but with the Washes remaining an attraction for ducks and swans wildfowling continues to be strong, and shooting and conservation have to exist side by side. Those fenmen who shoot see no contradiction in this and consider that their sport simply reaps a natural harvest of surplus birds; a harvest of about 1,000 ducks per year. After drainage the presence of dykes

[2] Approximate and to the nearest round figure, and given to me by the warden.

(Above left) A hunter with a deer rifle ascending a 'high seat' in Thetford Chase. These hides are built and maintained by the Forestry Commission, and are used for watching, photographing and shooting roe deer. (*H. Hitchmough / Shooting Times*)

(Above right) A roe deer peers out from amidst the woodland grass. Timid and alert, with excellent camouflage and remarkable hearing, roe deer are difficult to approach or even to glimpse. (*H. Hitchmough / Shooting Times*)

(Left) Wary and poised for flight, a fine red deer stag on a Scottish hillside – the epitome of Highland stalking. A 'three-quarters' shot such as this stag presents is not an easy one; the bullet is often deflected from finding a vital spot, and a long chase can follow. (*William Baxter/ Shooting Times*)

(Above) Wildfowling – flighting ducks at evening over decoys. A good water dog is essential if birds are not to be lost, particularly as most shooting takes place in half-light. (*John Tarlton*)

(Right) A remarkable photograph of a crossing grouse (flying left to right) a fraction of a second before the shot will hit it. The column of shot is visible ahead of the smoke from the discharge. Again notice the dog – birds are easily lost in bracken and heather. (*John Marchington*)

and ditches made the area important for domestic ducks as well as wildfowl and there were large flocks of farmyard ducks and geese. My own great-grandfather was a fenman and at the turn of the century his flock numbered nearly 2,000 geese.

Even after the arrival of shotguns many wildfowl were still trapped for sale, in decoys, when entire ponds and channels were covered with nets, and real and artificial decoy ducks were placed at their entrances to attract the wild birds. Some of the decoys are still used, but the caught birds are no longer killed and eaten, they are ringed and released. Now the pattern of fenland farming as well as fowling has changed, there are few domestic ducks and geese, and the great flocks on the Washes are virtually the only fenland fowl that remain.

The Washes themselves form a great wedge of land between long earth banks, some half a mile wide, over twenty miles long, and covering about 6,000 acres. They were created in the seventeenth century by a Dutchman, Cornelius Vermuyden, to drain the Fens, and the protective banks and the main drainage channels between them represent a staggering engineering achievement, especially as they were created by men using wooden shovels, wheelbarrows, horses, and carts. During the winter the area usually becomes a wasteland of floods and waterlogged soil, while in the summer the surface water drains away and the cattle of various farmers graze on the lush grasses, sedges, and reeds, under the supervision of 'wash shepherds'.

It is an area like no other; low and flat, with wide everchanging skies that give feelings and moods that are unique to the Fens. Each day and season brings changes, physical and visual, and each change affects the wildlife and the people of the Washes. Spring sees the start of the great annual migration northwards, as the ducks move off towards their summer breeding grounds. The Bewick's and whooper swans leave as well, for a journey that takes them 2,000 miles to northern Russia and the Arctic tundras, and afterwards the Washes seem empty.

Towards the end of March, after a long wet winter, I visited the part of the Washes managed by the Royal Society for the Protection of Birds, with the whole area still well under water. Most of the ducks had still to leave, but the swans had already gone. They were absent too from the nearby reserve of the Wildfowl Trust where each evening of their stay they are fed with wheat scattered along the edge of an artificial lagoon. Visitors can pay to watch the spectacle from wooden hides, and most enjoy the sight, as it introduces them to rare wild birds. To me, however, the swans seem far removed from the white, remote, and graceful birds that fly in with the autumn; they seem almost domesticated and the sight of them crowding to the shore to compete in the mud and water for corn, somehow seems to blur their beauty and takes away their independence and their dignity.

As I approached the reserve through the black fen fields, the landscape seemed inhospitable, bleak, and bare, with few trees and only occasional isolated and ugly farmsteads. But although the soil was still too wet for landwork, there were already clear signs of spring; lapwings in their erratic display flight with their piping calls matching their aerial movements, and hares running and sitting hunched up, already well into their March madness. The Washes were covered with water, shimmering in the bright sunlight, and it was warm walking with the warden at the bottom of one of the banks, out of the wind. Snipe flew up at regular intervals and two molecatchers slowly worked their way along the bank, checking and re-setting their traps – their work is essential, as the excavations of the moles weaken the banks.

In places osiers, alders and willow trees rose from the water and gateposts and wire acted as gibbets for assorted debris. The floods were gradually subsiding, for the high-water mark was shown as a line of grass, wood, bottles, and empty farmyard fertilizer bags, some decorated with an appropriate skull and crossbones. The water was light blue and dazzling, with a wide pathway of rippling gold and silver going away from the wind and into the sun. Flotillas of wigeon and teal were scattered at random over the water and others flew along the Washes, the sun catching their white wing bars as they drifted down unsteadily, to land in lengthening furrows of water; a pair of great-crested grebes swam close to one another, their necks briefly swaying in the unison of courtship. High over the bank came the strange humming sound of a snipe drumming, as it flew upwards and then swept down in a long arc, with the wind rushing through its fanned out tail feathers, and below the snipe in display, was a spinney of old leafless alders with several large twig nests high up in their branches. The heronry looked cold and exposed, but already some nests were occupied and incubation was in progress.

On land uncovered by the fall of water, the call of redshank mingled with the occasional whistle of drake wigeon, and close packed parties of dunlin appeared as light shadows over well grazed grass. Even the grass on the bank had been grazed, and at the water's edge it floated like clippings from a freshly mown lawn. As the morning advanced so the sky turned to a brittle blue and a line of high cirrus appeared as a fringe of white unkempt hair.

When the Washes flood the pintails are usually the first to arrive and they are present almost as soon as the water; the reason is simple, when they travel they fly at heights of up to five hundred feet, and so when moving along the coast or over the salt marshes of the Wash, the mass of freshwater in the Ouse Washes is clearly visible. When the water goes they are also the first to leave, with the pochards being the last to come and go. Pochards are amusing little diving ducks with grey bodies and chestnut heads; they are late arriving as they normally 'hedge-hop' from gravel pit to gravel pit, and so the message of the floods takes longer to register. Why they should remain for a fortnight after the main area of water has gone is a mystery.

At one spit of gravelly land, quite large waves were breaking on the shore and a solitary black-tailed godwit with long slender legs and bill stood at the water's edge. The sun came out briefly and the white wings of flying ducks matched the white flecked wave tops and the breaking surf. Swimming teal and wigeon flew up quite close to us, with droplets of water cascading from them, and the green speculum of a drake teal flashed gem-like with each downward wing beat. With the wind, the look of overall wildness, and the ducks wheeling about over the water, it was a stirring sight. Seen in isolation it seemed distant and remote; certainly not a man made phenomenon in over-farmed and over-populated East Anglia.

Crossing the railway bridge we passed another heronry with birds already sitting, and water stretched away on both sides for as far as the eye could see. Returning towards the warden's house we walked by the side of the Old Bedford River, causing a female wigeon to swim hurriedly away. It was a bird that had been shot by wildfowlers and could not fly. Many birds get wounded during the course of a season and great black-backed gulls regularly fly low over the water searching for easy kills. Earlier we had seen two other casualties; the half decayed corpses of two Bewick's swans.

By mid-summer there had been a dramatic change, for the wildness and desolation of the winter Washes had given way to a mellowness of appearance and feeling, a scene not of remoteness and running eyes, but of domesticity and warmth; wide rich pastures and herds of contented cattle, grazing and chewing the cud. It was a hot day, full of the smells of grass, water, and dust. From the bank, the Old Bedford River looked still and deep with pools of yellow water lilies about to burst into flower. We crossed a bridge to the Delph, for at this point the two drainage channels run side by side; willows grew along one of its banks, and a great-crested grebe was fishing, as was an old fenman, catching eels. Beyond the Delph, the Washes appeared as a broad, flat expanse of grasses, sedges, rushes, and cattle, extending out to the far banks of the tidal Hundred Foot Drain,[3] and beyond them was the grey outline of Ely cathedral. After the long winter and with feeding costs high, there were fewer cattle than usual, but those grazing, looked in fine condition.

To get to one of the hides we walked by the side of the Old Bedford River, while in the adjoining fields tractors were working and men and women were hoeing sugar beet by hand. The summer landwork in the Fens is long and hard and the hours worked would cause the average industrial worker to wilt, or to strike. But the work is not dictated by management whims and union fancies, it is governed by the hours of daylight and the amount to be done.

Thistles grew in profusion along the bank, and down by the water's edge the flags of yellow irises were beginning to fade. Yellow wagtails flew jerkily away from us, and a meadow pipit parachuted down in display flight, its wings and tail fanned out to control its unstable descent. From a hide overlooking the Washes the pastoral scene spread out before us in complete tranquillity; it was a patchwork of differing greens and uses. Many of the holdings are small and each farmer and tenant runs his land to suit his own requirements. As a result cattle go early onto some washes and eat the grass down quickly, while others are left for later grazing and some are used for hay. Each regime suits different birds; at one extreme the godwits and lapwings are attracted by the shorter grass of heavy grazing for their nests, while mallards and shovelers

[3] Also known as the New Bedford River.

seek out areas of longer grass for dense cover. Surprisingly, only a few nests get trampled on, and then many of the birds lay again.

The conservation bodies try to maintain and to manage the delicate balances in the Washes and their land too is let for grazing. Some areas of water and marsh have been created, as they are essential for the ducks and waders, and they also provide easy drinking for the cattle. Even the effect of the cattle in the water is important, and the mud churned up by many hooves provides rich feeding for the birds.

In front of the hide some Friesian cattle trudged about lethargically in a flooded depression, drinking, keeping cool, and swishing at flies with their tails. Lapwings fed among the mud and tussocks and the occasional quavering calls of redshanks were all that broke the silence. Two godwits suddenly flew up in agitation, with short, almost quivering wingbeats, their beaks long, their legs trailing out behind, and the sun catching their chestnut breasts. A bullock was too near their young, probably the chicks from a second clutch of eggs, and although it was dive bombed repeatedly, the animal remained unmoved and locked in lethargy. Then, for no apparent reason, the air was full of wings as many birds flew up from concealment. There were starlings, ruffs, redshanks, more godwits, snipe, and lapwings, with some calling out in alarm as if a predator had startled them. The cause of their consternation remained unseen to human eyes, but soon they settled down and peace returned. Three fully-fledged godwits landed to feed and a small group of teal splashed down in a neighbouring pool. Near them a shelduck with her large half grown brood sifted through thick black mud, and in the distance three herons stood along a ditch as if incubation had been successful. The water, mud, marsh and grazing held a great variety of ducks and waders and it is clear that throughout the year the Washes hold a wealth of wildlife.

Many ducks, mallards, shelducks, teals, and pintails had young, but the vast winter flocks of wildfowl and swans had returned to northern Europe and Scandinavia. All the visiting swans had gone, except one whooper and three Bewick's; they had remained in the Washes, unable to fly, as body-borne shot[4] had prevented their

[4] On Monday 24 February 1975, over three weeks after the finish of the shooting season, twenty-three wounded birds that could not fly were seen in the osier bed not far from the warden's house. There were five teal, twelve wigeon, three mallard, two pintail and one tufted duck.

migration. As we returned to the warden's house at mid-day, the eel catcher too was returning for his dinner.

Like fowling and fishing, eeling is another of the Fen's traditions, for eels can be found in large numbers. Again the skills of eel-catching once provided many livelihoods, but nowadays they are practised by just a handful of men for pocket money as well as pleasure. The eeler who fishes along the dykes uses nets and has spent the whole of his working life in the Fens, farming, fishing, mole catching and eeling. Now in his retirement he spends most of his time after eels and as he goes to check his nets he leaves his ninety-two year old father sleeping in his van.

Each week-day morning he crosses the Old Bedford River using a bridge of planks on floating oil drums, to walk down to the Delph where he moors his small flat-bottomed boat. It felt unstable to me, but he claims that he has never fallen overboard. For propulsion he uses a homemade double-bladed kayak paddle, and for navigation among the lilies and willows he has a long pole with bent over pitchfork tines at one end. When I went out with him his golden labrador Prince swam to the far bank, making redshanks fly, and a mallard flapped into the water, feigning injury, to draw the dog away from her young. The eel nets were staked close to some willows, with the stakes sunk deep into the mud; they were strung out vertically and led the eels into a large trap, like a keep net, with a 'chair' in each one to allow the eels to get in, but which prevented them from getting out. He makes his own keep nets from pieces of netting and wire rings; at one time he used to make them with wire netting and bicycle wheels. In the first net three or four eels slithered about, proving that the method worked; but I could not understand how or why the eels should follow the ordinary fish-net into the keep net. The next one was empty, however, except for the head of what had once been a large roach; it seemed as if eels had been present but had managed to escape, the fish had swum in and had been eaten.

His experiences of eeling make him disbelieve the 'experts' who claim that eels only breed in the Sargasso Sea, for he has caught many large eels, including one weighing five pounds, but he has seen others 'barely as big as a matchstick'. As a result he thinks they live and breed where he catches them. He is also sure that eels have two brains, one at each end, and that the quickest way to kill an eel is to cut its tail off. He states that his theory is proved by the fact that the eels often try to get out of his nets tail first, and some have even entered the water the same way after jumping out of his boat.

He considers that the story of eels travelling overland is also totally false and he has never seen a live eel out of water: 'Even if a drag line scoops 'em out with the mud, you find dead eels on the land side of the mud. If they could travel overland and smell water they would go the other way, back into the dykes. The trouble is people read too many books, and most of them are rubbish; I've never read a book in me life. You get bird watchers over here with their binoculars and books; if they see a bird do something unusual, that's not in the book, then the book's right and the bloody bird's wrong.'

In the old days he also caught eels by 'bobbing'[5] with wool or silk stockings as well as with weighted night lines. He would never fix the lines to the bank or cork floats, 'otherwise people would find them', instead he would fix them to corked beer bottles; 'people will fish out cork, but they will ignore a bottle'. He has also successfully used a 'gleeve' in the past, a special long handled multi-tined fork, something like a trident; it is forced down into the mud in the hope of impaling eels. Some old fenmen claim that eels can be caught by submerging a box full of 'hen's innards'. Holes are made in the sides, and after the eels have gorged themselves they become stuck in the holes. The eel catcher describes this method as 'bloody nonsense; horse squit'. One claim with which he does agree, however, concerns the strength and quality of eel skin; 'my mother always wore eel skin garters to prevent rheumatism', and eel skin could also be used to link the two lengths of wood in a flail, as it was considered to be more durable than leather.

He caught about a dozen eels that morning and as we returned along the bank with his catch, Prince suddenly froze, almost pointing; the dog sprang forwards, sinking his front paws and nose into soft earth and emerging with a mole. The eel catcher claims that he is also the most expert and knowledgeable molecatcher in the Fens, and the dog has evidently learnt some of his master's skills. The eels were put into a large wooden box already containing about thirty others of various sizes. The box was then secured to the

[5] The same as 'clatting' in Devonshire.

bank of a deep pit, and because of its perforated sides it was left floating, but almost completely submerged; the pit where the catches are stored covers about four acres and was formed when the River Authority dug out clay to reinforce the nearby bank after a bad winter. The eels can remain alive in the box for many weeks, and when the eeler has about a hundredweight he telephones a dealer to collect them alive. In late summer it takes him several days to get enough, but in the spring one morning's work is often sufficient.

My other two visits to the Washes were after the shooting season had started; once with the warden, and once with Mark, a keen wildfowler. The first was early in September to see what changes had occurred after many of the birds had become 'legitimate quarry'. The warden had seen few ducks during the day, but even so he had heard several shots, particularly from a private wash where shooting day-tickets can be purchased. Because of the availability of shooting even people with no knowledge of wildfowling can shoot, and consequently some shooters seem to shoot at anything with wings and feathers.

As we walked along the roadway to the Washes thousands of swallows and sand martins were milling around in the air and perching along the telephone wires. One sand martin was pure white, and as soon as it flew it was followed by swallows that frequently swooped down at it. Being so conspicuous it seems likely that sooner or later it would be picked out by birds of prey.

The pasture land was still, baked brown by the dry summer, and covered with scorched grass and dark patches of seeding docks and dying rushes. Heavy black clouds began to form a threatening anvil to the north, but no thunder or lightning followed. A tufted duck swam across the Delph, unusually low in the water, and the warden thought that it had been shot and wounded. We went through a gate, held together with wire and string and began to walk over the grazing land. Half-way across we had to stop and retrace our steps, for a bullock was almost submerged in a small dyke. It had just a small strip along its back free of stinking mud, and even its head was black with slime. The shepherd was telephoned, but a neighbouring farmer arrived first, for every evening he checks his cattle and the dykes to prevent casualties. He put one end of a rope around the animal's neck and hitched the other to his Land Rover. He revved the engine and the animal was slowly heaved out. No damage was done, although the bullock coughed and stood unsteadily for several seconds. Many cattle get into the dykes during the summer, but most are recovered without mishap.

At the Hundred Foot, the tide was coming in fast and three wildfowlers were trying to cross in a small boat. It was so low in the water that a capsize seemed imminent. The fowlers realized their danger and threw their three dogs overboard, a curly-coated labrador, a spaniel, and a golden retriever that did a backward somersault into the water. Somehow the crossing was made safely, and, as they jumped ashore, they looked like remnants of a resistance army. Again the dressing up, the guns, and the hazards, were obvious and important parts of their sport. If they saw no ducks that night they already had plenty to talk and laugh about afterwards. Often, when the Washes are in flood, the actual shooting is done from boats, which greatly increases both the danger and the humour of wildfowling. They all had broad Fenland accents and spoke with contempt about 'the day-ticket holders who shoot at bloody anything'. The dogs were eager to be on their way, and the group dispersed; one man said that he was going to try and flush a couple of tufted ducks that he had seen regularly on a drainage channel before the start of the season. At various places over the Washes guns fired periodically, but we saw no ducks, nor what had been fired at.

The visit with Mark was more successful, for being in November there were plenty of 'quackers' about. Although Mark lives several miles away from the Fens he is a keen wildfowler, and the small syndicate of which he is a member hires a six-acre plot in the middle of the Washes. The wash itself had been cut for hay, so Mark stuck three sticks into the ground and strung dead grass over them to form a small makeshift hide. Almost immediately eight mallard approached us flying in a straight line, just in range. As they flew overhead Mark fired and missed, and fired again, rolling over on his back as he did so. One duck veered away from the others and flew over the artificial flight pond of the day-ticket shoot on the adjoining wash. It immediately faced a barrage of shots and lost height, as if hit, and flew down to land on the bank of the Hundred Foot River, a quarter of a mile away. The three camouflaged shooters hiding around the flight-pond had no dogs, and despite the fact that the duck had been hit, they made no effort to go and look for it. At Mark's suggestion I went to search for the bird, but with no dog it was impossible. As I returned another mallard flew over the guns, but several shots failed to bring it down.

The wind was cold and the light began to fade. High up I suddenly saw eight whooper swans flying silently. They were the colour of hoar frost against the darkening sky and flew with grace and easy wingbeats in a wavering, slanting line, straight over the guns, but no shots were fired. Elsewhere gunfire came from all over the Washes, sounding like November the Fifth, and from the tall alders of the heronry regular shots rang out as pigeons flew to roost.

The light went rapidly, and as it did so we heard wigeon, the distinctive whistle of the drakes and the susurrant sound of rapid wing beats as sixteen flew over us in a perfect V formation. They flew from the direction of the elms; Mark fired one shot, but missed, as the 'quackers' were flying too fast. Two more whistling chevrons flew by at speed, slightly to the side, and Mark let them go. They flew directly over the day-ticket wash and more shots rang out; after one there was a splash and the sound of a man wading to retrieve a duck, and spent shot fell around us like a shower of rain. The moon shone out intermittently with watery cloud regularly dimming its brilliance. More ducks flew over, though I did not see them, but just heard their wingbeats. Shooting in this light would have been by reflex only, with no chance of positively identifying the birds. Despite this our neighbours fired several more times. With the wind, the moonlit darkness and the sounds of flying ducks, I could understand the wildfowler's feelings of excitement and anticipation, although it is a sport that I could never enjoy. Mark had not shot a duck and had used five cartridges, and for him, even without a duck, the visit had been worthwhile. He dismantled his makeshift hide and we walked back towards the causeway and his car.

I have always had a strong liking for ducks, muscovies have for many years been part of the farm, and my first bird-watching expeditions took in a gravel pit which sheltered tufted ducks and pochard. Consequently, I would find it hard to shoot wildfowl even for the pot, and to suddenly open up at birds so beautiful and free just for sport is something that is not for me. Nevertheless, I have met many wildfowlers who are pleasant and agreeable men, knowing much about the ducks they shoot, as well as about their conservation. Yet it is also true that the behaviour of others cannot be defended, for many people shoot at any birds they see, in range or out, and completely disregard the law.[6] Some have even been seen shooting on Sundays, a crime no longer important to most people on Sabbatarian grounds, but important for the ducks as Sunday is a day when harassment stops and they can settle and feed in peace.[7]

Many wildfowlers are attracted to the Washes by the numerous articles and books that have romanticized and popularized both the sport and the area, and with day-tickets available virtually anybody can shoot. As a result it is not really surprising that tests carried out with X-rays on captured ducks and swans have shown that a third of the birds in the winter wildfowl population carry lead shot in their bodies, which in round figures means that 20,000 birds have been hit and not brought down. What is even more disturbing is the fact that the same high percentage applies to swans as well as ducks. Indeed, some people consider that one-third is a low estimate and that the actual figure is well over 40 per cent. There are numerous eye-witness accounts of swans being shot at, and one man who knows the Washes well considers it fair to say that if a flock of Bewick's swans was to fly along the Washes in broad daylight, on a Saturday, the birds would come under fire. The wardens have seen men raise their guns at protected birds only to be warned by friends: 'Be careful what you shoot, the wardens are over there.' Some wildfowlers become so frustrated after a duckless day that they shoot at anything, and even the noticeboards along the bank of the Hundred Foot Drain have been shot.

It has been estimated that of all the shots at least a quarter are fired when it is too dark to identify the birds, or to pick them up, and at the height of the shooting season 25,000 cartridges are being used on the Washes in a month. From this figure and the number of wounded birds it is clear that ducks are being shot out of range. Whereas responsible fowlers are satisfied with four or five shots and a duck, others get through whole boxes of cartridges. On one

[6] Birds found shot in the Washes include herons, mute swans, Bewick's swans, goosanders, hen harriers, lapwings, ruffs, short-eared owls, fieldfares, and redwings, as well as a single great-crested grebe, whooper swan, and skylark.

[7] The shooting of wildfowl on Sundays is banned in certain areas by a special bye-law, the Ouse Washes being one of these areas.

occasion the warden met a wildfowler as he left the Washes at midday.

'How did you get on?' he asked.

'The best day's sport I've ever had', the wildfowler replied, 'I've only come off because I've run out of cartridges. The best day's sport I've ever had, I think I winged a teal.'

'How many cartridges did you use?'

'A hundred. The best day's sport I've ever had.'

Even the shot fired contributes to another growing problem on the Washes, for each cartridge contains up to 200 lead pellets; this means that large quantities of lead are being spread over the whole area. As a result many of the mallards, shovelers, pintails, teal, and the three types of swans, pick up shot as they sift for seeds and grit, and like grit, the shot is retained in the gizzard. This in turn leads to lead poisoning, to lethargy, and death, and it is estimated that 400-700 birds die each year on the Ouse Washes because of lead shot. Between 5 and 8 per cent of the pintails die annually because of lead poisoning, and 20 per cent of all the dead Bewick's found by the wardens and sent for analysis have died from the same cause.[8] In other centres there are similar difficulties and although wildfowling conducted responsibly is a valid sport and a good way of getting a dinner, two problems have to be faced. Something has to be done to reduce the incidence of lead ingestion, and controls must be imposed to rid shooting of those 'marsh cowboys' who every weekend dress up for their Saturday's sport and behave as if they are at war.

Many wildfowlers consider that shooting inland is nothing but 'duck shooting', whereas real wildfowling can only be experienced on the foreshore.[9] There the salt, wind, tides, and mud, provide more chance of shooting geese, and 'goose fever' can drive a wildfowler many miles in the hope of a shot at a greylag or pink-footed goose. Geese seldom stay long on the Ouse Washes, the area is too narrow to give them security. Feral Canada geese, and Norfolk

[8] Of four Bewick's swans found dead on the Ouse Washes on 24 November 1974 and sent to the Wildfowl Trust at Slimbridge for post mortem examinations, two had died from lead poisoning, with shot in their gizzards, but not in their bodies. One had died from 'shotgun trauma', with six shot in the body and a multiple wing fracture, and the other was suspected lead poisoning although no shot was found.

[9] The area of shore between the high and low watermarks, traditionally (like swans) the property of the Crown.

introduced and bred greylags are the most common, but their visits are usually brief.

The winter foreshore is a most inhospitable place, often bleak and cold, and yet some fowlers will make numerous journeys until they get a morning or an evening flight that makes their many failures seem worthwhile. Indeed, I went on one typical day to the salt marshes of the Wash with Mark; we crouched low in a cold, oozing, salt creek until the light vanished, but we saw and heard nothing, except one straying blackbird. Another wildfowler claims that when he started his sport he visited the coast at regular intervals from September to January before he had a shot, yet he prefers the foreshore to any other type of shooting.

In an attempt to sample foreshore shooting, with a high chance of seeing geese, I travelled up to Inverness to be taken out by a wildfowler of great skill and experience. It was a cold February morning when my host knocked me up at 5.00 am; pitch dark, with snow falling steadily. As we drove along winding roads the snow swirled in the car's headlights, and the black labrador, Mole, spent the journey sitting in the rear seat with his front paws draped over the front seat, looking eagerly out of the front window. We passed signposts bearing names that I had heard before only as remote places mentioned in gale warnings and shipping forecasts, and as we approached the coast the snow turned to slush on the road.

A few weeks earlier there had been well over 1,000 greylags in the area, but now the fowler thought that there were fewer than 100, because of harassment. The main cause of their disturbance had been the activities of two men on the dole, who had shot at roosting geese and had even tethered wounded birds to act as decoys. Although it is illegal to offer geese for sale, they had sold the shot birds to customers in local pubs.

By the time we arrived at the wide bay the light was gradually increasing. It was bitterly cold walking over the mud flats, with the sea well out and the wind driving rain over the desolation. It was an area of mud and weed, with the corpses of old cars well rusted and almost buried. My hide was erected in front of some unidentified amputations from wrecked cars; it was only two feet high and consisted of wire and khaki material over four small rods. Mole and his master went about 100 yards further on; their low hide was made from a strip of flexible metal, draped with camouflage netting, that from a distance merged into the dark weed surrounding it.

Even with wellington boots and waterproof trousers it was cold, uncomfortable, and damp. Oyster catchers and other waders flew over and a pack (a wildfowler's term) of wigeon went wide to our right. Movement ahead caught my attention; geese were flying in a long low irregular line from the land, almost loping through the wind on lazy wings. Few sights can match that of flying geese or swans and they seemed almost drawn towards the fowler's hide. As they were almost over him he fired; one fell and the others flared upwards, calling out in alarm. He fired again and one of the highest birds plummeted down as if dead. The remainder continued in disarray, calling anxiously as they went, before settling into a ragged, wind-tossed V as they flew off over the bay.

My host thought that he had killed two birds, for the first goose looked dead and the second was lying on its back with its 'paddles up'. Several minutes passed without movement in case more geese should arrive, but none came over, and Mole was sent to retrieve. As he set off enthusiastically towards the 'deadest' goose, the bird stood up, shook itself, flapped its wings, and slowly and laboriously left the ground. Mole pursued, but gradually the bird gained height and flew off after the others. At the sea the frustrated dog gave up his chase and returned to retrieve the other goose, which was dead in a pool of shallow water. As there were no more geese we returned for breakfast.

By the time I left the wildfowler's home to return south, the Highlands had turned completely white, with mature pines by the roadside heavy with snow, sending miniature avalanches crashing from their branches. It was a gentle, soothing scene after the bleakness of the foreshore, full of whiteness and woodland, mountains and fast-flowing streams. In occasional low lying fields, sheep seemed content in their thick wool and some chewed at turnips, left out in their rows for fodder. Where one valley side rose up majestically, red deer stags could be seen as distant specks. Some were trying to graze by scraping the snow away from the heather with a front hoof, and several looked absurd and awkward having cast one antler.

Out of the mountains I passed the Perthshire Loch Leven where large numbers of geese from Iceland spend each winter, and where many wildfowlers congregate.[10] When shooting begins great black-backed gulls start to patrol the loch, as they have learned to link gunfire with easy feeding from dead and dying birds. The loch also provides evidence that many of those who shoot geese are just as irresponsible as those people in the Ouse Washes who blast away at all birds. Over Christmas and the New Year there is usually a three-week break from shooting on the loch, yet after the lull, the accumulation of freshly dead geese that have struggled to the loch to die shows that inaccurate and out-of-range shooting takes place in the surrounding areas.

As well as firing from wildfowlers, the geese also face much harassment from farmers; for the sight of a flock of large birds landing in a field of recently sown corn can be extremely worrying to the landowner or tenant concerned. The presence of ducks creates similar worries, as they can appear to graze fields almost bare. Usually the anxiety is ill-founded for the grazing often seems to have a beneficial effect, stimulating growth and spreading duck manure. Indeed, in the days of widespread mixed farming, sheep were often driven into fields of growing cereal crops to graze, and the yields at harvest-time were not adversely affected.

It would be wrong, however, to claim that wildfowl do no damage to farming, for when the land is wet, the large footed and heavy birds puddle about in the fields, and growing corn can die as a result. One year, we were suddenly plagued by large flocks of mallard which flew in at dusk every evening onto six acres of winter wheat, and they turned the whole field into a quagmire. Several local people tried to shoot them, without success, and only one duck was killed. The land was so wet that the corn was grazed and then trodden down into the slurry, and in the spring no wheat reappeared. Harassment, out-of-range shooting, and 'accidental' poisoning with sprays or chemically dressed corn, are not the answers to such a situation. What is required is a proper conservation service offering advice, practical help, and compensation; such an innovation would not only aid those who suffer crop damage, but it would also benefit the wildfowl.

10 The greatest numbers are usually between 8,000 – 10,000 pinkfeet and 4.500 – 5,000 greylags. It is estimated that the Icelandic summer population of these birds is over 70,000 each and they all winter in Great Britain.

Chapter Eleven

To Drown a Worm

Fishing is by far the most popular of all blood sports, and there can be few men who, in boyhood, failed to take a rod, line, net, or jam-jar down to the local pond or stream, in the hope of catching a fish, big or small. Wet feet, muddied trousers, and parental annoyance were often the penalties for abducting a few sticklebacks or minnows, but the exercise always seemed to be worthwhile. As time passed and experience grew, the would-be fishermen moved on to larger fish and learnt the art of angling in fresh water; they graduated from 'tiddlers' to roach, dace, perch, and even pike. With the onset of work, many gave up their sport, but with the advent of wage packets others became even more enthusiastic and developed their fishing still further. Some were able to take in game fishing as well as coarse fishing, and at every summer holiday they could take their rods with them down to the sea.

Today the same process is continuing and by every river bank or mill pond, small boys can be seen with their optimism and long rods as they try to catch fish. When bites are few and boredom sets in they even take live fish from their buckets or keep-nets to impale them on large hooks to use as live bait for pike, and from their ranks a new generation of dedicated anglers is assured. Yet, like all blood sports, the reactions to fishing are surprising, for although fishing is unavoidably cruel, and despite the fact that most anglers fish solely for enjoyment, it is the one blood sport which is subjected to hardly any criticism. Even the secretary for the League Against Cruel Sports has written: 'The League has no plans to actively campaign against fishing'.

Fishing, like hunting, is as old as history itself and throughout the ages of Man, nets, spears, and traps have been used to catch fish for food. Now, with necessity gone and vast and efficient fishing fleets catching all our requirements, fishing still takes place with rod and line. It is a sport that has developed over several hundreds of years, in which the knowledge and skill of the fisherman is pitted against the wariness and the natural needs of the fish.

I started fishing in my childhood days, like most of my friends, and we often assembled down at the brook with nets, jam-jars, cotton, worms, and bent pins, in the hope of returning home with a fish. On several occasions we even dammed a small tributary stream that flowed into the brook, so that below the barrier, sticklebacks and millers' thumbs became marooned on sand banks, and we could catch them more easily. They were then transferred to an old bath in the farmyard, and even water snails and caddis flies joined them and were looked upon as great prizes. Gradually, with experience and pocket money, rods, nylon lines, barbed hooks, floats, and weights, equipped us still further, and armed with bread, cheese, and bright red worms dug from a heap of cow muck we offered the fish treats that we hoped they would not resist. Much to our annoyance they often spurned our generosity, which was hardly surprising, for the activity on the banks and bridges would have frightened them well away. When we took more care we were often successful in catching quite big fish, which made us even more determined, and the next stage was to journey into Cambridge to fish in the River Cam. We fished at a place where undergraduates and foreign students punted in the summer, close to an old quay where elderly men could remember barges unloading their cargoes. There we competed against each other, to see who could catch the most fish in a morning, and we would haul out small brown gudgeon at regular intervals. One year we were so keen that we even started fishing before the season had begun, and several annoyed fishermen strode over to warn us away.

Along the brook's banks we fished in the early morning, the late evening, and all the hours in between, and we caught anything from half-inch tiddlers to medium-sized roach. Larger fish also inhabited the pools of the brook for we often saw them, but they could never be caught. Pike sped away in a swirl of water when their basking sessions were disturbed on sunny afternoons, and with them went their expressions of malice and evil which made us hate them. Sometimes they even seized small fish as they were wound in, and we viewed their cannibalism and rows of savage needle-sharp teeth as being far worse than our deception and our tempting, barbed hooks.

Shoals of roach swam from shallows to deep water, and dace

darted beneath the surface of their own favourite pool, and on warm summer nights ripples would break the stillness as fish rose to suck in flies. For me, as time went by, the need to catch fish slowly faded. I was satisfied and my senses were refreshed simply by sitting out in the peace and solitude of the brook; it was enough just to sit and watch my red-tipped float drift on the faint current, and I could enjoy quietude, contemplation, and the ancient atavistic attraction of water. Sometimes other fishermen joined me in the peace; herons drifting in on wide wings, to stand long-legged and patient, and occasionally the turquoise flash of a kingfisher would be reflected in the water. Other life, independent of fish, also depended on the brook, and the rushes, scrub, and meadows around it. Warblers would go about the business of raising their broods in the reeds; mosquitoes and dragon flies would dance out their fleeting day long lives, and at dusk others too, took to the wing; bats flew frenetically and erratically in pursuit of food, and owls hunted with grace and beauty, in complete silence. As life went on around me I would become lost in my own world of thought and contentment, and it ceased to worry me whether or not the float responded to the actions of a hard, hungry mouth. It was an appreciation of fishing that had nothing whatsover to do with fish.

My last morning's fishing occurred on a bend in the brook, where we sometimes swam in summer. I was dangling a worm in the water, hopefully suspending it just above the bottom, at the deepest point. I did not really like fishing with worms, for they always seemed to squirm and writhe as the hook pierced their bodies. Neither did I believe the story that they felt no pain, for their reactions indicated acute discomfort. In addition I disliked handling them at the end of an unsuccessful morning, for they would be limp and soggy, confirming what an old uncle always maintained, that fishing was simply an extravagant way of drowning worms.

The signs of autumn were all around me as I fished, and its distinct damp mellowness filled the morning air. The hedgerows of hawthorn and bramble were showing the rich colours of winter's advance, and clusters of blackberries hung, dew-coated, among the jewelled strings of spiders' webs. The last swallows of summer skimmed low over the water, and the young heifers and bullocks from the meadow wandered over to the fence to stand and stare.

Soon the float began to move and bobble and I struck. The line tightened and the top of the rod bent as I wound in a small perch that struggled fiercely for its freedom. It was an attractive fish, with broad vertical stripes and a spined dorsal fin, but the hook and barb were embedded deep into its throat. I used a long metal disgorger to heave, push, and pull, the hook before I eventually ripped it out. I returned the fish to the water and caught several more by casting in the same place, and each time in slime and blood I had to heave out the half swallowed hook. After that I decided that I could enjoy the brook and its life without the ritual of barbs and worms.

For others, however, fishing continues to be a popular sport, and a pastime in which the worries of work and home can be forgotten. The fisherman can leave his factory or high-rise flat, forget the stresses, strains, and non-stop rushing of modern-day civilized living, and for a few hours he can 'drop out'; he can get back to nature and pit his wits and skill against wild creatures. Each weekend during the season, coachloads of fishermen spill out into the countryside from our large industrial centres, as coal miners and foundry workers and people of all other trades briefly respond to the echoes of their ancestral past. The enthusiasm for fishing is particularly obvious at the start of each new season, for hordes of fishermen emerge with keep-nets, bait boxes, rods, and rests, and some even get up to fish in the early morning darkness. One such fisherman had no luck and, from fatigue and boredom, he dropped off to sleep as he fished; he dropped off the bank as well and fell right into the river.

Because of the popularity of fishing, clubs and private individuals have bought up the fishing rights of most of the best water available along the banks of streams, brooks, rivers, and lakes. Even ponds and gravel pits are bought up and stocked with fish so that fishermen can sit and dangle their maggots, worms, cheese, luncheon meat, broad beans, and various other delights. Virtually any pond or disused gravel pit can have fishing potential, and one Sunday afternoon I went to watch a schoolmaster fish in a gravel pit where he spends much of his spare time. He and several friends acquired the rights when the pits were overgrown and contained little life; they cut the rubbish from the paths, removed the debris, dragged out broken branches, and dug out decaying leaves. Now they have fishing which gives them good sport, for the pit holds perch and rudd and large carp which they introduced and which now breed freely.

It was a cold, clear afternoon with a cool east wind and small white clouds scudding across the wide sky. Initially, my companion used yellow grains of tinned sweet corn as bait, without much success, and his float, a simple length of quill, gave no indication of interested fish. In a small lagoon, near some reeds, coots preened and fought and then a splash and a widening ring of ripples suggested that carp might be starting to feed. We changed our position and slowly advanced along a small headland, but even with caution a fish saw us and its indistinct form shot towards deeper water. Two others moved languorously over dark weed, cruising without purpose. The schoolmaster baited his hook with more sweet corn and re-cast. We sat and waited but no fish could be seen and the cold soaked through my clothes and into my bones.

After a time the fisherman changed his bait to bread, and almost immediately the quill bobbed up and floated flat on the surface, it then started to move away. He struck, and the empty hook flew out of the water. Again the hook was baited with bread and as the float began to move we were so eager and expectant that our coldness disappeared. He struck, again he missed, and soon all the float's unnatural movement stopped.

We changed our position and he reverted to sweet corn; straight away the float disappeared, the rod bent, and I thought that he had hooked a large fish. When it broke the surface it was a perch, small but vigorous. After the next cast the float seemed to tremble, as if other fish were nibbling at the bait, but they were obviously small and no more positive bites came. The light sharpened the shape of the willows as the sun sank to the west, gulls flew over, fired in bronze, and a large flock of field-fares, newly arrived for the winter, continued their journey inland.

Back at our original starting point the schoolmaster cast again, hoping that fish had at last found the handfulls of sweet corn that he had thrown in as ground bait on arrival. Several inactive minutes passed and then suddenly the float bobbed momentarily and disappeared. He struck, the tight line sliced through the water as the fish fought against the hook and unnatural restraint. Gradually its effort weakened and it was wound in; it was a carp, and despite its fighting spirit it weighed only half a pound. As the hook was taken from its mouth the fish's small yellow-rimmed eyes seemed to be watching us, and once returned to water it quickly swam away. Carp were introduced into this country several centuries ago as food for the table but now, despite the millions of freshwater fish that are caught each year, tastes and necessity have changed, and nearly all the coarse fish caught by rod and line are immediately put back into water.

In the same way as my friends and I once fished against each other, to see who caught the most, so up and down the country each week-end, coarse fishermen compete with each other to see who can land the heaviest catches. At some matches just a few members of a club participate, with the winner receiving a small memento, while at the other extreme, many hundreds take part for large prizes. Indeed, fishing competitions are becoming so popular that many predict that angling will grow into a major spectator sport. At one competition in the Vale of Evesham for Britain's top twenty anglers, a crowd of over 15,000 was attracted to watch and to spend its money at a nearby carnival. Some even say that fishing will become an important television sport and point to the fact that a float is no smaller than a golf ball, yet in the early days of televised sport, golf was not considered because of the size of the ball. Now television companies pay vast sums to show golf tournaments, and the day might well come when viewers will have to sit through an action-replay of a float disappearing beneath the water.

It is the club and competition fishing which does invite some criticism, for often many country people cannot fish on their local water, as the fishing clubs have purchased all the rights, and they also tire of the bus loads of factory workers and city dwellers who line the river banks each week-end and who treat the countryside like a gigantic litter bin. As they fish, they eat and drink their way through the day, leaving their beer cans, waste paper, and empty pie packets along the banks. Some also suggest that in any case competition angling is cruel, for in their eagerness the anglers treat their fish with little respect and injury is often caused.

Like most sportsmen, however, each fisherman considers his particular pastime to be completely humane. Coarse fishermen maintain that their sport is good because they put all their fish back: 'It's the game fishermen who are cruel as they crump their salmon and trout on the head.' The game fishermen say it is the coarse fishermen who are cruel: 'Match fishing is not a sport it is a glorified gamble. We kill our fish quickly and cleanly, they hook their fish and then put them back; that is cruel.'

Percy Anderson, a middle-aged fisherman, is a well known match angler who competes in many competitions. Although he has a cockney accent, he has never lived in London, and when he is not fishing he runs his own fishing tackle business in Cambridge. He does not regard fishing as cruel, 'for you often catch the same fish twice and you wouldn't if it had been hurt or frightened.' He started fishing as a boy and has developed his technique and knowledge of fish to such a level that he has won both the European and the All-England individual championships. Among fishermen he is famous and with his long hair and large cigar, heads turn whenever he takes up position on a river bank. As I talked to him in his shop he told me how he had started when he was very young: 'You just get hooked on fishing', he said, without acknowledging his pun. Several times our conversation was interrupted by small boys who walked into the shop, and I had to wait while he served them with pints of maggots.

Although he fishes competitively he still likes to go out in the early morning, 'specimen fishing' for really big fish. He puts his success down to a mixture of skill and luck, but he does not think it possible to do well without being 'dedicated and professional'. Consequently he believes that the average fisherman could be in an ideal spot, but he would not match the catch of an expert fishing in the same place. He makes no secret of the fact that to him the prize money is important, and when he won the First Division of the National Championship in 1974 it was worth in the region of £2,000, excluding the advertising and the offers to speak and write that also followed.

In a large competition there can be as many as 750 anglers competing and putting money into a pool, and there may be independent bookmakers present as well. Percy often puts £10 on himself and he estimates that it costs him £400 a year to fish and to compete. For the ordinary person wanting to start fishing, adequate equipment could be bought for £5, but for good reliable gear it would cost between £50 and £60. He sees nothing cruel in catching fish and putting them back and he speaks contemptuously about continental fishermen, 'for the bloody foreigners kill all they catch'.

I went to watch him compete in the Middle Ouse Angling Championship, which took place along several miles of the Great Ouse one Sunday in late summer. By 8.30 am, the time of the draw for positions along the river bank, the small grass common where the officials' tent had been erected was packed with cars and people. There were new cars, old vans, and all the men were in anoraks, waterproof clothing, and a variety of waders and wellington boots. Some were buying their entry tickets, and a queue had grown at a small table, where each entrant paid £2.50 into the pool, while others were buying hot dogs from a refreshment caravan, and groups of old acquaintances had formed to discuss past achievements and future hopes. There were almost 500 competitors altogether and there were accents from all over the country – Hampshire, Wigan, Stockport, Chelmsford – and one man had even driven down from Alloa in Scotland, a round trip of over 700 miles.

Percy thought that bream would win the competition, a large fish that swims in shoals, but from the number he had drawn he was not optimistic about his own chances. Gradually the groups dispersed as the fishermen drove off to their stretches of the river and I helped Percy carry his equipment to his peg, which was several fields away. He had a large wicker basket to sit on, which contained various pieces of equpiment, as well as a bag full of bait, mostly maggots, casters, and some worms that he had acquired from a friend. I carried another bag full of bits and pieces, as well as his heavy rod case which contained five rods. With so much equipment he was ready for any eventuality and condition of water, while some competitors were loaded up so much that they looked like sherpas setting out on some great expedition.

Once at his peg he set up a rod and sorted out his bait, mostly casters, the small dark red pupae of blow flies, and yellow, brown, and white maggots. All the anglers seemed to have a large supply of maggots, coloured by their diet, and most had spent between £8–£10 on bait – the British maggot industry must be one of the most rapidly expanding in the country. Once ready he sat and waited, like the others, and as far as the eye could see along the bank there were fishermen at twenty-yard intervals, some sitting behind large green umbrellas to keep out of the breeze. Percy's immediate neighbour on one side was another fishing tackle shop owner, who only takes part in competitions occasionally, and on the other was an expert bream fisherman from Leicester who reckons to win £1,000 each fishing season.

At eleven o'clock a shrill whistle blew and the fishing started. At various places competitors lobbed in great balls of cloud bait which splashed into the river like depth charges; rather than attracting the fish, it seemed to me that such mass activity would frighten most of them away. The river, about forty yards wide and with a steady flow, was quite deep, so deep in fact that the fisherman from Leicester decided to ledger for bream.[1] Percy took his time and cast into mid-stream, and then produced a special catapult made from a metal hoop with a handle, and four strands of rubber joining a leather disc. The leather was designed to hold half a handful of bait, and with this contraption he catapulted casters around his float with ease and accuracy. His other neighbour decided that his maggots for ground bait were being eaten by small fish before they got to the bottom. He therefore produced a metal container which took the maggots down to the bottom and then opened. I was amazed at just how far human endeavour and ingenuity would go, simply to enable men to triumph over fish.

By dinner time it was obvious that in places fish had triumphed over men, for one or two competitors had already given up. One had abandoned his rod and had gone to sleep on the bank and another, who had travelled seventy miles, was very disconsolate – he had spent £10 on bait, but had only caught three gudgeon. The competitor near a disused textile mill was said to be in an ideal position for bream, but he was not catching much. Two of the small fish he had caught were floating upside down in his keepnet with their gills gasping.

Percy kept trying all day, periodically changing his float and depth, and trying different baits. His reactions were fast and as the small float bobbed in the wind-created ripples he had to concentrate hard. He caught a steady stream of small roach, the largest being about half a pound. He was doing better than his neighbours, showing that when fish are scarce, skill is important. The Leicestershire fisherman admitted that he had used the wrong tactics and had wasted his day.

At four o'clock, the whistle blew again and all fishing stopped. A man with a bucket, a spring balance, and a polythene bag in

[1] Fishing on the bottom, using lead weights.

which he put any eels that had been caught, walked along the section weighing the catches. Percy pulled his keep-net out of the water and emptied his fish into the bucket. He had four pounds two ounces, a pound more than any of his immediate neighbours and for a time it looked as if he might qualify for one of the minor prizes. Then another keep-net was hauled up and among the small roach was a large barrel-shaped chub, a dark, big-mouthed fish, flopping about in the alien air, which must have weighed three pounds on its own. The next fisherman had done even better, he had 'got among bream', and several of the large, deep-bodied fish, once eaten by monks, took his weight up to twelve pounds. Lemonade cans drifted by on the current and some waste paper was caught up in the rushes, and as it was clear that Percy would now win nothing we joined the others in the long, loaded plod back across the meadows to the cars. News travelled fast along the river bank, for before the weighing had been completed it was said that the winner had been fishing several miles away and had caught many bream. He was said to have landed almost twenty pounds of fish, and he had also netted the first prize of £114.

Chapter Twelve

To Float a Fly

Because of its mass appeal, coarse fishing is usually thought of as a working-class sport, being cheap and readily available to most people, whereas game fishing, mostly with dry and wet flies, for trout and salmon, is generally regarded as a pastime for wealthy landowners and the 'upper class'. Not only is the sport of fly fishing thought to be better in quality than coarse fishing, but so too are the surroundings in which it takes place. Trout are found in fast, clear rivers and in streams that rise in chalk, whereas salmon, as they go to spawn, swim through some of the richest mountain scenery in the British Isles. As a result the cost of the limited amount of top-class game fishing reflects the demand, and the best water is generally reserved for those fortunate enough either to own the banks, or to possess deep pockets.

But even so, with changing social and economic conditions the division of fishing along class lines is not so clear-cut as in the past, for all classes can, if they wish, obtain the type of fishing they want, and cheap day tickets are even available on some famous Scottish salmon rivers.[1] Although he prefers coarse fishing, Percy Anderson also enjoys fishing with dry flies. As he says, 'Game fishing used to be a gentleman's sport, but now with reservoirs and high wages, more working- and middle-class people fish for trout and salmon than upper-class fishermen.'

In Scotland there are stories of free fishing being available for the residents of certain villages, on just one day each year; when the men and boys go down into the water with buckets and even pitchforks to hoist out as many salmon as possible. But although the stories persist, the tellers can never quite remember the actual name of the village concerned or the day on which the spectacle can be seen. Similar stories exist about villages near continental salmon rivers, but again, fantasy and wishful thinking are more common than actual facts.

[1] Salmon fishing can be experienced on the River Spey at £1.25p per day.

Even in lowland England, however, fishermen can now enjoy the excitement and satisfaction of fly fishing, for many reservoirs have been stocked with rainbow and brown trout, and streams with clear water and a steady flow in their higher reaches have been turned into trout streams, with the introduction of reared fish. Some owners put wire grilles in the water to stop their fish straying, yet those that do escape often grow fat on the bread and scraps thrown to them by people who adopt them almost as pets. One woman, with a small stream flowing through the garden of her water-mill home, has several rainbow trout that have escaped from adjoining water. She throws them food and claims that, until its recent disappearance, her favourite would recognize her and swim out from under a bridge every time she approached. She believes that fish can think and that their relationship was based on more than food. Several times the fish's former owner tried to catch it with his imitation flies, but without success, as the pampered fish had grown to prefer kitchen scraps.

Those who enjoy game fishing consider it to be far more rewarding and skilful than dangling worms and maggots, although it is also said that 'any fool can catch a salmon if the conditions are right'. Indeed, the real attraction of game fishing seems to be a combination of factors; the surroundings in which it usually takes place; the fact that when hooked, both trout and salmon fight with surprising strength and determination; and also simply because they are most attractive fish, both to look at and to eat. The romantic aura that surrounds the salmon is also important, for each fish that returns to fresh water to breed has travelled many hundreds of miles and has survived numerous natural and man-made hazards. Each salmon starts its life in the shallows near the headwaters of a mountain stream and then journeys down to the sea. It lives as an ocean fish for up to four years, and then returns to the estuary of its home river, a creature of great beauty, strength and size. Then an irrepressible force urges it through raging river torrents and over obstacles, until its birthplace is reached and spawning occurs. The now weakened fish dies or drifts weakly down to the sea, where it may recuperate until drawn again to fresh water; but new life has been assured. One of the great mysteries of natural history is that salmon do not feed once they enter the rivers, and of the number that arrive in spring only about one third survive to reach the sea again.

Because of their size and the quality of their flesh, salmon are always in great demand for the table, and it is not unusual for fishermen to get as much as £1 per pound for salmon. Consequently not only are salmon taken legitimately by fishermen, but they are also poached. When the water is low and fish are waiting in estuaries for rising water to enable them to 'run' upstream, men will take them legally and illegally. In the pools of rivers and streams nets are used,[2] as are gaffs, and large fish hooks that are just dragged through crowded water, 'foul hooking', in the hope that a barb will penetrate and hold flesh. Even tins of carbide are used in remote areas when the police and water-bailiffs are thought to be absent, for the carbide removes the oxygen from the water and the suffocating fish float helplessly to the surface.

Trout too are poached with nets, worms and artificial flies, and some are taken by 'tickling'. A fish can be tickled when it is found resting under an overhanging bank or in a narrow stream; a hand is worked along its belly, until it is suddenly whipped out. Tickling is an art that requires much skill and knowledge and one enthusiastic and well respected trout fisherman has tickled many trout during his long sporting career. He received a shock one day when he came across a resting otter, and he still has a long scar on the palm of his right hand to prove it. He thinks that there is no sport to compare with dry-fly trout fishing, for unlike coarse fishing the quarry is located by the rings of water made by the fish as it rises to take flies off the surface. The marked fish then has to be stalked with skill and patience, until the artificial fly can be placed just upstream of it and the trout can be deceived into taking the disguised hook. In fly fishing the conflict between the hunter and the hunted is intensified by the setting in which it takes place, where the beauty of the river and its peace brings out the ancient urge to take a wild creature. Often as he has fished for trout he has witnessed other dramas too, and during the nesting season he has seen angry swans hold ducks under water to drown them.

To see trout fishing at its best I went down to Hampshire, to the River Test, in late April, where I was told that I would see

[2] The mouths of rivers are netted legally from roughly April to September, according to the river. This, together with trawling at sea, disease and low water, are the chief causes of salmon decline over recent years.

skill, and a chalk river famous throughout the angling world for the quality of its fishing and fish. The journey took me to the village of Nether Wallop, to meet Dermot Wilson, a fly-fisherman of repute, who teaches fishing and who sells equipment from the large old water mill where he lives. The morning was still, clear, and hot, with new foliage giving a haze of green to the trees, and the land was gently rolling, with hedges, spinneys, and fields of arable and livestock. The villages too were largely unspoilt, and the whole area made a sharp contrast to other country areas where pressures of both agriculture and planning have harshened the landscape and the people.

Nether Wallop itself lies in a small valley with the Wallop Brook running through it. Several of the nearby villages also have the suffix 'Wallop' to their names, and it is said to have originated from a family of famous Wallops who once lived in the area. One Wallop of history played a prominent part in defeating the French in battle; they were 'walloped'; and another less distinguished member of the family was a boozer and a drunk; he liked his 'wallop'. The village also has another claim to fame, for Dr W. G. Grace always insisted that his cricket bats were made from Nether Wallop willow.

The old mill, a large, impressive brick and timber building, stands just inside the village, surrounded by running water, with the mill race burying itself deep into the foundations. It was an ideal setting from which to start a day's fishing – willows and shaded water, a strong current and stony shallows, and the reflected light and rippling music that only flowing water can give.

There were not many fish to be seen rising in the water of the mill, so we drove through several small villages to the Test. Dermot's favourite river is the nearby Itchen, where nearly all the brown trout are truly wild, and he considers that there are too many reared fish in the Test for the angling purist. He stopped the Range Rover near a weir, where the river rushed over concrete into a swirling, foam-topped pool. Large trout live in the cauldron and at week-ends they cut easily through the powerful rush of water to thrive on the spare sandwiches of day-trippers. We walked through a small field to his fishing hut where the water was clear and clean – the 'gin clear' water of a river rising in chalk. Nearby a small copse spread almost to the water's edge and on the other side cattle grazed contentedly and drank from the low bank, a traditional piece of English landscape, timeless and tranquil, which wound into the distance for as far as the eye could see.

As there was no fish activity we sat in the sun, hoping that flies would soon begin to hatch. After a rest and a drink, we strolled along the far bank, but there was nothing, only the occasional ring of water as fish rose. But the activity was irregular and did not give much hope. When walking back, Dermot cast several times to trout we could see beneath the surface, working his fly backwards and forwards through the air with deft movements of his wrist, and carefully gauging distance and direction before dropping the small artificial fly onto the water. But few real flies were hatching and the imitation, of hook and feathers, was left well alone. At times he went down on one knee to get the correct angle and action for his cast, but still the trout showed no interest.

We tried a small tributary stream next and at a bend a trout was rising regularly. Dermot judged the distance perfectly and dropped the fly exactly where the fish had risen. It rose again and was briefly hooked before slipping off to freedom. Further on, where the water ran fast and clear over bright shingle and where thick beds of starwort bent with the current, he waded in. He cast long, up to a small arched bridge, working his fly until he dropped it into the shaded water below the bricks; the surface broke, the fly disappeared and he had a fish. This time the hook held firm and he played the fish to his landing net. It was a small wild brown trout, delicately spotted and streamlined for its life in clear flowing water. It was big enough to eat and he cracked it over the head with his wooden priest.[3]

Back on the main Test it was peaceful, the sun had climbed higher, the cattle were chewing voluptuously in the warmth, but weed cutting was going on further upstream and strands of loose weed floated by, caught in the current; a situation that Dermot thought would spoil the hatch and the fishing.

More expanding rings of ripples betrayed feeding fish, and by their size and regularity, Dermot guessed that they were not trout but grayling. Getting on one knee he again cast straight over the fish and on the second cast he was successful and played in a fine two pound fish. Grayling are also of the salmon family,

[3] A priest is a small cosh for killing fish.

being silver-blue and beautiful, but unfortunately they are not always welcome in trout streams as they tend to bully the trout.

All at once conditions improved and by late afternoon trout were rising all along our stretch of water. Dermot then decided to let me feel the fighting power of a freshly caught trout, for he hooked a fish and handed me the rod; instantly I felt the old excitement of my childhood return, as I responded to the feel of the tight line and the hooked fish. The trout ran, eased, and ran again, and suddenly the rod ceased to bend and the line hung limply. The fish had got away and I was disappointed by my effort.

Almost immediately another one was hooked and I clumsily brought the two-and-a-half pounder to the landing net, where it was quickly despatched with a blow on the head. Its tail was rounded, showing the wear suffered against the walls of the concrete pool where it had been reared. We returned to the fishing hut to sit in the sun and talk, and a beam of brightness flashed by the copse as a kingfisher flew up the small tributary stream. It had been a restful, yet stimulating day, with all the ingredients of peace, expectancy, and urgency that makes fishing so appealing to so many. If I had been an American the day would have cost me £70 with a limit of four fish; I had been Dermot's guest, I had enjoyed my day, and later I experienced for the first time the pleasure of eating freshly caught trout.

Salmon fishing is said to be less skilful than fly-fishing for trout, as a fly, lure, or spinner can simply be pulled through the water until a salmon is found. Peculiarly, salmon do not actually feed when in fresh water and so why they suddenly seize a bright object cast in front of them is the cause of much debate. But to the dedicated salmon fisherman the reason is not important; all that does matter is the fact that salmon do take artificial baits, and it is their power, size and beauty that makes salmon fishing such an exciting sport.

Lionel Sweet, an elderly Welsh fisherman, agreed to try and catch a salmon for me. In fishing circles he is highly regarded and has won many prizes for casting in both Britain and Europe. In competitions he has cleared over sixty yards with a cast, while in practice he has exceeded eighty yards. His party piece is to keep four artificial flies airborne at the same time, using two rods in each hand, with a fifth rod and fly strapped to his right foot.

When I arrived in Usk, his small tackle shop was cluttered with fishing equipment and in a cramped back room two girls with lilting Welsh accents sat tying flies, skilfully using silk, hooks, and feathers. He was not too optimistic about the chances for the day, for as it had not rained for several weeks, the water was low, and the fish were not moving. A fisherman from Ross-on-Wye strolled into the back; his fishing was different on the Wye and he had caught two salmon that morning as well as his own foot, making a hole in one of his waders with his gaff. The Wye was still good for salmon because of the tidal influence, which allowed the salmon to advance and retreat with the movement of high and low water.

The stretch of the Usk that Lionel decided to try was rural and quiet, meandering through a mixture of uncut hayfields and meadows of grazing cattle and black-faced sheep. The trembling songs of curlews rose and fell with their flight and a heron flew slowly upstream. The banks of reddish soil were wide, and stony spits and headlands divided the river into shallows, pools, and short stretches of white water. As we walked to a large pool, trout were rising, with the sun catching the ripples, and beyond the river and the low flat fields were trees, and a range of high, rounded hills.

There were more white-topped waves where the water gushed from the pool, as rocks forced it through a narrow mouth, but behind the barrage it widened, and darkened with depth, and two fallen willows rested half-submerged by the far bank. Lionel started to fish using a large red wet-fly, which settled on the water and then drifted below. It was quite different from dry-fly fishing, with the cast being long, across the water and downstream so that the current would drag the fly to the middle; the effect of this action meant that as progress was made along the pool, the fly quartered the water, A mallard duck with a large brood of quarter-grown young disappeared among the roots of one of the fallen willows, and some sand-martins, delicate and brown, skimmed the water, while others flew to their nest holes in the banks. Pied wagtails bobbed and bowed at the water's edge and suddenly a large splash shattered the peace, bubbles moved outwards with ripples from the centre of the pool. Lionel thought that it must have been a salmon.

He gradually worked his way along the pool towards the centre. As he cast, his fly repeatedly whistled over his head and then with a whiplike action he pitched it back towards the water,

A trained peregrine falcon plucking feathers from a hoodie crow it has just killed. (*Philip Glasier* for the 'Survival' Anglia programme 'The Lure of the Falcon')

A punt-gunner out after wildfowl. The key to success is stealth – hence the craft's low free-board and the gunner's furtive attitude. (*Shooting Times*)

A stoat caught in the toothed, spring-loaded jaws of a gin-trap. (*Shooting Times*)

A rabbit in the last stages of myxomatosis. (*David A. Cowans/Shooting Times*)

leaving a fine spray of moisture in the air. The fly fell near the willows and almost immediately a large streak of silver flashed beneath the water and swerved upwards towards the fly; tension and excitement heaved in my stomach, until another glint of silver showed that the salmon had veered away. It was a large fish, but it paid no further attention to the fly.

In the faster water where the pool narrowed, another big salmon leapt high, to flop down belly upwards with a great splash. Lionel said that it was probably trying to rid itself of lice. Salmon suffer a great deal from parasites; and earlier in the day the fisherman from the Wye had seen a salmon drift by with eel-like lampreys stuck fast to it,[4] slowly sucking life away. As rain began to fall, the temperature dropped and the hills became hidden by low cloud. Lionel decided that our luck would not alter, and dismantled his rod.

As the sun settled behind the hills he decided to try again; the day had changed, it had become warm and humid and many trout were rising. Despite the change no salmon could be tempted in the pool and we walked on to shallower, fast flowing water, where Lionel decided to try for trout with a light-coloured dry fly. Flies were hatching in large numbers and swarmed in great clouds over the water. Looking along the river towards the sun the whole air over the water seemed to be alive with translucent movement. Despite the hatch, the trout were not interested in the artificial fly and Lionel cast repeatedly with no luck.

A heron called out harshly and flew off lethargically, dark against the glowing sky. Sand-martins still flew and three dunlin beat fast and low upstream, flying just above the water. Bats hunted in the dusk and Lionel informed me that in the past he has hooked both bats and swallows as he has fished. Five ducks passed overhead, their urgent wingbeats whistling in the quiet of evening; a cool breeze sprang up, and within a few minutes the clouds of flies had gone.

Lionel decided to have one more try, with a darker fly, again after trout. Almost straightaway he was successful and landed a fish of about one-and-a-half pounds. He took his hat off and dried the fly in his hair, and another small fish was taken with the next cast. Crunching gristle sounded as the hook was worked out in the

[4] It is more likely that they were hag-fish, which belong to the lamprey family.

poor light and the fish lay feebly on its side when returned to the water. With encouragement it slowly swam off to the middle of the stream, but I found it hard to believe that it had experienced no fear or discomfort.

Chapter Thirteen

To Catch a Shark

With large numbers of anglers sea fishing is also popular, using rods and lines from the shore as well as from boats. No licences are required and there is no close season, so sea fishing can be enjoyed the whole year round; consequently the angler on holiday does not have to give up his sport during his annual fortnight by the sea and the ordinary holidaymaker can also pick up a rod and line to fish.

Mackerel are found in large shoals during the summer in most coastal areas and mackerel fishing is a popular holiday pastime that requires little skill or equipment, yet it provides fishermen with good sport; for mackerel are in the tunny family, and although quite small, they 'put up a good fight'. I went mackerel fishing with a baker, who lives in the village, and who spends many of his summer week-ends and days off water-skiing on the Wash at Hunstanton. He fishes in a most unorthodox way, for he does not drift for hours in a rowing boat with his line trailing, hoping to run into a shoal of mackerel; he gets into his speed boat and goes looking for the fish. 'Look out for the gulls diving', he said as we set off, ''cause that's where the fish will be.' It was warm and calm, with a watery sun struggling to break through the mist; but even with my binoculars I could see no signs of diving birds.

He accelerated sharply away from the shore and we planed along parallel to the coast, leaving a long line of shimmering water showing our trail. Suddenly wings glinted as white feathers caught the sunlight – 'gulls' were wheeling in the air and diving headlong into the water. On seeing a fish they seemed to pause, tuck in their wings, and fall like stones, their place of entry being marked with white spray. When they emerged, sea showered from them as they became airborne, and most had caught small white-bait, which they ate, or took towards the shore.[1] They were not

[1] The mackerel also feed on the shoals of whitebait.

gulls, but Sandwich terns and gannets, whose aerial grace and beauty seemed to give a new dimension to flight, as they soared, wheeled, and dived. We sped to them; the fishing baker cut the engine and grabbed a rod with six feathered hooks at intervals along the line.

The line was thrown overboard and at the first tug upwards the rod bent and flashes of silver glinted below us. The baker's method had worked; he had found the 'gulls' and we were immediately among the mackerel. He hauled in the line and four fish struggled as they were hoisted into the boat, which rocked with our activity. He quickly got them off the hooks and cast again. More fish were immediately taken, and they flapped about in a frenzy of death at the bottom of the boat. They bled quite freely through the mouth and gills, and died quickly once exposed to air. Most fish seem to linger a long time before they die, but mackerel are marginally more fortunate.

I flung a line over and twice all the hooks were taken and it was hot, hard work, hauling in the fish to cast again as soon as possible. In a quarter of an hour we had over thirty mackerel safely aboard, we were plastered with blood and lose scales, and the whole boat stunk of fish. We rested briefly and twice a seal surfaced quite close, to look at us, sniff, and then submerge. There are many common seals in the Wash and their large soft eyes and their expressions of sadness make them the favourites of naturalists and animal lovers. They breed on the nearby sand banks and when their numbers get too great the population is reduced by shooting. Occasionally bodies are not recovered, and when they are washed up on the shore, or orphaned seal pups are found, there is usually a great outburst of public outrage and anger.

By the time we were ready to resume fishing the birds had gone and so had the mackerel. We steered in wide circles but found nothing; a few terns flew by and occasionally they dived, but we could find no great concentration of birds or fish. Two arctic skuas flew over and briefly chased a gull, before continuing out to sea. As we cruised the water seemed to be full of sediment.

'What's that stuff?' I asked.

'Turds in a tempest', the baker replied, 'probably from the Hunstanton sewage outfall.'

Apparently, although being a popular place for family holidays, the east coast is also an area where much neat sewage flows into the sea. (Despite this, the conceit of the British is such that we always insist that it is 'the Ities, the Frogs, the Wogs, Wops and the greasy Dagoes', who are the really filthy races on this planet.) As the morning wore on a few more terns dived and we took our total number of mackerel to forty; it had been a much better way of fishing than waiting to be found by the fish.

It is the sea too that provides the largest fish to be caught by anglers, and in the last twenty years a total of over 70,000 sharks were caught in British waters, among them some of a frightening size.[2] Most of the large sharks are caught off the South Coast with Looe in Cornwall being the centre. It is an attractive little town with whitewashed cottages and hotels perched on either side of a small steep-sided valley, where the rivers Looe and West Looe flow into the sea. My landlady was glad shark fishing had become established: 'About twenty boats go out each day, and it's really put Looe on its feet'.

As the small boats were chugging in at the end of a day's fishing, I went and booked a place for the following day on a three-and-a-half ton boat, the *Prosperity*. With time on my hands I wandered down to the sea to watch the remainder of the boats return. Two youths were fishing from rocks, and one hooked a herring gull, causing a great commotion as they tried to catch the bird and remove the hook. Each year, on salt and fresh water, many birds are damaged by fish hooks or become tangled up in discarded lengths of nylon line.

At nine o'clock the next morning both the tide and the boats were out and so the four holiday fishermen and myself were taken in a small dinghy to the *Prosperity*, which was anchored 100 yards from the shore. We boarded from the starboard side, for Cornish fishermen are extremely superstitious and they say it is unlucky to board from the port side. Many of the older fishermen will never start a fishing season on a Friday; they will never wear green, and lilac flowers never enter their houses; all are said to bring misfortune. A youth, the skipper's trainee, was already on board, and the skipper arrived a few minutes later, a small man with a black fisherman's jumper, a fisherman's gait, and a tousle of gingerish

[2] The British shark records are: for blue – 218 pounds caught at Looe in 1959. Mako – 500 pounds caught at Looe in 1971. Porbeagle – 430 pounds, Guernsey in 1969. Thresher – 280 pounds in 1933 at Dungeness.

hair. Although he was barely five feet tall, Bonzo Butters had a personality of huge and extrovert proportions, together with a broad accent, full of rich and rolling 'rrrrrs'.

As we got under way the sea was choppy and those of us who wanted to move about the deck crawled or sprawled as if drunk. The youth directed our course from the wheelhouse, while Bonzo stood on the deck with his feet rooted firmly to the wooden boards and his body swaying to the movement of the boat. The day before it had been rough, and by the time he had reached the shark waters all the fishermen had been so sick that he had turned the boat round and sailed straight back to Looe. 'Now then', he said, 'as you are all men, if you want a piss, do it over the side, it's easier. But for goodness' sake remember not to do it into the wind. Scottish fishermen do it into the wind with their mouths open, as they say it's a shame to waste good whisky – but we don't. You can go anywhere on the boat, but don't fall overboard. If you do, then for Christ's sake come up holding your rod.'

Bonzo informed me that he came from a long line of Cornish fishermen and had started fishing as a boy, 'long-lining for mackerel' with his father and uncles. Then, they fished without radar and they depended on their senses, physical and common, to tell them the whereabouts of fish. Some old fishermen claimed to be able to smell mackerel, and the presence of gannets and storm petrels indicated large shoals. He said that the way a gannet dived showed the sort of fish in the area. If it hurtled straight down from a great height it was after pilchards; if it was not so high or straight it was homing in on sprats, and if it flew along and entered the water at an angle it was after mackerel. Once a gannet dived down and took a mackerel that had been put out as shark bait. Then the fisherman had gone to the 'fighting chair', and instead of the line going deep into the water as with a shark, it had gone vertically upwards, over the boat. A Dutch fisherman had stood watching in amazement, periodically pointing and saying 'goose, goose'. The gannet was eventually pulled down, and when released if flew off apparently unharmed.

We ploughed on through the swell at eight knots, with the bows rising and falling so sharply that several times I briefly lost contact with the seat. My companions, a policeman, a fireman, a warehouseman, and a factory worker, all wore the traditional English holiday uniform of bright red, sun scorched faces, light shirts, flannel trousers, and sandals or plimsolls, and they looked more like customers for candy-floss than for sharks.

The sky cleared and even the high wisps of cirrus melted away, as the sea gently flattened. We were further out than the Eddystone Light, which was a small speck to our left, and the shore was about seventeen miles behind us. The engine was stopped and the lone sail was left up to encourage drift. Four shark rods were produced by the frail-looking youth, and some feathers for mackerel were dropped over the side. The shark rods were quite short with strong lines and large hooks. Two of the hooks were baited up with dead mackerel and thrown out, each one with a different coloured cork float to establish ownership if a shark was hooked, and the rods were strapped to a rail at the back. The other two were to be secured at the front and by the time the last hook was ready for baiting, two mackerel had been caught. They were impaled while still wriggling and thrown overboard as live-bait. Two bags of 'rubby-dubby' were then lowered over the side and made secure. Rubby-dubby is an oily mess of chopped-up fish, which, as the boat drifts is said to leave a trail of scent to attract sharks.

Nothing much happened as we waited for a bite; the fishermen fished with mackerel rods and caught a few mackerel and whiting, and I sat in the fighting-chair, enjoying the sun. Bonzo gave instructions that as soon as a shark was hooked the owner of the rod was to unstrap it and take it to the fighting-chair, a small revolving wooden seat with a holder for the handle of a rod, designed to make the struggle with a large fish much easier.

After two hours, most of the active angling had stopped for dinner, with the shark lines drifting out from the boat. As we ate the fireman thought he saw a shark. Sure enough a crescent shaped dorsal fin had broken through the surface of the sea as a large fish swam past the boat. The fin was not slicing effortlessly through the water, but flopping from side to side. 'That's not a shark, that's a sun fish', Bonzo informed us, 'that won't take the bait.' As the fin moved by, the large blue shape of the fish could be seen just below the surface; they are deep-bodied oval fish, growing to a length of eleven feet and a weight of two tons.

A fulmar cruised by effortlessly and then several storm petrels appeared skimming daintily over the water. 'Look at they', Bonzo observed, 'Mother Carey's chickens.' Still no sharks appeared, but it was pleasant out there drifting in the light breeze with the sea and the sun. The warehouseman had once worked for the Forestry Commission controlling pests, and I asked him if he had ever used ferrets on rabbits.

'My goodness, you must never use that word on a Cornish boat,' Bonzo interrupted, 'that's another thing that brings bad luck.'

'What word? Ferret?'

'No.'

'Rabbit?'

'There, you said it again. We'll never get a bloody ol' shark now.'

'You don't believe that do you?'

'I don't, but a lot do. You listen to this.'

Bonzo went to his radio transmitter and called up another shark boat.

'I say, Roger, you'll never guess what these buggers on my boat are talking about – we'll never get any fish now.'

'What – not Underground Chickens – you take care.'

'There you are,' Bonzo beamed, 'that's what they call them ol' furry things you were talking about. Some of them call 'em "bush congers". Some captains would have packed up straight away and gone home as they think that the mention of them things will make their boat capsize. The only way to break a curse is to piss in a bottle, put needles in it, put the cork in and wave it round your head three times saying "break the curse" each time, and then throw it overboard.'

We had a bottle, but no needles, yet the boat remained upright. Both Bonzo and the boy shook the bags of rubby-dubby at regular intervals, but nothing was attracted and at 3.30 the bait was hauled in. When a shark is caught, it is gaffed and lifted aboard and placed below deck to be taken ashore for weighing. On one occasion Bonzo claims to have caught a shark that gave birth to forty-two live young ones as it died in the hold; they were thrown overboard and swam off quite normally.

As we headed for the harbour the chat among the other skippers indicated that some had been successful. The sea was almost mill-pond calm, and inland from the distant cliffs the white scars of the kaolin quarries gave the appearance of sweltering desert or snow. Despite being sharkless the fishermen were not unduly disappointed, and none seemed sorry at having spent £7.50 for no actual sport, other than the mackerel.

Those fishermen in other boats who had been successful would be heading for the weighing machine of the Shark Angling Club of Great Britain, and if any of them had a shark of seventy-five pounds or more, caught unaided, they could then become a member of the club. The day before, a German had caught one of eighty-five pounds; it had been duly weighed and he was photographed, grinning, by the suspended corpse. Blue sharks are the ones normally caught, graceful, streamlined fish, the same metal blue as the open sea. As there is little use for shark meat, after the ritual and the expense of capture, death, and weighing, many of them are taken back out to sea and dumped overboard.

Chapter Fourteen

Falcons and Fighting Cocks

Two of the oldest surviving field or blood sports involve birds; falcons and hawks flying free in their natural element, and fighting cocks who do battle wearing sharp metal spurs, in a situation that is artificial and contrived. Both have been traced back to very early times; falconry to 2,000 BC, and cockfighting to at least 1,000 BC, and both have their origins in Asia and the Far East. During the Middle Ages the sports flourished in Britain, with falconry being a favourite recreation of the aristocracy, and cockfighting taking its followers from all classes.

Since then both have declined. The art and practice of falconry fell away with the introduction of shotguns, when game could be shot, and also with the enclosure of land, when wide open tracts of countryside were divided up by rows of trees and hedges. As a result falconers found it difficult to keep up with their birds, the quarry was given more opportunity to avoid capture, and even the birds of prey themselves found it easier to return to the wild because of the new landscape. Indeed, with the popularity of shooting the only falcons or hawks that were allowed to fly were made of cloth, and in the early years of this century my grandfather still went shooting, aided by a large silk kite, made to look like a hawk. He would walk with his back to the wind with the kite flying well out in front; the partridges and pheasants would then skulk in the grass or stubble, at the sight of the large hovering bird, until flushed by the walking guns. Cockfighting's decline came with the development of the 'puritan conscience', which suggested that the needless fighting and spilling of blood for the edification of gamblers was cruel, barbaric, and evil. Because of this, cockfighting was forbidden by law in 1849. Despite their decline, however, both sports still survive, one legally, and the other well outside the law, and whereas the supporters of other country sports can be measured in thousands, and even millions, those people who fly falcons, or who attend cockfights, are very few in number.

The attraction of falconry is easy to see, for hawks and falcons possess a beauty and a wildness which some sportsmen and naturalists find irresistible, and in consequence they respond to the challenge of training the seemingly untrainable, until their own bird can be flown free, as if wild, yet at a call, or after a kill or the throw of a lure, it will return to sit on the gloved fist of its master. This regard for birds of prey is found in a lesser form with most people interested in wildlife and the countryside, for the birds' nobility and mastery of the air leaves a lasting impression on those fortunate enough to see them.

My encounters with birds of prey have been brief and quite unremarkable, yet their images remain clear in my mind. A childhood holiday in Cornwall, when buzzards perched on almost every telegraph pole over Bodmin Moor, while others wheeled effortlessly on wafts of hot air, high above. A fleeting glimpse of a peregrine sitting on a fence post at the side of a high mountain road in Wales, before it flew off into the mist. I had another view of a peregrine while going by small boat to the island of Skomer off the Pembrokeshire coast; briefly, it came near us, but then it flew off over the water towards high, sea-pounded cliffs. It was on Skomer too, that I got unexpectedly close to a sparrow hawk. I was on the island to see the vast seabird colonies of guillemots, razorbills, kittiwakes, and puffins, and also just to enjoy the sea, the isolation, and the rugged beauty of the small but delightful island. On my way to sit in the sun, down by a rocky inlet, I took a short cut through a low ridge of granite, and there, on a ledge, perched the hawk. It sat and stared at me for several seconds, its yellow-irised eyes fiery and hypnotic. With its talons, its primitive aquiline beak, and its look of anger, I felt that I was looking on a creature overlooked by evolution and that I was seeing a living relic of the earth's wild and primeval past.

My own particular favourite bird of prey is the kestrel, a small falcon, whose fanned tail, chestnut wings and hovering flight as it hunts over hedgerows and open fields is a pleasing part of the rural scene around me.[1] The only falcon that I have ever owned was a kestrel, and to see its small but powerful talons, its hooked beak, and its deep brown eyes, was to gaze at a rare composition of innate savagery and soft beauty. I found it with a broken wing,

[1]The kestrel is also known as the stannel or windhover, and is one of the few birds that can hover, stationary, for extended periods.

which healed with the help of sticking plaster and brown paper, and one morning after partial recovery it escaped and flew to freedom. At first I was tempted to train the young bird, for kestrels can be taught to fly to a lure, and to return to the fist. But it soon became obvious that I could not give it the time that was needed. Perhaps this too partially explains why falconry has declined, for each bird needs to be handled and flown for at least an hour every day, and so the sport can only be attempted by those with the time and the dedication to succeed.

Somehow a farm manager in Norfolk has found both the time and the self-discipline, and he has trained and flown a number of falcons and hawks.[2] He prefers to fly hawks and so regards himself as an austringer rather than a falconer; although for the sake of simplicity the word falcon is often used to describe these birds of prey. At the front of his house a number of hawks, owls, and falcons perch on small wooden blocks on fine days, while at the back, many species of wildfowl, wigeon, pochard, and geese wander about the garden. Even as we sat in his living room, several Canada geese advanced to the french windows to watch us inquisitively.

He has always been interested in birds, eggs, and nests, and at one time he used to shoot, but now his shooting has stopped and his spare time, if not his life, is devoted to birds of prey. He has trained many birds, but started with a kestrel, Kessy, that he taught to stoop, rather than hover. It was his favourite bird and he kept it for eighteen months, until it died of TB. During its short life he flew it at several types of quarry including bats, and once it even killed a half-grown Brent gosling. Other birds have killed creatures far heavier than themselves; he owned a Lanner Falcon[3] and claims that it once killed a hare, and now he has a goshawk (with a name meaning 'the divine wind') which, although it weighs only 2 pounds 6 ounces, can fly at 45 mph and has killed a rabbit weighing over 4 pounds.

With the help of his son he has successfully bred kestrels in captivity, and has trained them so that on release they have been able to fend for themselves. Now, the birds are often seen hunting

[2] Falcons have long, pointed wings, dark eyes, and longish tails, and tend to kill their prey by stooping on it from a height at great speed. Hawks have long tails but short, rounded wings and yellow eyes. They cruise at low altitude and catch their prey by pouncing on it or by pursuit.

[3] The Lanner falcon is no longer a visitor to the British Isles, and has not been since the last century, though it continues to inhabit some of the countries bordering the Mediterranean.

around the farm, and some have also bred locally. Ultimately he thinks that breeding will be an important part of falconry, both to prevent birds being taken from the wild, and to provide a reserve stock in case the wild population is again threatened by the use of toxic chemicals, as it was in the sixties. He considers that all birds used for falconry, including those bred in captivity, ought to be licensed, but at the moment licences are only required for wild and imported birds.

At the Falconry Centre near Newent in Gloucestershire, the director is confident that soon it will be possible to breed several types of birds of prey in captivity, including the peregrine falcon. He is a big, bearded man, who once worked as a professional falconer and who has been deeply involved with falcons, hawks, and owls since he was a boy. The Centre itself lies in a pleasant country setting, spoilt only by the rows of dead elms, destroyed by the ravages of Dutch Elm Disease, which to that part of the country has given a dead-winter look to many hedgerows and copses, even in mid-summer. The birds are housed in a mews,[4] and when I visited, one falcon was flapping and straining at its leash for freedom, but the jesses[5] around its legs held firm. To me, the sight of a bird tethered and wanting freedom is undignified and sad, particularly when the plight of a captive bird is compared with the splendour of one flying free.

Falconers say that this is part of the challenge and the appeal of falconry, to train birds to fly as if wild, and then to return to their master. An assistant at the Centre demonstrated the point by taking a Lanner falcon into a field. He removed the jesses and cast the bird into the air. It climbed and then planed over us, cutting through the air with absolute control. The falconer began to swing his lure, made of bird's wings on a length of string, and the bird glided round, tucked in its wings and accelerated down in a stoop that was both awesome and breathtaking. As it closed in, the falconer flicked the lure away and as soon as the bird realised

[4] The name of the place where hawks or falcons are housed. In the Middle Ages, the horses on which the falconers rode were also kept in the mews. Today many place names retain the word, showing the former use of the building or place concerned. On State occasions there are still frequent references to the 'Royal Mews', which has not seen hawks or falcons for many years. To mew means to moult, and to mew a bird is to cage it when moulting.

[5] Leather straps fastened to the legs of a hawk or falcon.

that it had missed, it opened its wings, to cruise easily upwards, climbing on the uplift of its own momentum. Several more times the bird plunged down towards the lure and then cruised upwards until finally the falconer allowed it to catch the lure. The falcon seized it in its talons and was fed as a reward.

In lowland areas, hawks and falcons are flown mainly at rooks, partridges, pheasants, pigeons, rabbits, and moorhens, but the finest form of falconry is said to be flying trained birds at grouse. It was late August when I went up to Sutherland to see a falconer after grouse. For most of the year he lives in the West Country, but from August until December he stays in his remote crofter's cottage with his dogs and falcons. Like most falconers, his interest in falconry started when he was a boy, at boarding school. While there he trained a sparrow hawk, and his mother sent him helpful parcels from time to time; most of the year they would contain pieces of meat, but at harvest time they would be full of dead mice. He has since developed his skill and knowledge until he has become one of the most experienced and skilful falconers still practising the sport. He, too, hopes to breed his own birds quite soon and one of his falcons has already laid a clutch of fertile eggs. Unfortunately a fault then developed in his incubator and they were ruined.

He is completely dedicated to his sport, devoting several hours each day to his birds, and he is in the fortunate position of having all the time he needs. The small white cottage where he spends his autumns was once a genuine croft, which he has converted into a comfortable home, overlooking heather-covered hills. For the afternoon's exercise he loaded up his car with his three dogs, and the cadge, on which perched two hooded falcons. The cadge was a simple wooden frame that could be carried easily; in the past men were employed to carry the cadge and it is possible that, from the meaning of the word 'cadger' as it is still used today, they often pestered their wealthy employers for gifts and tips.

We drove along a narrow, winding road at the foot of a valley, occasionally passing small crofts and run-down buildings that gave an indication of the difficult life and hard financial facts facing those still crofting. The fields of the valley floor were of grass and uncut oats, and in one untidy yard an old binder stood rusting, next to a lean-to shed containing the croft's new, though second-hand combine-harvester. Beyond the fields, heather and hardy mountain grasses covered the rising land and sheep wandered free. The road wound its way upwards at the side of a small mountain stream, and as we passed the last croft, built right next to the road, hens scattered, children stared, and a working border collie briefly set off after the car.

Just beyond a cattle grid we stopped and the dogs spilled out, English pointers, fine, intelligent and aristocratic-looking dogs, two black and grey, and the other brown and white, and all eager to get on with the search for grouse. One of the darker dogs was a thirteen-year-old bitch who, despite her failing faculties, still wanted to hunt for game. The falconer put one of the hooded birds onto his wrist and the movement briefly set the bells in motion. It was a tiercel[6] Mediterranean peregrine, a species closely related to the British peregrine.

The heather was high where we started out, up to our knees in places, and once away from the grass fields of the valley floor the hills were ablaze with brilliant purple. It was hard work walking, and with each stride pollen puffed out in sweet-smelling clouds. The dogs searched keenly for scent as we worked our way slowly upwards, but they found no trace of grouse. As we gained height, our surroundings seemed perfect, despite an overcast sky; the smell of heather and highland grasses, the sound of bumblebees working and dogs hunting, and the sight of purple hills, the green valley, and the winding stream leading to a shimmering loch and a grey expanse of sea.

One of the dogs, with its nose held low and its tail working, suddenly pointed, 'freezing' with its neck and head stretched forwards as if it had located grouse. The two other dogs saw it and moved in on the point, until all three were still and pointing to an area just ahead. The falconer removed the leather hood and jesses from his tiercel and cast it into the air for free flight. It was a magnificent bird, with slate grey wings, a buff coloured breast broken by dark horizontal bars, brown penetrating eyes, and a beak and talons made for tearing flesh.

The falconer ran to the opposite side of his dogs, making a warbling whimper to his tiercel and waving his arms, wanting it to 'wait on' above him. With the wind running up the slope

6 A male falcon, so called from the old French word *tierce*, meaning a third, as the tiercel is roughly a third smaller than its mate. Like duck, falcon is a female term.

the bird soared and then planed, high, away from us. It had seen a wild bird of prey beyond the nearby hilltop. The wild bird was a kestrel and the two birds rose effortlessly on the current of air and then swooped towards each other as if wanting a closer look. Two of the dogs, impatient for action, crept slowly forwards, 'wait on', the falconer shouted, and he again called the peregrine.

The brief meeting of the birds was over and the distant sound of bells grew nearer until the tiercel was overhead. It was a remarkable sight, a scene of mutual trust and cooperation – the dogs pointing, the falconer directing, and the peregrine watching high above, almost stationary on the strong current of rising air. All was quiet as we waited tensely for the approaching climax. 'Get in, get in', the falconer shouted as both he and the dogs rushed forwards; a grouse flew, the tiercel folded its wings and fell in a stoop of astonishing speed and frightening splendour. The grouse had obviously seen falcons before and quickly dropped back into the heather, as talons missed it by inches. The tiercel opened its wings and swept upwards again, and as soon as it had reached its full pitch the grouse flew once more. The peregrine turned and fell in another controlled stoop and the clutching claws touched the bird as it again went into the heather, but the tiercel had lost its impetus and had done no damage. As the falconer approached, the grouse flew yet again, but the tiercel was still low, and instead of stooping it pursued the grouse fast and low into the wind. On equal terms the grouse had the greater speed and the two flew down into the valley. The dogs were still pointing, as if other grouse were skulking in the heather, and as he made off to recapture his bird he ordered them to 'stay there'. A blue mountain hare loped along a sheep-run up to the summit and stopped on the skyline to watch us, with its long rounded ears working backwards and forwards. The wild kestrel returned and twice it swooped down towards the hare as if in play. The hare seemed to know that because of its far greater size it had little to fear, but both times it ducked its head as a precaution; it then ambled off, out of sight, and the kestrel also lost interest and flew away.

Down in the valley the falconer had located his bird perching on a stone wall, so he called it and produced his lure from his canvas shoulder bag. Thinking that they were missing something, the dogs could contain themselves no longer and made off towards their master, and as they moved a whole covey of grouse exploded into the air in front of them and went with the wind over the hill top.

The tiercel was recaptured and the falconer and the dogs had to make the long journey back up the hill. The reaction of the grouse demonstrated that it had seen birds of prey before, and that an experienced bird could escape death. In fact the mountainous regions of Scotland make up an area of Britain where birds of prey remain reasonably numerous, and one of the falconer's most memorable experiences involving wild raptors occurred there. He was watching a small flock of geese fly up a long valley with mountains on both sides, when suddenly a golden eagle fell in a tremendous stoop, from a height of several hundred feet above them. The skein scattered in all directions as the geese realized their danger, and the eagle pulled out of its dive. In all probability the attempt had not been serious because of the size of the quarry, but the stoop had been spectacular and from a height that few other birds could have matched.

Back on the hill the dogs started hunting again and almost immediately they moved in on another point. The hood of the peregrine was removed and the bird quickly flew to gain height, and glided in a large half circle towards its master as if eager for more grouse. When instructed the dogs dived in and a whole covey of grouse whirred into the air. The tiercel tucked in its wings and fell again in a dive of impressive velocity and control, but the grouse had started too early, however, and the bird missed again. The grouse went with the wind behind them, flying low and following the contours of the land until they rounded a rocky outcrop and were hidden from view.

The peregrine flew in pursuit, but soon lost them; instead it suddenly seemed to find its freedom, for ignoring the cries of the falconer it rested its wings on an updraught and rose steeply until it had gained a height of several hundred feet. It swept in wide smooth circles away over the valley, its pointed wings and long tail cutting effortlessly through the air. For several minutes it seemed to feast itself on the eddies and upcurrents around it, before suddenly planing down on a long low glide to perch on a high rock where it rested and preened. Again the falconer had to resort to his lure and then make the long trek back to his car to change birds.

He returned with an American Peale's falcon, a bird also very much like a peregrine, and we made for the top of the hill. At the summit the heather was shorter, but the extra altitude and the uninterrupted vision gave an even more splendid view, with the nearby hills dipping down to a long black tarn, and beyond, to an inlet of the sea, where a causeway separates fresh water from salt and salmon assemble to move upstream at high water. A faint call came in on the breeze and two small specks could be seen flying inland towards the higher mountain peaks; they were said to be two Great Northern divers.

We walked along the small undulating plateau of the summit until the young brown pointer again stood motionless. The two other dogs bounded over towards the point and soon all three were frozen with unwavering concentration. The hood was whisked off the falcon, which began to climb with quick winnowing wing-beats. Before it had managed to 'wait on', however, the grouse flew, for no apparent reason, and the falcon had no chance to stoop. Instead, it satisfied itself with several sweeping dives and climbs, as if enjoying its own aerial ability, and then it flew down to the lure.

When the dogs pointed again the falcon seemed determined not to miss a second chance. It went high to wait on, but then started to fall, as if anticipating the 'get in' to the dogs. When it had descended to about sixty feet, a large covey of grouse burst into flight and flew off downhill and downwind. The falcon turned, tucked in its wings still further and hurtled down in a vertical descent of awesome ferocity. As it closed in on the birds its wings opened, its talons struck, and a grouse went bowling into the heather. It was a drama of savagery and grandeur, sophistication and total wildness, and the bird's death was part of an act that has held Man fascinated for many centuries.

The falcon glided up to lose speed and then dropped back to where the grouse had fallen. When we ran up to it, its talons were firmly fixed in the bird's breast, and with its wings fanned out, it tore at its victim's head and neck to feed. The falconer slowly retrieved the body and rewarded his bird with a deep-frozen, day-old chick. One grouse had been killed, and although its death had been sudden and violent, it had contained considerable beauty.

Death when it comes in cockfighting is also savage, but the sight of cocks, spurs, and gambling 'sportsmen' can contain little beauty. Because cockfighting is illegal it is very difficult to see, but 'mains'[7] still take place quite regularly, particularly in wealthy sporting circles and among gypsies and didecoys.[8] Because of the secrecy with which the fights are conducted, the cockfighting farmer whom I located was unable to get me an invitation, but I have no doubt that fights still take place, and the condition of his gamefowl, and the spurs he keeps hidden away, seem to confirm the fact. I have also met a man who claims to have attended a main in Scotland; it was held in a large remote barn, with lookouts posted, and a large audience paid £2 each to get in.

When I first visited the farmer, a workman mentioned his cockfighting interest in a whisper, and pointed out a long low building that had once housed the pit and where benches had been placed around the walls for the comfort of the spectators. Two years ago the police caught several people attending a cockfight in the north of England. The farmer had intended to go, but had been prevented at the last minute, and so he luckily avoided prosecution. He attends fights in both the north and the south of England, and the sport is said to be particularly strong in horse-racing areas, where there are plenty of isolated buildings, and gambling sportsmen. The contradictions and inconsistency apparent in other blood sports are also to be found in cockfighting, for one of the keenest supporters and participants is said to be an eye surgeon from Surrey.

Despite his workman's whispers, the farmer spoke quite openly about his cockfighting, and his main reason for taking part seems to stem from the fact that 'nobody is going to tell me what I can or cannot do.' The spurs used are long, thin, and curved, with a razor sharp point at the end. The cock's own spurs are cut and the leather strap of the metal spur is fitted round each leg, with a hole fitting the cock's tailored spur to keep it in place. The farmer also had some practice spurs, with pads of soft material instead of metal spikes, so that the birds could do themselves no damage. The fights are carried on to the death, and to make them longer and more 'sporting', each cock has its comb and wattle[9]

[7] A main is a match between fighting cocks.

[8] A word used for travelling dealers and scrap merchants, implying that they are not true gypsies and cannot be trusted.

[9] The red, fleshy appendage hanging from the throat of a cock.

cut off with scissors, so as to prevent its opponent seizing them.

To add authenticity to his talk, the farmer took me to see the pens of gamefowl in his garden; they are handsome birds, originating from India and looking like large and flamboyant bantams. Many of the cocks were minus their cones and wattles and one still bore the scars and tatters of a fight a few weeks earlier. He showed me another cock, the brother of whom was said to have killed two opponents in half an hour at the same cockfighting session.

The birds he breeds are in great demand and recently two didecoys turned up unannounced in an old car and informed him that they wanted to buy a black fighting cock. He refused to sell. 'We'll give you twenty pounds for a pair,' they told him, and he promptly accepted. As he showed me his birds he was obviously proud of their condition and appearance, which made his liking for a sport that is undeniably cruel extremely difficult to understand. Apart from being friendly and open about his bloody pastime, he was also generous, and gave me a pair of gamefowl. They will wander free around the farmyard, they will not fight, and the only threat to their peace will come from prowling foxes.

Without any doubt cockfighting is a 'blood sport', and even the old cockfighting farmer admits that it is cruel. It is a survivor of the ancient fighting sports, that at one time provided popular entertainment outside taverns and on the roadside. Bulls, bears, and badgers were all baited and subjected to much suffering. The bull or bear was tethered and taunted and then dogs were set on to it; in some towns metal rings still exist where the unfortunate beasts were tied. The animals were forced to fight, with no chance of escape, and the anger and violence provided a gory spectacle for gamblers as well as for ordinary onlookers. Dog fighting was another violent and cruel sport, and one East Anglian woman has told me that occasional organized dog fights still take place in Norfolk, although she was not prepared to say where or when.

Other unpleasant pastimes can also still be found. In the highlands of Scotland red deer are sometimes coursed by deer hounds, with two dogs being set after one deer, and when, and if, the animal is caught, the dogs pull it down and savage it to death. It is said to be the entertainment of a few wealthy sportsmen and dog breeders, and the end of such coursing, with only two dogs and a large quarry, cannot be pleasant or quick.

Badger digging too, continues to take place, and if persistent I would have had little difficulty in getting to see a dig in the West Country. Some diggers still extract the cornered animals with large tongs, and death can come by driving a metal hook, like a bale hook, into the badger's skull. Such an end to such a creature is both senseless and criminal. Badger digging as a sport developed many years ago, before mass entertainment provided other alternatives, and when the activities of the occasional 'rogue' badger tarnished the reputation of the whole race. Now, however, it is known that badgers do little harm to game or domestic fowl, yet old prejudices die hard and punishments for breaking the law fail to deter.

Chapter Fifteen

Ethics and Indignation

My various travels, from Cornwall to Sutherland and from the Wash to Wales, have provided me with many memories of places, people, and wild creatures. They have shown me the importance of our forests as wildlife reserves, and how, despite 'progress' and development, there is still much beauty to enjoy in these small overcrowded islands. They have introduced me to deer at close quarters and enabled me to see my first wild badgers. To stand silently outside a sett at dusk as a badger shuffles almost into you is an unforgettable experience. I have also witnessed at first hand many sports and skills that have become traditional activities of the countryside. But although I have met men and women passionately devoted to their sports, I have met others who consider them to be barbaric, cruel, and based on class and privilege; consequently they feel that blood sports have no place in modern society. They point to the legislation which outlawed the fighting sports of the past and want new laws to ban blood sports, particularly those which involve the use of hounds.

Yet strangely, from all the sports that I have seen, the 'cruelty' caused by hunting has not been obvious. I have seen creatures in great fear and pain, but not through the work of huntsmen and their hounds. It also seems wrong to compare blood sports with fighting sports, for they are in no way alike. The animals used for fighting were captive and tormented, while field sports involve creatures living free; the situation usually resembles that of the hunter and the hunted, which is an integral part of nature, the fittest survive, and the old, weak, and sick fall as food to predators. In a natural situation deer would be hunted by packs of wolves and run down, and in times of food shortages foxes might even experience a similar fate. In the wild, foxes have been seen coursing hares, and peregrine falcons kill grouse, pigeons, and many other birds. Yet through the evolutionary process deer, hares, and birds have developed features to enable them to survive and stamina, speed, and flock behaviour are all the end products of this development. Consequently, if sports such as hunting and falconry are cruel, then so too is nature; a hypothesis that I cannot entirely accept. Such a view would also condemn the work of some conservationists who want to reintroduce the wolf and the lynx to areas where they have been extinct for many years; indeed, it could even be argued that such animals are themselves 'cruel' and that their survival should not be encouraged.

There is no doubt that in many highly developed countries there are great pressures on the countryside, and so wildlife has to be managed, to keep populations healthy, to encourage rare species to breed, and to limit the numbers of those creatures that become too numerous, and it does seem that some blood sports have a genuine role to play in this management. Even many opponents of field sports accept the need for management, but consider the fear, anxiety, and pain caused by hunting to be unacceptable. To me this is a subjective view, which sees the fear and suffering of animals through human eyes and in human terms. It gives human feelings to all soft-coated, warm-blooded mammals (except rats), and is largely indifferent to creatures with feathers or cold blood, although their senses and nervous systems may be extremely highly developed. It is the 'cuddly bunny syndrome', based on sentiment, emotion, and wishful thinking; thus coursing is cruel because a soft brown hare is involved, yet falconry, which is almost an airborne version of the same thing, gets little critical attention, nor does fishing, which is undoubtedly the 'cruellest' sport of all. But although animals experience a wide range of emotions and feel pain like human beings, it is unlikely that they experience fear and anxiety in exactly the same way; consequently it is foolish to base judgements concerning field sports on the human view of fear and pain.

In collecting information for this book I experienced fear just once, during my trip to Scotland to see goose shooting. Arriving early I decided to go up into the Cairngorms for a day, in the hope of seeing ptarmigan. It started to snow but I still left my car and began to walk into the bad weather. I saw the ptarmigan early but kept climbing higher, intending to walk in a wide half-circle to return via the ski slopes.

As I went up I passed into cloud; visibility lessened and there were no signs of rock or vegetation below or around me – everything was white. Fallen snow merged into a mist of falling flakes and I was completely enclosed in whiteness. I trailed my stick to add to my footprints and still I went on, thinking that I would soon be able to descend to the ski-runs. Boulders appeared and then I briefly descended. I caught a glimpse of a sheer rock face falling away to my left and of a distant valley floor hundreds of feet below, but then cloud again engulfed me. Suddenly the terrain began to descend steeply, but all I could see was a uniform whiteness and my strides could not be guided by vision. After three and a half hours I again moved below the clouds and rested in a wide, rolling wilderness of white.

In front of me the ground rose steeply into cloud, as it did behind me and to my right, and to my left was a great jutting crag of rock which plunged straight down and out of view. I had no idea where I was, so I consulted my compass and decided that the only sensible thing to do was to retrace my steps before the light began to fade.

The weather seemed to be getting worse, snow was falling faster, the wind had increased, my beard was a mass of solid ice and my face burned. The line of my footprints, that I thought had been straight, meandered backwards and forwards erratically through the mist. Over the rocks and boulders the compacted snow was treacherous, and as time and distance wore on so my tracks grew fainter as they were worn away by the wind and filled with snow. I strained my eyes searching for every faint imprint in the snow, but all around me it was again nothing but white, pressing in on me with claustrophobic force. It was what mountaineers call a 'white-out', with visibility virtually nil, and everywhere the same oppressive whiteness. I felt for the compass in my top pocket, but it was not there. Despite the cold I was now sweating and I frantically searched my other pockets; finding it in one of them the panic left me.

I had to go west, but the west of my compass seemed all wrong. I put it down in the snow. It made no difference, for I was sure that where it pointed north it should have read south. Conflict started up in my mind; it was a cheap compass that had been given to me as a small boy. I felt it must be wrong and that I should ignore it, but at the same time reason told me that compasses did not go wrong. I decided to follow its westerly direction, and after what seemed like hours of wading through the snow, but which was probably no more than forty-five minutes, I felt a downward step, and soon visibility gradually improved. I went steadily downwards. Somewhere I had crossed the watershed, for a small stream flowed south. I briefly went up into the mist again until the land dropped away to the north and I recognized a flat area of ice and frozen marsh, and the ridge that would lead me down to a stream, the ski lift, and my car. My steps slowed, my legs felt heavy and I experienced a great sense of relief.

As I walked slowly down through the wind and drifting snow I decided never to go looking for reindeer,[1] ptarmigan and mountain hares like that again, for my trip had been one of folly. Back at the car I felt a peculiar sensation of fear at the thought of what could have happened; a night lost in a snow storm; death after walking blindly over the edge of a precipice; a fall on slippery rocks and a broken limb, and nobody searching for me as I had told no one my plans. All the unpleasant possibilities flooded through my mind and I felt physically and mentally exhausted.

I had returned safely, but it was an awareness of the possible alternative conclusions to my journey that caused me mental anguish. The following summer I retraced my steps and saw that I must have wandered within a few feet of a quick but brutal death, and even now, when I think of my stupidity, I experience a very strange sensation, almost a numbness that grips the mind and the pit of the stomach. Such a condition is unlikely to occur in the minds of animals, for they live largely in the present and animal anxiety is directly related to the situation in which they find themselves. In the human mind, however, it is a knowledge of the past and an awareness of the possibilities for the future that cause the most mental suffering.

My feelings and reactions in the snow were similar to those of an East German refugee who now lives in our village. When she fled across the border at the end of the Second World War she did not feel fear as she passed through forests at night to avoid Russian soldiers, and it was only after she had reached safety that she experienced a great nervous reaction. Then she could think of what might have happened and about the enormity of her decision to leave her home country. In fact she felt less fear fleeing through the woodland than she did crouching down

[1] Reindeer were introduced experimentally in the Cairngorms several years ago.

in an air raid shelter, for there, cramped into a confined space, feelings of real fear accompanied the drone of heavy bombers.

So it is with wild animals, when they are free, with a number of alternatives open to them, they feel no great fear. They react to create what the scientists call an adequate 'flight distance' between themselves and the enemy. If they cannot maintain a sufficient distance they are caught and killed, but if their flight is successful then normality quickly returns. Consequently a hunted deer or fox can feel discomfort through physical exertion, but if it evades the hounds, it seems likely that its behaviour speedily returns to normal. If, however, an animal is held in a cage or a snare and its movements are restricted, then it experiences great stress and anxiety. My own fox's behaviour seems to confirm this; on the occasions that she has run free, she has appeared to be quite untroubled, even when pursued, but when she is in her run and a stranger approaches, her behaviour is completely different. Because her movements are limited she crouches down in a corner and actually trembles with fear.

Pain can create fear, as anybody who has tried to aid an injured domestic cat or dog can testify, but in hunting the actual time between an animal getting caught and being killed is very short. It seems likely, therefore, that the quarry feels little real anxiety, and pain is quickly over. Because of this, much of the dislike of hunting is based on impulse; an understable emotional reaction, but one which is based on the false assumption that the hunted animal is subjected to great suffering, during the chase or when being driven.

I have seen fear and pain in wild creatures, but strangely they were most obvious in sports and methods of control that most people seem to accept. Yet my memory of them is clear; the screams of wounded hares at the hare shoot; the shattered limbs of some of the rabbits during the night shooting; the mackerel as they were impaled for shark bait; and the thought of the vixen in the snare still fills me with sadness. On one pheasant shoot I saw a bird fly on after shot had broken both its legs, causing them to hang down limply, and the shock and suffering felt by that bird must have been great. In pigeon shooting, too I have seen much suffering. It is a sport-cum-method of control in which pigeons are shot as they fly onto crops or go up to roost. In order not to disturb the flight the hit birds are not retrieved by dogs or shooters until shooting has finished, which means that wounded pigeons can be left where they have fallen for several hours.

But of all the sports that I have seen, fishing is without a doubt the most cruel, yet it is also the most popular and even young children are allowed to participate with no supervision. In angling, highly developed and sensitive creatures are hauled struggling into an alien environment; they face barbed hooks, the use of gaffs, keep-nets, and the touching of cold delicate skin with warm dry hands, and there is no doubt that if a hooked fish screamed like a wounded hare, then fishing would have been banned long ago. The RSPCA states quite definitely that fish feel pain and distress, caused by playing the fish on the end of a line, by heaving it out of the water on a hook, and by sometimes leaving it to die slowly. The actual fight of a fish is an indication of its fear, and by fishing on light tackle to make the fight last longer, fishermen simply use that fear to improve their sport. The suffering of a small fish being used as live-bait must also be extremely great. Just as the cruelty in fishing is obvious, so are the reasons why it is seldom attacked. Being cold blooded and silent, fish do not activate the 'cuddly bunny syndrome' and, as fishing is readily available in both town and country there are at least 2¾ million fishermen, many of whom are working-class. The angling industry also has an impressive financial turnover which with the hire of water, the cost of bait and equipment, and so on, is between £196 million and £220 million per year.[2]

Class is a significant factor in objections to blood sports, and there is no doubt that at one time hunting, shooting, and fishing were the preserves of the wealthy and the well-bred. Things have altered, however, for economic and social changes have brought country pursuits within the grasp of nearly anyone who wishes to participate, as is evident from the existence of shooting clubs, wildfowlers' associations, and the Banwen Miners' Hunt and others of its type. Although living upper-class caricatures still abound on the hunting field, usually arrogant imitations of the old aristocracy, many ordinary people with rustic accents and wellington boots can also be found. Indeed one kennelman considers that things have gone too far: 'Even scrap merchants now hunt', he told me, with obvious disapproval. There are also numerous stories of the

[2] The National Angling Survey 1970. Other estimates of the number of fishermen have been as high as 4 million.

most unlikely people hunting; a northern chimney sweep who rides a donkey, and an old farmer who mounts his ungroomed moorland nag in his working clothes. When his local hunt meets in his village he turns out as if he has ridden straight from work, and on one such occasion a young onlooker shouted out to him, 'Good morning, Mister Thompson. Where are yer harrers [harrows]?'

But although class continues to be an underlying issue, in reality it is largely bogus and irrelevant, and the main objection ought to be a moral one – that birds and animals should not be ill-treated or killed for sport. The blood sports objector at the fox-hunt that I followed is a scientist doing research into the causes of cancer. He objects to hunting because of its trappings and what he sees as the 'snobbishness and the overbearing manners of the hunters.' But he also thinks that running after wild animals really is cruel. He agrees with controlling pests and killing animals for food, but in his view, death must have a specific purpose and should not be achieved just for fun. When he has been troubled by foxes on his few acres at lambing time he has shot at them and admits that they can be a nuisance, but he likens controlling them with hounds 'to taking a musket to kill a butterfly', Another of his objections is one of trespass, and he has been warning the hunt away from his land for twenty-four years; yet meets are still held close to his holding every year and the foxes invariably run near or over his paddocks. For the Christmas Eve trespass he received £50 compensation, though he wants 'the nuisance of hunting controlled by law.'

I found him to be a friendly man, with strong beliefs and a deep interest in the countryside, yet at the same time I could not understand how he considered shooting to be more humane than hunting. In fact there seem to be great inconsistencies with most of the moral objections to blood sports; it is apparently immoral to eat shot or hunted deer, that has given meat and enjoyment to the hunter, but it is permissible to eat rump steak from a bullock that has been de-horned, castrated, and which has never seen a green field. Similarly, some people object to purchasing driven pheasants, but they see nothing wrong in devouring a mass-produced, caponized cockerel; cruelty to foxes is condemned but the feeding of anti-coagulants to rats and mice, and the squirting of clouds of nerve gas at insects is condoned. Live baiting for pike is wrong, yet we eat fish from trawlers that die of suffocation, and crabs and lobsters that meet their ends in boiling water. Many huntsmen hunt because they like it and because it is traditional, they are thought to be immoral; but many people who eat meat do so because they like it and because it is traditional, yet their behaviour is generally thought to be moral.[3] Old ladies complain about huntsmen destroying wildlife, but over the years they have fed much of the world's whale population to their overweight, neutered pussycats, and now they are even feeding canned New Forest ponies to their pets. It is interesting to note that although many find the activities of the New Forest Buckhounds unacceptable, they account for only one or two deer each year. Yet despite the numerous notices warning of the presence of deer, ponies and cattle, over forty deer are killed on the roads of the New Forest every year, in addition to about three other large animals a week.[4] All over the country the annual carnage to our wildlife caused by motor vehicles is enormous, including many hedgehogs (that can easily be avoided), foxes, deer, and badgers, yet criticism of this careless destruction is rarely heard. As a result I find the niceties of moral selection difficult to follow.

There are other interesting double standards as well; many modern wildlife films show creatures that are not truly wild, hunting creatures that are not free. Thus it is said to be wrong to hunt an otter or a fox with hounds, yet films showing otters catching fish, eels, and moorhens; weasels catching mice; wild cats catching rats; sparrow hawks catching sparrows; and a jay wrecking the nest of a small bird have all been shown on television. The fish, moorhen, mice and rats were all released in confined spaces so they could not get away, and for one film the jay was actually taken to the nest and released in front of the cameras. The films were made essentially for television, ie for money and enter-

[3] In the present state of world food shortages a very strong moral case can be made against feeding cereals to livestock. It is a very wasteful method of converting vegetable protein to animal protein for the benefit of pampered stomachs. If vegetable protein went immediately for human consumption, far more stomachs would be satisfied.

[4] In 1972 sixty-four deer were killed on the roads running through the New Forest but the normal yearly figure is about forty.

Domestic animals killed by cars in the New Forest					Known injured animals	
Year	Ponies	Cattle	Donkeys	Pigs	Ponies	Cattle
1972	120	33	2	nil	15	9
1973	110	28	3	3	13	15

tainment, as the way cats catch rats or jays eat eggs have been recorded many times before.

The prevalent anti-blood sports attitude also shows itself in other ways. Each Twelfth of August much is made of the great 'slaughter' of grouse by wealthy sportsmen, yet to make the idea of killing domestic animals more acceptable 'slaughter houses' are now pompously called 'abattoirs'. There is also no doubt that if a film was made of the activities inside a slaughter house, showing some of the 24 million gallons of blood spilt annually so that we can eat meat, the outcry would be just as great as from a film showing the bleeding of a dead stag after a hunt. But of course films of mass slaughter would be too realistic for many people to stomach, for they prefer to buy their Sunday joint neatly wrapped in cellophane paper from the supermarket, and the last thing they want to see is a link between their purchase and a living animal. In addition, if a stag is hunted and two or more shots are used to kill it, great headlines appear in the popular press about 'cruelty'. Yet such 'cruelty' is common in slaughter houses and there are numerous stories of 'humane' captive-bolts failing to kill, and of pigs falling into scalding water before they are dead. Yet when such reports appear in newspapers they are always kept small and inconspicuous. One recent story in the *Daily Telegraph* read:

> A bullock which remained alive after being shot with a humane killer, yesterday ran into a road from an abattoir, scattered pedestrians and charged into Epping Forest. A helicopter called in to search for the animal spotted it in the front garden of a cottage in Sewardstonebury, near Chingford. There police marksmen fired two shots from a revolver into the bullock's head but it still remained alive and ran into the back garden. Finally they cornered the beast and fired two shots from a shotgun behind each ear before it fell dead. It had run 2¼ miles.[5]

If such a story had involved huntsmen and a deer, questions would have been asked in Parliament, and abuse would have been heaped 'on the barbarians who inflicted such untold suffering'.

In fact, even in the straightforward production of meat and milk cattle suffer, for there is a very strong bond of attachment

[5] *Daily Telegraph* 13/11/1975

between a cow and her calf; yet within a few days of birth they are separated, and the bellowing of the mother, which may last for several days, shows her anxiety. Then, at the end of a cow's useful life she is taken out of the herd and sent to market. When this happens on the farm we try to keep the distress down to a minimum, but even the act of separating a cow from the rest of the animals causes some mental stress. The animal then has to be forced, with sticks and shouting, into a cattle truck and the apprehension is obvious. More sticks and shouting face her at the cattle market, where she is driven and prodded, before being loaded up again for the slaughter house. There too the cow will be ill at ease, for the smell of blood and disinfectant will join the shouting and hitting. Yet most people enjoy drinking milk and eating meat, although both have by-products of stress and anxiety.[6]

Because of her feelings for the cows and calves, one girl who used to visit the farm on her school holidays became a vegetarian. She would watch the calves being fed and the cows being milked, and she grew so attached to them that she stopped eating meat. Halfway through her teens beef returned to her diet as she got bored with forever eating cheese and eggs; she got tired of overhelpful waiters saying, 'It's nice to have cheese with your Sunday dinner, isn't it?' whenever she went out, and she also stopped associating the meat on her plate with the live animals in the farmyard.

Even strict vegetarians retain a capacity for self-deception. Some adopt a superior intellectual posture and object to the slaughter of all animals, but at the same time they will readily accept eggs and milk products, both of which produce a surplus of unwanted males that have to be killed. In addition, they wear shoes, which are not made from the hides of geriatric animals that have been allowed to die peacefully in their sleep.[7]

The Christian position is equally confused. Some Christians argue that hunting and shooting are merely lingering habits from man's animal background; that may be, but there seems little doubt that in the development of human society, hunting played a

[6] Experiments have been conducted showing that pigs and sheep can also experience great stress when loaded up into trucks as a normal part of the meat producing routine. However, my attempts to get further information met with a lack of cooperation from the Government bodies concerned.
[7] There are a few 'vegans' who will touch no animal products.

very important role, demanding mutual help, order, and communication. Now the refined end products of man's early efforts have mainly become traditional pastimes, yet the very qualities and disciplines which were needed and which enabled man to begin his march away from his primitive beginnings are now condemned. To me, it seems wrong to condemn activities simply because of their association with basically animal behaviour; sexual debauchery, gluttony, drunkenness and slothfulness, are all extreme conditions of animal overindulgence, yet few people would want to ban sex, food, drink, and rest. All in excess are harmful, but controlled and in moderation they are essential as well as pleasurable. There may well be a time, too, when hunting for food again becomes necessary, for all but the most optimistic mortals would not rule out the possibility of nuclear devastation, or a new lethal virus sweeping through an over-populated world. Then, any survivors would have to hunt and kill for food, and already there are 'civilized' people in the over-developed West who would starve to death in such a position, although surrounded by rabbits, deer, pheasants, and wildfowl. They would not know how to hunt, snare, or trap, and they would realize too late that man and his animal nature are not completely incompatible.

The President of the League Against Cruel Sports is also a Christian. He is a Methodist Lord; a charming, compassionate man of great wit and sharp intellect. He objects to the cruelty and class of blood sports, but he also adds what he describes as the supreme Christian objection, 'that is that we are bound to love God's creation, and I find it very difficult to believe that anyone who indulges in field sports really is practising love to the creature which is hunted.' He also believes that legislation should outlaw hunting and that such laws would not be an affront to individual liberties: 'There is no such thing as liberty, there is only ordered restraint. Our liberty consists of a community acceptance of certain principles, and unless these principles are accepted there is no such thing as liberty. The only liberty for the Christian is to obey God, and I think that if you obey God you can't go hunting.'

But there are numerous Christians who disagree. A Forestry Commission District Officer in the New Forest is a practising Non-Conformist; he is a large gentle man, and his love of deer has helped to pioneer the successful deer management policy of the area. He shoots deer with a rifle, and does not hunt, but he thinks that such decisions should be left to the individual. His small daughter rides, and if one day she asks to ride with the new Forest Buckhounds, he will not stop her.

In the village of Steeple Bumstead in Essex, there is an old style hunting parson who, although over seventy years old, still rides regularly to hounds: 'It's a great thrill to be going full belt with hounds in full cry in front of you, boy, it's like Mr Jorrocks says: "It's the image of war with only 25% of its disasters".'[8] He sees no conflict between his Christian beliefs and hunting. 'Hunting's cruel if you look at it in cold blood, but, you see, a fox is a predator who is only being served out with the same gravy that he's dished out far and wide. And if you keep hunting them they'll get further and further out into the wild and live on moles and rats and all that. They're alright out there. Love doesn't come into it, a fox is a wild animal, he's no human being; he's the destroyer being destroyed, a question of the survival of the fittest. If you gave up fox-hunting the fox population would disappear altogether, it would get murdered and poisoned.'

One old countryman gives Biblical authority for his point of view, referring to the birth of Jesus he said: 'If God had been a vegetarian he would have ordered the angel to rouse a bunch of market gardeners, and of course the first disciples were fishermen.' In fact huntsmen even have their own patron saint, Saint Hubert, but like all things connected with blood sports, his position is peculiar. In AD 683 he was hunting in a forest when his hounds put up a stag. Between its antlers was a large luminous cross which made the hounds cower down and Hubert's horse rear up; the stag then disappeared. From that day on Saint Hubert never hunted again. He did not learn his lesson, however, for in AD 727 he died following an accident while fishing from a boat on the Meuse. Whether the accident was an act of God, fish, or stupidity is not known, but it does seem that Saint Hubert ought to be the patron saint of the Hunt Saboteurs' Association and not of hunting.

But although it is difficult to make a straightforward moral assessment of blood sports, the task is made more difficult by the immorality of some organized groups, both 'pro' and 'anti'. Indeed, if there was an equivalent to the Trade Descriptions Act to cover

[8] What Jorrocks actually said, and the hunting parson significantly omitted, was '. . . it's the sport of kings, the image of war *without its guilt*, and only five and twenty per cent of its danger.' (My italics).

their pronouncements, many individuals would rarely be out of court. Some of the more obvious errors, given as 'anti' facts, are that hares and foxes do no damage, that hunted deer and coursed hares are 'torn to pieces', and that some animals and birds are being hunted and shot to the point of extinction. It is also sometimes suggested that blood sportsmen are cruel; it is true that some are arrogant and insensitive, as are some of the objectors, but I found most to be normal people with normal feelings, and many of them were good naturalists. A lot of them even went so far as to tell me that they got little satisfaction from the actual kill in their sport. What they did enjoy, however, was the skill the sport involved, and it was the practice and demonstration of their skill that gave them pleasure, and shooting, riding, fishing, and controlling dogs or hounds, all require a great deal of genuine skill.

Another erroneous suggestion is that hunting and blood sports bring out 'blood lust', and that those who watch or participate can be mentally damaged and 'de-humanized' by the experience. Few reputable psychologists would support such a theory, nor would many butchers or slaughter house workers, and I certainly do not feel damaged after having hunted. Although I had never hunted before, and am most unlikely to hunt again, I have to admit that with the adrenalin flowing, hooves pounding, and mud flying, it was for me a most exhilarating and dangerous experience, and I have no doubt that most people who enjoy physical sports such as rugby, football, tennis, and cricket, would enjoy hunting. It is also possible that when Hunt Saboteurs run to intercept hounds or try to anticipate the movements of a hunt, they are, in fact, enjoying the same feelings that they condemn in huntsmen.[9] It has to be said, too, that if watching one animal kill another is degrading, then the same applies to a person who watches a cat with a mouse, a blackbird pulling a worm from a suburban lawn, or a thrush smashing a snail on its anvil. To me the most degrading and undignified sight – degrading that is to both the spectators and the animals involved – is the use of performing lions, tigers, bears, elephants, and horses in circus acts.

Unfortunately, many blood sportsmen are just as misleading, and they deliberately sweep unpleasant aspects of their sports under the carpet. Thus the cruelty of self-lock snares, the fact that high-

[9] Some of the activities of the Hunt Saboteurs directly interfere with the freedom of others. Because of this their activities should be restricted by law.

density pheasant rearing results in the killing of too many wild predators, and the transportation of foxes are all vigorously denied, yet they are all easy to confirm. Such people see any admission or concession, not as a sensible advance, but as a major defeat, 'the thin end of the wedge'. Many also say things just as absurd as their opponents; that foxes and deer like being hunted, that shot stuns a wounded bird or animal and deadens pain, that hunts are doing a public service, that otter hunters help to conserve the otter, and that most wounded swans have been shot on the continent. None of these statements can be substantiated. They also try to destroy the credibility of those who actively object to hunting and shooting. It is suggested that they are politically motivated and that all they need is a hair cut, a cross-country run, and a cold shower, to make them into real men. In fact, many objectors are extremely sincere in their views, seeing blood sports as cruel and themselves as campaigning against a genuine modern-day evil. Slurs are even cast against objectors personally: when Harold Wilson declared himself against coursing, a story was put about that he was going to give the Russian prime minister a pair of Purdey twelve-bore shotguns costing £6,600 each. As shooting hares is far more hideous than coursing the story was widely reported in sporting circles, yet it was completely without foundation. Consequently it is sometimes far easier to make moral judgements about the organized 'pros' and 'antis' than it is about the sports themselves.

Because the issues are confused and contradictory, it is both strange and an indication of intellectual arrogance, that some people want the state to act against blood sports, even though the facts are so blurred in the minds of so many. Apparently, despite our traditions of freedom of thought and action, it is considered that the individual is incapable of making up his or her mind, and that the state must interfere. Legislation on such comparatively unimportant matters would therefore represent yet another erosion of individual liberties and one more step towards the day when the state becomes master of body and mind. The situation is made more remarkable by the fact that in other spheres, and for other reasons, restrictions are being lifted. In what passes for art, literature, and entertainment, the movement is towards more personal choice and responsibility, although no real choice is often available. If viewers find television programmes too violent it is said that they can switch off, if they find the sexual content unacceptable, they are told not to watch, and in any case it is argued that such experiences do not adversely affect those who view them. Yet with blood sports a completely different set of standards is demanded.

Some legislation is required, however, not to ban blood sports, but simply to extend the protection and preservation given to wildlife. That legislation should not be negative, it should be positive, to ensure the survival of our flora and fauna, but it should also take into account the influences and traditions of the past. Consequently, in considering the future of field sports, the main questions should not concern fear, pain, and abstract morality, which are subjective and not easily defined, but should examine whether or not the sports concerned are undertaken to obtain food or to limit numbers; they should find out if there are any practical alternatives, and they should look for any links with conservation. Using these criteria, and retaining the aim of keeping suffering to a minimum, it is possible to come to conclusions based on common sense and on the long-term interests of the creatures themselves.

The two activities that are carried out entirely for sport and which cannot be justified on any grounds are otter hunting and shark fishing. Otter hunters claim that they do much to conserve the otter; but as the breeding of otters is difficult to influence either in the wild or in captivity, the only aid huntsmen can give otters is to limit their enthusiasm while hunting. Some hunters argue that they keep a record of the otters they see; that does not conserve them, and as I saw in East Anglia there is no real way of establishing whether the hounds are responding to an otter drag or to the scent of some other mammal. The main influences leading to the decline in otter numbers are disturbance and pollution and again otter hunters do little to combat either, and actually increase the amount of disturbance, not only to otters, but also to various breeding birds. (The problem of human disturbance to wildlife goes far beyond river banks; with free access for the general public in many of our forests, roe deer kids are killed and injured by the pet dogs of Sunday afternoon strollers, birds are upset and their eggs stolen, and rare wild flowers are trampled on and even picked.)

Despite this, otter hounds are attractive creatures with an

interesting past. Most otter hunters, too, are not the blood-thirsty villains of the countryside that they are thought to be, and hunting is rather like a pleasant alcoholic romp through the reed beds. Even so, the sport cannot be defended, particularly in the slow flowing rivers of lowland England where the otter is scarce. The Ministry of Agriculture does not consider it to be a pest in any part of the British Isles, nor do most fishermen, who see the protected heron as a far greater nuisance. Consequently otter hunting should not be banned as such, the otter should simply become a protected animal. If otter hunters wish to continue, they should be restricted to hunting mink and coypu, after the main nesting season for waterbirds is over. Serious consideration should also be given to efforts to encourage the return of otters, by reducing the amount of disturbance on some waterways by boatmen, anglers, and various other individuals. These flock to water in their thousands every summer and cause a far greater disturbance than a few huntsmen and their hounds.

Shark fishing, too, takes place solely for sport, and I found the fact that many of them are just killed, weighed, photographed, and dumped back into the sea, extremely distasteful, for despite their reputation, sharks are magnificent creatures. I had a very amusing and enjoyable day on the shark boat, but I cannot defend the sport; again the simple solution would be to protect sharks in British waters. Little can be done about other forms of angling which are, in the main, traditional and skilful, whereas shark fishing is recent, and even a novice can land a shark once it has been hooked.

Because anglers have formed a significant pressure group to fight against pollution, angling has been beneficial to many of our rivers and streams, and each year action is taken by fishing clubs against many of those who foul our waterways. There are issues in the sport which need to be watched, however. Many fishermen themselves are worried by the growth of match angling and clubs should make certain that codes of conduct are observed to ensure a minimum of suffering and waste. With artificial spinners and imitation fish being available, live baiting is another practice that ought to be stopped.

Hare hunting and coursing are the other sports that are not carried out for food or control, although coursed hares can be eaten. But I can not get excited one way or the other about beagling or the activities of harriers, to me they just seem highly eccentric and absurd pastimes. If many of those hares that are killed by hounds were not hunted they would probably be shot, and once more it seems that the question of participation should be a matter for personal choice and not of legislation. The Windsor Forest Bloodhounds offer an alternative form of hunting, and they follow the scent of a man. One follower says: 'This has all the enjoyment of hunting without the immorality; you have exercise, skill, drama, snobbery and fresh air, but no blood. It is the obvious modern alternative. The additional advantages are that you can avoid crops, motorways, airports, other people's pets and back gardens.' He admits that hunting can be enjoyable, but says: 'Hunting, like rape, can be fun for some people, but it is immoral', and his sport provides him with a moral alternative. Hound trailing, in the Lake District, is another sport in which there is no death, for the hounds follow a trail laid by a runner, alone and unaided, and the first one back wins money for its owner. Unfortunately, hare hunters do not enthuse over such substitutes.

With coursing the problems are more simple. Firstly, hare shooting is more cruel, and secondly, no legislation will ever stop coursing, as is evident from the continuation of cock-fighting, and the real choice is between lawful organized coursing, and illegal, unorganized coursing. In the former there are rules and standards; but in the latter there can be no checks, just a few people and their dogs in an isolated field. In such a situation a hare could be caught and not killed, and it could be several minutes before a human presence ensured death. At organized coursing most hares in a similar situation would be quickly killed, and so ironically the one animal to suffer from legislation to ban coursing is the hare, because of more shooting and illegal sport. It is also likely that with changing social, agricultural and economic conditions, left to itself coursing would slowly fade away. When it is under attack, then both interest and support are increased.

Most of the other blood sports have strong links with conservation and there is no doubt that without the fox hunter the fox would have been extinct in most parts of the British Isles long ago. Many 'antis' cite, as a case against fox hunting, the fact that 'fox hunters preserve foxes', but this is the very essence of sensible conservation, a combination of encouragement and control. In America, where hunting took place mainly for commercial reasons, the buffalo was shot almost to extinction, and in Britain the draining of wet places has meant that the common frog is no longer common in many areas. It is not eaten or hunted, so there is no lobby screaming hysterically about cruelty to frogs, the 'cuddly bunny syndrome' lies dormant, and as a result the common frog is suffering the worst of all possible fates – it is being forgotten.

Where hunts exist there are usually foxes, and if hunting was outlawed, the pheasant and the keeper's snare would reign supreme, with the likelihood that the rural fox would become extremely rare. Even now, in the Fens, hunting does not take place, and it is an area where the fox is uncommon. At the Ouse Washes no special measures need to be taken to protect nesting wildfowl or waders from mammalian predators, except occasional mink, and whenever a fox shows itself, numerous fenmen reach for their guns.

It is said that the other forms of fox control are more humane and that huntsmen should only follow drag hounds. The other ways of killing foxes are certainly more efficient than hunting, but the amount of injury and real terror is far greater. If fox hunting was stopped, it also seems unlikely that those anxious to outlaw it would take any active steps to conserve or to control foxes. Consequently the day when the British fox will be in the greatest danger, will be the day when hunting is outlawed.

From the point of view of the fox hunter, drag hunting is a poor substitute for the real thing. I had a ride with the Cambridge University Drag Hounds, and contrary to one view, they are not a group of transvestite undergraduates who chase choir boys, but 'young gentlemen' who pursue a runner with hounds and horses. The runner trails a sack containing scent which, in the past, was aniseed or straw soaked in wolf's water (at £2 a gallon), but on the day I rode it was a sack containing pieces of fox. My horse spent the half hour of the hunt alternately refusing jumps, running through them or going out at the side. The drag followed a cross-country course in the grounds of a large house, and halfway round the hounds caught up with the runner and his sack. The whole hunt then had to stop and wait while the youth plodded on. After my experiences following a wild fox it was an anti-climax, lacking the uncertainty and the spontaneity of real hunting.

The red deer of Exmoor are also preserved and managed by those who hunt them, and it is interesting to compare their status with that of other red deer in England. In Devon and Somerset they are healthy and secure, but in the Breckland where there are no popular traditions of hunting wild deer, the red deer is under pressure from poachers and shooting landowners. Pursuing a stag to the point of exhaustion so that it can be shot has little appeal for me, but hunting in the West Country does seem to be in the best long-term interest of the deer. Some say that, if hunting stopped, the deer would be shot to extinction, as all control would go, and the main interest would become a straightforward commercial one, while others maintain that the deer would remain. To me it would be folly to take the risk of change. The situation involving the men and deer of Exmoor would be helped if stag hunting received more objective coverage in the media. At the moment, if football matches were covered in the same way, reports would be limited to broken legs, fouls, players spitting at referees, and mob violence in the crowd; the cry would then go up: 'Ban football'.

In Scotland there is no real alternative to stalking. Deer farming is possible on marginal land, and I saw a successful experiment being conducted by a young vet at Auchtermuchty, in Fife, which suggested that deer could be a better proposition than sheep or cattle. But to farm the whole of the Highlands would be unpractical and too expensive. Yet although hunting and stalking are legitimate when viewed in the context of conservation and of the past, deer of all species do need more protection from poachers and shotguns, and the punishments for all forms of poaching should be made more deterrent. To prevent much unnecessary suffering the Deer Act should be extended to make all deer shooting with shotguns illegal, even with buck shot, except when dealing with an injured animal or a deer standing at bay. Deer drives should be forbidden, and only those with special licences should be allowed to kill deer, or sell venison, and records should be kept of all transactions.

It is probably because of my experiences as a boy, seeing roe deer killed with shotguns, that shooting remains a sport that does not appeal to me. Yet many shooting men are obsessed with their sport and their lives seem to be based on the philosophy 'isn't it a lovely day, let's go and kill something'. I do not understand such an outlook, nor that of a sportsman from the Isle of Man who advertised in the shooting press for springtime rook shooting anywhere in Britain, with an offer to pay for his sport. Shooting rabbits, hares, pigeons, and pheasants all cause some fear and suffering, but again it seems to me that participation should be a matter of personal choice, for there are important links between shooting and conservation. At the same time, efforts should be made to make sure that shooting is conducted sensibly and in such a way that stress and pain are kept to a minimum. Dogs and pickers-up are essential and shooting purely for the sake of large bags should be discouraged.

If shooting stopped, the impact on the countryside would be enormous, both from an amenity and from a wildlife point of view. In areas of intensive cereal production it is the shooting and hunting interests that retain trees and hedges for fox and pheasant coverts, and they also plant belts of new woodland. As a result, in the 'prairie lands' it is the hunting or shooting farmer that preserves the traditional look of the countryside. Such a landscape is not only valuable for country sports, but it is an important visual amenity for everyone, and the trees and thickets provide refuges and breeding areas for many woodland birds.

Wildfowlers, too, can claim with some justification that they contribute to the conservation of wildfowl. They provide or preserve much important habitat, they have financed work into the diet of wildfowl, they have reintroduced greylag and barnacle geese into various parts of the country and the Wildfowlers' Association of Great Britain and Ireland (WAGBI) has even exerted pressure on the government to prevent any extension of goose shooting in Scotland. But the work and high standards of the responsible wildfowlers and organizations cannot obscure the damage done by those who shoot at birds out of range, and who kill and wound protected birds. Consequently, special permits should be issued to those who want to go wildfowling; permits that are only issued to satisfactory applicants and which are easy to withdraw. All those wanting to shoot would have to produce comprehensive references from officers of responsible wildfowling clubs affiliated to WAGBI, confirming their competence to shoot, and each applicant would have to undergo a test in wildfowl and wader recognition. Such measures would rid the sport of many 'marsh cowboys', shooting standards would improve, and much injury and wanton destruction would be prevented. It should also be an offence to shoot wildfowl without a dog to retrieve wounded birds. Furthermore special legislation is required to forbid the use of cartridges containing lead pellets in areas of heavy shooting, especially if those areas are of great ecological importance. It should not be beyond the technical ability of cartridge manufacturers to introduce a satisfactory alloy substitute that would not poison birds if retained in the gizzard. Those people who still practise the ancient art of punt-gunning are too few in number to cause concern or to warrant restrictions.

Falconry is the other real minority sport, and any move to outlaw a skill that is so old and so beautiful would in itself be an act of irresponsibility and pettiness. As the removal of wild birds can only be undertaken with a licence, the main threat of wild raptors comes from theft, pollution, egg collecting, and pigeon fanciers who see them as pests.[10] Some pigeon owners now pay thousands of pounds for their birds, and seem to want to exterminate any wild hawks or falcons that might threaten their prize-winning pigeons. One man in the north of England recently paid £7,000 for a pigeon; it was not killed by a wild peregrine falcon, but by his neighbour's cat.

Regardless of personal feelings about blood sports, their overall effect on the countryside is undoubtedly beneficial. They encourage landscape that is attractive and add much richness and variety to the wildlife and to the traditions of the countryside. The present populations of foxes, deer, pheasants, French and English partridges, various ducks and geese, rainbow trout and many other species of fish, all owe much to field sportsmen, both past and present. In addition it was sportsmen who reintroduced the capercaillie to Scotland, and who took grouse to Exmoor, and the only species to have suffered through sport is the Great Bustard. As a result, if field sports were made illegal, many thousands of people who actively help to manage and preserve wildlife and wild places, admittedly for their own vested interests, would cease their activities, and it is doubtful whether the state or those who actively campaign against them would fill the gap.

In fact, despite all the lip-service paid to wildlife conservation, the actual contribution made by politicians and government is small, and most of the work and finance comes from private individuals, landowners and sportsmen, as well as from organizations dependent on voluntary contributions, such as Naturalists' Trusts,

[10] An article in the *Pigeon Racing Gazette* of October 1974 was entitled 'The Working Man's Enemy: the Menace of the Falcon', by 'Icarus'. It even seemed to suggest that pigeon fanciers should illegally shoot peregrine falcons.

the Royal Society for the Protection of Birds and the Wildfowl Trust. Even now, efforts are being made to re-establish the Great Bustard on Salisbury Plain, and there too it is the work of private individuals who have formed a trust. Public authorities in which government does have some control, such as those for water, agriculture, and forestry, put their own narrow interests before all else. Although the Forestry Commission tries to fulfil its obligations to wildlife, albeit as a secondary consideration, other bodies see no further than maximum efficiency in food production and land drainage. Even the Countryside Commission seems to see the countryside in terms of recreational facilities alone. Because of this, what is really wanted is an actual government department for wild life conservation, with the power and the resources to protect species, to control them, and to offer practical advice, management schemes, and financial help to landowners. In an area like the Breckland red deer management should be under one authority, with shooting severely restricted and money paid out for damage. Other properly coordinated schemes in various parts of the country are needed for deer, wildfowl and various other wild creatures from toads to badgers. Such a department could also offer help with the control of rabbits and pigeons, as well as with the maintenance of trees, hedges and wet areas, which cost ordinary farmers much in time and money. For too long farmers have been expected to run their farms almost like charities, providing cheap food for little return, while at the same time they have paid out of their own often inadequate pockets for landscape management and wildlife control. It is hardly surprising that many farmers have taken the easy way out; that they have uprooted trees and hedges, and drained all their areas of marsh in the name of economy, efficiency, and necessity. Yet the countryside and its wildlife riches are of benefit to the whole community and everyone should be prepared to foot some of the bill to retain them.

Because the delicate balances and links of the countryside are generally misunderstood, it is not surprising to find that many people want field sports abolished. But with increasing pressures for new towns, roads, recreation facilities, and efficient agriculture, it is vital that these balances do not get disturbed. Consequently, I do not believe that the blood sports controversy is basically rich versus poor, immorality against morality, or 'baddies' against 'goodies' – it is a straightforward case of ignorance against understanding and town versus country. With a large number of people the views expressed are based purely on emotion, and even many of those who move into new village estates take their essentially urban outlooks with them, for they do not understand the countryside or country traditions, and to them country sports are simply 'barbaric and degrading'. Their contempt stems from a union of the 'cuddly bunny syndrome' with pseudo-intellectual suburban morality; Oscar Wilde gave us the 'uneatable' and the 'unspeakable', these people provide us with examples of the 'unthinkable'. To them the importance of continuity and selective predation is lost, as are the origins of factory-farmed food and their scrambled battery eggs for breakfast. They do not understand that some things have to die so that others may live; they are blind to the appeal of tradition; and even in their everyday language they fail to recognize the phrases that are still in regular use which show how deep our sporting heritage goes, whether we like it or not.[11]

My own position regarding blood sports remains unchanged. I continue to take no part in organized killing, simply because I prefer to watch wild things than to kill them, for as I cannot give life I have no wish to take it away. My feelings for birds and animals, domestic and wild, are undoubtedly based on a mixture of sentiment and the 'cuddly bunny syndrome', but just because participation in these pursuits would be wrong for me, I do not believe that it is automatically wrong for others. In addition, I shall continue to retain my own double-standards; if rabbits and pigeons damage crops I shall reluctantly take up a gun, and I shall still eat shot pheasant wherever possible, for the thought of reared 'broiler pheasants' is quite abhorrent.

In the future, the dates for hunting, shooting, and fishing, will not govern my year, but it will be influenced by the natural succession of seasons. In spring and early summer I will hope to see a vixen and her cubs around the earth in the large field, and later, on warm evenings, I will wait for badgers to emerge from their hill-side sett. In the autumn it will be the fascination of the fallow deer rut that attracts, and in winter there will be wild low-

[11] To ferret out; to let off the hook; to rise to bait; to run with the hare and ride with the hounds; lock, stock, and barrel; hook, line, and sinker; to go off at half-cock; a flash in the pan; to slip the leash; to give someone their head; to be in at the death; to turn at bay; to draw a blank; to run for cover; to flush out, etc. Just as the word 'cadger' comes from falconry so too does 'boozer', for 'to bowse' means to drink in hawking parlance.

land skies, the chance of ice, and the occasional skein of geese. At all times I will let the dogs chase rabbits and down by the brook I will hope for a glimpse of an otter. When the hunt meets at one of the local pubs I hope too that I will be there, for the sight of hounds and horses and the sound of many hooves along the hard road surface is soothing, appealing, and satisfying. Later, when the hunting horn is heard, faint and far-off, I shall not feel anger, I will simply feel reassurance, for I will know that at least the hunters still have something to hunt.

Acknowledgements

In writing this book I received valuable help from a variety of people and organizations, from as far apart as Auchtermuchty, Looe, Nether Wallop, and Steeple Bumstead. A full list would fill too many pages, but because necessity requires some omissions, this does not diminish my debt of gratitude. Among the organizations and their representatives who gave me much assistance were the League Against Cruel Sports, the British Field Sports Society, the Game Conservancy, the Forestry Commission, the Ministry of Agriculture, the Universities Federation for Animal Welfare, the Royal Society for the Prevention of Cruelty to Animals, the Royal Society for the Protection of Birds, the Home Office, the Hunt Saboteurs' Association, the Mammal Society, the Wildfowlers' Association of Great Britain and Ireland, the British Deer Society, the Norfolk Naturalists' Trust, the Cambs and Isle of Ely Naturalists' Trust, the Red Deer Commission, the Nature Conservancy Council, P. A. Gouldsbury of the Gamekeepers' Association (now part of WAGBI), John Williams of the Masters of Otterhounds Association, John Kirkpatrick of the Association of Masters of Harriers and Beagles, Rex Hudson of the Masters of Basset Hounds Association, the Hon. A. D. Tryon of the Great Bustard Trust, the National Anglers' Council, the Salmon and Trout Association, the Anglers' Co-operative Association, and the Anglian Water Authority.

Many individuals, both for and against field sports, were generous with their time and hospitality. I spent many hours listening to Jim Ling who worked on the farm for many years, and to Arthur Sewell from the next village; both have died since the completion of the book. They were fine old countrymen and are sadly missed. My thanks too go to Alan Bednall for the loan of his horse Remo, and to Linda Robarts who had to catch it several times and who gave me the benefit of her riding experience. To the White Horse Riding Stables at Cambridge for my first hunting horse and to Moss Bros. of London for the boots and for the head gear in case of disaster. Mr Peter Thelwall, Chairman of the Cambridgeshire Hunt, gave me much help as did Michael McNulty, the kennelman, Marshall Ingle the terrier-man, and Eric Brand his assistant.

Help came with every sport; Mr and Mrs H. Gingell of the Cambridgeshire Harriers, Jack Poile, kennelman of the Trinity Foot Beagles, John Humphreys of the De Burgh Basset Hounds, John Hare, Mrs P. Bailey, and Hartley Hawes. Officers of the Forestry Commission assisted with deer; Fred Courtier in the New Forest, and in East Anglia, Mr John Fletcher, Rex Whitta, Tony Reeman and Derek Rand. Also Miss Pam Field and Mr E. R. Lloyd of the Devon and Somerset Staghounds, G. Sellick of the Tiverton Staghounds, R. H. Buttle, Dr John Fletcher, and R. Balharry of the Nature Conservancy. Those who helped me with otters were Harvey Cole, Master of the Dartmoor Otterhounds, Derek Myhill the secretary, May and Les Drake of Otterton, Mr Charles Corner of the Eastern Counties Otterhounds and Mr Philip Wayre of the Norfolk Wildlife Park.

My shooting uncles, Cyril and Roy Crow, taught me much about shooting, as did Den Northrop, Bernie and Brian Sewell, Noel Cunningham-Reed, Will Garfit, Charles Coles and T. H. Blank, the Director, and the Research Director, of the Game Conservancy, and several gamekeepers, past and present, Walter Lake, Bert Baker, Charlie South and Freddie Carter. Fred Pearson of the Fenland Wildfowlers' Association gave me assistance, as did Arthur Cadman, Peter Conder, the former Director of the RSPB, Clifford Carson, the Warden at the Ouse Washes reserve, Jeremy Sorenson his predecessor, Gareth Thomas, and Jim Hall the Farming and Wildlife Adviser.

Fishermen were also very co-operative, Mr M. W. Talor, Mr Maurice Green, the former editor of the *Daily Telegraph*, Percy Anderson of Cambridge, Dermot Wilson of Nether Wallop, Lionel Sweet of Usk, Jim Whitehead, Roy and Clare Robarts, and Mr D. Fleming-Jones, Fishery Officer at Grafham Water. Falconers who came to my aid were T. H. Brookes, Philip Glasier, and Stephen Frank.

Others too, rich and poor, famous and unknown gave me help of various kinds. They include The Rev the Lord Soper, Marcus Kinball M.P., the Rev E. H. Wheeler, Raymond Brooks-Ward,

Mick Brown, Jim Docwra, Michael Goodchild, Hector Naylor, Charlie Waters, Bridget Wood, Prof W. H. Thorpe, Teresa Brown, Sir Newton Rycroft, A. J. Keep, Dr Richard D. Ryder, J. A. Hodginson, P. J. Long, John Heath, John Robbins, Jane Barham, Dr Brian Heap, Marcus Webb, Stephen Clare-Higgs of the Lords Bridge Farm Riding Stables, Kevin Macdonald of Game Finders, 'Pack' Odams, Toby Buchan of Davis-Poynter Limited, Hettie Gorton, and Nan Anscombe.

I am grateful to the editor of the *Shooting Times* for permission to reproduce two articles as part of the text, and for help with illustrations. A few days before his cowardly murder, I also received permission from Ross McWhirter to quote from the *Guinness Book of Records*.

Bibliography

The following small selection of books and pamphlets for further reading would help anybody wanting to study details of wild creatures and blood sports more closely. Some also help to explain our emotional attitudes towards certain animals.

A Field Guide to the Mammals of Britain and Europe – F. H. Van Den Brink (Collins)

British Mammals – L. Harrison Matthews (Collins)

A Field Guide to the Birds of Britain and Europe – Peterson, Mountford, and Hollom (Collins)

Collins Guide to British Birds – R. S. R. Fitter and R. A. Richardson (Collins)

Collins Guide to Animal Tracks and Signs – Preben Bang and Preben Dahlstrom (Collins)

Animals after Dark – Maxwell Knight (Routledge and Kegan Paul)

Town Fox, Country Fox – Brian Vesey-Fitzgerald (André Deutsch)

Wild Fox – Roger Burrows (David and Charles)

The Belstone Fox – David Rook (Hodder and Stoughton)

Memoirs of a Fox-Hunting Man – Siegfried Sassoon (Faber)

Fables of Aesop – several versions

The Elements of Hunting – R. S. Summerhays (Country Life)

Jorrocks's Jaunts and Jollities – R. S. Surtees (Cassell)

Wild Hares – Henry Tegner (John Baker Ltd)

The Leaping Hare – George Ewart Evans and David Thomson (Faber)

Beagling – J. Ivester Lloyd (Herbert Jenkins)

Beagling – W. Lovell Hewitt (Faber)

Modern Greyhound Racing and Coursing – Roy Genders (Sporting Handbooks Ltd)

A Review of Coursing – Owen Stable Q.C. and R. M. Stuttard (British Field Sports Society)

The Report of the Lords Select Committee into Hare Coursing – 1976 (HMSO)

Living with Deer – Richard Prior (André Deutsch)

The Fallow Deer – W. A. Cadman (HMSO)

The Roe Deer – J. S. R. Chard (HMSO)
East Anglian Forests – Edited by H. L. Edlin (HMSO)
New Forest – Edited by H. L. Edlin (HMSO)
The Wild Deer of Exmoor – E. R. Lloyd (The Exmoor Press)
Exmoor National Park – Edited by John Coleman-Cooke (HMSO)
Deer Stalking in Scotland – G. Kenneth Whitehead (*Shooting Times* Library)
Highland Year – L. MacNally (J. M. Dent)
Bambi – Felix Salten
The Running of the Deer – Ewan Clarkson (Hutchinson)
Ring of Bright Water – Gavin Maxwell (Longman)
Tarka the Otter – Henry Williamson (Macdonald)
'*Otters, signs of revival*' – J. Ivester Lloyd (article in *The Field*, 6/9/1973)
The Private Life of the Rabbit – R. M. Lockley (André Deutsch)
Rabbits and their History – John Sheail (David and Charles)
Rabbiting and Ferreting – E. Samuel and J. Ivester Lloyd (BFSS)
Rabbit Control in Woodlands – E. V. Rogers (HMSO)
Brer Rabbit – there are several versions of Joel Chandler Harris's stories.
Fifteen Rabbits – Felix Salten
Watership Down – Richard Adams (Rex Collings)
The Complete Book of Game Conservation – Edited by Charles Coles (Barrie and Jenkins)
The Shooting Man's England – Patrick Chalmers (Seeley Service)
British Game – Brian Vesey-Fitzgerald (Collins)
So you want to go Shooting – Anthony Jackson (Arlington Books)
Rough Shooting – W. A. Cadman (David and Charles)
A Wealth of Wildfowl – Jeffrey Harrison (André Deutsch)
Report on Wildfowling in the Ouse Washes – S. C. Madge and J. Sorenson (internal report for the Royal Society for the Protection of Birds)
Wildfowl and Agriculture – RSPB publication
Birds, November – December 1975. An article in the magazine of the RSPB by Gareth Thomas, a research biologist
Angling – RSPCA publication
Fishing with Mr Crabtree in all Waters – Daily Mirror Books
Salmon Fishing – Eric Taverner and Jock Scott (Seeley Service)
The Trout – W. E. Frost and M. E. Brown (Collins)
The Compleat Angler – Izaak Walton (Everyman, Dent)
Shark Fishing in British Waters – Trevor Housby (Gentry Books)
A Manual of Falconry – M. H. Woodford (A. and C. Black)
Falconry – Gilbert Blaine (Neville Spearman)

The Peregrine – J. A. Baker (Collins)
A Kestrel for a Knave – Barry Hines (Michael Joseph)
The Goshawk – T. H. White (Jonathan Cape)
As the Falcon Her Bells – P. Glasier (Heinemann)
The Capercaillie – C. E. Palmer (HMSO)
Tales of a Devon Village – Chapter One: The Badger Dig – Henry Williamson (Faber)
The History of Hunting – L. G. Pine (The League Against Cruel Sports).
Victims of Science: The use of animals in research – Richard D. Ryder (Davis-Poynter)
Animal Nature and Human Nature – W. H. Thorpe (Methuen)
The Hunting Hypothesis – Robert Ardrey (Collins)
New Agricultural Landscapes – The Countryside Commission
Farming and Wildlife: A study in compromise – Derek Barber (RSPB)
Wildlife Conservation in Woodlands – R. C. Steele (HMSO)
Report of the Technical Committee to Enquire into the Welfare of Animals kept under Intensive Livestock Husbandry Systems. (HMSO Command number 2836).
Report of the Departmental Committee on Cruelty to Wild Animals (HMSO Command number 8266).
The Humane Control of Animals Living in the Wild – (UFAW)